Advances in African Economic, Social and Political Development

Africa is emerging as a rapidly growing region, still facing major challenges, but with a potential for significant progress—a transformation that necessitates vigorous efforts in research and policy thinking. This book series focuses on three intricately related key aspects of modern-day Africa: economic, social and political development. Making use of recent theoretical and empirical advances, the series aims to provide fresh answers to Africa's development challenges. All the socio-political dimensions of today's Africa are incorporated as they unfold and new policy options are presented. The series aims to provide a broad and interactive forum of science at work for policymaking and to bring together African and international researchers and experts. The series welcomes monographs and contributed volumes for an academic and professional audience, as well as tightly edited conference proceedings. Relevant topics include, but are not limited to, economic policy and trade, regional integration, labor market policies, demographic development, social issues, political economy and political systems, and environmental and energy issues.

More information about this series at http://www.springer.com/series/11885

Gbadebo O. A. Odularu ·
Mena Hassan · Musibau Adetunji Babatunde
Editors

Fostering Trade in Africa

Trade Relations, Business Opportunities and Policy Instruments

Springer

Editors
Gbadebo O. A. Odularu
Department of Economics and Finance
Bay Atlantic University (BAU)
Washington, DC, USA

Mena Hassan
Trade Policies Review Division
World Trade Organization
Geneva, Switzerland

Musibau Adetunji Babatunde
Department of Economics
University of Ibadan
Ibadan, Nigeria

ISSN 2198-7262 ISSN 2198-7270 (electronic)
Advances in African Economic, Social and Political Development
ISBN 978-3-030-36631-5 ISBN 978-3-030-36632-2 (eBook)
https://doi.org/10.1007/978-3-030-36632-2

This Springer imprint is published by the registered company Springer Nature Switzerland AG
The registered company address is: Gewerbestrasse 11, 6330 Cham, Switzerland

Foreword

As the World Trade Organization (WTO) marks its 25-year anniversary, the global trading system has helped transform international economic relations across its 164 Member States. Trade liberalization under the multilateral trading system has led to a significant reduction of trade barriers, reinforced regional integration and helped open global markets. The 2030 Development Agenda highlights that trade is an engine for inclusive economic growth and poverty reduction. Moreover, trade is an enabler which has economic cross-cutting positive effects and has significant linkages to other sectors. So, for countries to fully reap the benefits of trade, it is necessary to adopt approaches which aim to mainstream trade into their national sustainable development strategies.

The African continent is remarkably rich with its enormous natural resources and diverse cultures. It is the second most-populous continent with the youngest average population among all the continents. Agriculture remains the key driver of most economies in Africa. However, petroleum, minerals and the services sector are main contributors to the continent's GDP. In addition, African countries are members of several regional economic groupings as well as the most recent African Continental Free Trade Agreement (AfCFTA). The AfCFTA entered in force in April 2019 and is aimed at boosting intra-African trade, deepening Africa's regional and continental integration and further developing the industrial and services sectors of the economies of African countries.

Nevertheless, Africa's share in world merchandise trade remains very low at 2.7% in 2018; over the past ten years, Africa's share in world exports declined from 3.5% in 2008 to 2.5% in 2018, the lowest regional share. Moreover, the African continent continues to suffer from very high trade costs and doing business environment remains cumbersome. The WTO Trade Facilitation Agreement will enable the simplification, modernization and harmonization of export and import processes in Africa. Africa faces an urgent need in tackling poverty, enhancing inclusiveness and fitting the continent into a rapidly evolving global digital economy. The continent has huge investment needs in terms of both of physical infrastructure and human capital, as well as to improve governance. Although increasing efforts are being made for export diversification and to enhance cross-border market access in

Africa to enhance the benefits from regional value chains, still too many businesses lack access to sub-regional and continental markets. In fact, while regional trade accounts for about 70 per cent in Europe and 60 per cent in Asia, it accounts for only 18 per cent in Africa. The low level of intra-Africa trade remains one of the most critical stumbling blocks to Africa's economic transformation aspirations.

How Africa adopts the appropriate trade policy instruments and strategies towards navigating the regional and global trading landscape, as well as steering its development path is the main topic of this book. Authored by African academics and practitioners, I hope that it will be a useful resource for decision- and policy-makers who have a stake in Africa's economic development. In addition, I hope this book will contribute to knowledge sharing and spark new ideas and stimulate actions to develop innovative solutions, which are urgently required for the advancement of Africa's economic prosperity in 2020 and beyond.

Dr. Yonov Frederick Agah
Deputy Director-General
World Trade Organization
Geneva, Switzerland

Contents

Abbreviations

AIDI	Africa Infrastructure Development Index
AFTA	ASEAN Free Trade Area
APEC	Asia-Pacific Economic Cooperation
BE	Business Environment
BTE	Border Transport Efficiency
CEMAC	Central African Economic and Monetary Community
CIF	Cost, Insurance and Freight
DCNT	Draft Consolidated Negotiating Text
EAC	East African Community
ECCAS	Economic Community of Central African States
ECOWAS	Economic Community of West African States
EDA	Economic Development for Africa
EPZ	Export Processing Zones
FTAs	Free Trade Areas
GATT	General Agreement on Tariff and Trade
GDP	Gross Domestic Product
GRA	Ghana Revenue Authority
GPHA	Ghana Ports and Harbors Authority
IGAD	Inter Governmental Authority on Drought and Development
IRTG	Improved Road Transport Governance
ICT	Information Communication and Technology
NTBs	Non-Tariff barriers
OECD	Organization for Economic Co-operation and Development
PI	Physical Infrastructure
PTAs	Preferential Trade Areas
RTAs	Regional Trade Areas
RECs	Regional Economic Communities
SADC	Southern African Development Community
SSA	Sub-Saharan Africa
WDI	World Development Indicator

Introduction: Trade Relations, Business Opportunities and Policy Instruments for Fostering Africa's Trade

Mena Hassan, Gbadebo Odularu and Musibau Adetunji Babatunde

Context and Purpose

The African continent is remarkably rich with its natural resources and diverse cultures and is the second most populous continent, behind Asia with the youngest average population amongst all continents. Agriculture remains the key driver of most economies in Africa, but petroleum, minerals and services sectors are main contributors to the continent's overall GDP. In addition, African countries are members of several regional economic groupings as well as the most recent African Continental Free Trade Agreement (AfCFTA), which entered in force in April 2019, in order to boost intra-African trade, enhance Africa's regional and continental integration and further develop the industrial, manufacturing sector of their economies.

This note represents the opinion of the author, and is the product of professional experience and research. It is not meant to represent the position or opinions of the WTO.

M. Hassan (✉)
Trade Policy Analyst, World Trade Organization (WTO), Geneva, Switzerland
e-mail: mena.hassan@gmail.com

G. Odularu
Department of Economics and Finance, Bay Atlantic University (BAU), Washington, DC, USA
e-mail: odularu@comcast.net; godularu@live.com; godularu@bau.edu

Socio-Economic Research Applications and Projects (SERAP LLC), Washington, DC, USA

Center for Research on Political Economy (CREPOL), Dakar-Yoff, Senegal

Trade, Economics and Agribusiness Division, SSCG Consulting, Birmingham, UK

American Heritage University of Southern California (AHUSC), Ontario, CA, USA

M. A. Babatunde
Department of Economics, University of Ibadan, Ibadan, Nigeria
e-mail: tunjiyusuf19@yahoo.com

G. O. A. Odularu et al. (eds.), *Fostering Trade in Africa*,
Advances in African Economic, Social and Political Development,
https://doi.org/10.1007/978-3-030-36632-2_1

Nevertheless, Africa's share in world merchandise trade remains very low at 2.7% in 2018; and over the past ten years, Africa's share in world exports declined from 3.5% in 2008 to 2.5% in 2018, the lowest regional share (AfDB 2019). Moreover, the African continent continues to suffer from very high trade costs, and doing business is difficult (Odularu and Alege 2019).

Trade relations and business opportunities are becoming increasingly crucial to all societies and their economic activities, especially in this digital era. Thus, recent and ongoing trade policy discussions and decisions in this rapidly changing world require appropriate trade facilitation instruments, in order to understand the underlying trends and drivers of trade, but also to set the direction of trade outcomes for the future.

Against this background, international trade theory and policy reforms motivate the major questions that this book attempts to unravel. The centrepiece question that this book endeavours to answer is: What trade policies and instruments enable Africa to foster trade, promote economic growth and raise its standards of living? The answers are reflected in the purpose of this book, which are, to provide frameworks on how trade facilitation instruments play a role in fostering Africa's trade. The issues examined in this book are both relevant and timely in the sense that they focus on doing business in Africa, regional integration and trade facilitation which are at the forefront of both sustainable business development policy and intellectual discourse across African countries. This book provides a comprehensive analysis on trade and business opportunities, capacities, issues, challenges and lessons, with a special interest in sustainably enhancing Africa's business ecosystem in the digital age. It examines the contributions of trade facilitation-related policies, programmes, tools and initiatives towards fostering trade and business opportunities in the face of increasing non-tariff barriers, asymmetries and opacity that highly characterize the African business landscape. The authors recommend innovative conceptual frameworks, appropriate initiatives and workable policy recipes towards making Africa's business environment more friendly and attractive.

Selection and Organization of Chapters

This book comprises ten chapters. Each chapter presents compelling discussions on the opportunities to improve trade policy processes in order to foster trade outcomes in Africa.

The initial six chapters focus on trade facilitation landscape in Africa. In so doing, it discusses the enormous business opportunities and trade relations that will foster Africa's trade and enhance its capacity to overcome the massive challenges and needs that are posed by their ongoing regional integration efforts. They also discuss evidence-based policy recommendations on Africa could benefit maximally from the One Belt One Road (OBOR) initiative and infrastructure.

The subsequent last four chapters examine critical dynamics relating to the trade facilitation side of the fostering trade equation, including the ongoing US-China trade issues, US-Africa trade relations, aid-for-trade, corridor development, regional integration and digitization policy issues that fosters the adoption and usefulness of trade facilitation tools, and the deployment of emerging technologies to leverage data for realizing its trade potential.

More specifically, while Chap. 2 of this book provides the big picture on the state of play, implementation challenges and policy recommendations for Africa within the World Trade Organization (WTO) Trade Facilitation Agreement, Chap. 3 focuses on leveraging trade facilitation application tools for overcoming sanitary and phytosanitary (SPS) challenges in the continent.

Chapter 4 presents an empirical-based analysis on how trade facilitation instruments promote bilateral trade in sub-Saharan Africa. The authors examine the bilateral trade challenges being faced in Africa and also recommend evidence-based, workable and analytical trade facilitation tools to overcome these hurdles.

Chapter 5 focuses on trade liberalization as an innovative tool for facilitating trade in West Africa. The authors explain how trade data can be deployed to analyse trade challenges and serve as the basis for informing trade facilitation policy processes, as well as expand the adoption of trade facilitation instruments amongst trade practitioners.

In Chapter 6, OBOR initiatives are reviewed as effective trade facilitation instruments for connecting Africa's infrastructure, thereby enhancing Africa's trade potential. The chapter presents OBOR's business case and opportunities, as well as the need for Africa to adopt the appropriate OBOR initiatives based on its evidence-based needs, best practices, robust governance structure and clearly measured metrics.

Chapter 7 discusses what Africa stands to benefit from the ongoing US-China trade tensions and Chap. 8 expatiates on the future of US-Africa trade relations and business opportunities in the face of growing policy reforms with a focus on the Proper Africa Initiative.

Chapter 9 takes a different tactic towards fostering West Africa's trade by reviewing the growing role of Aid for Trade in enhancing corridor development, trade expansion and regional integration.

In this last chapter, the authors bring an international perspective to strengthening the role of digitization in fostering Africa's trade and business opportunities in this fourth industrial revolution era. This concluding chapter emphasizes how Africa could leverage on existing digital trade analytic systems, rather than building from scratch, especially in a global space that is characterised by increasingly scarce resources.

Finally, this book does not attempt to provide a comprehensive discussion on fostering Africa's trade relations and business opportunities in this digital age. Rather, it endeavours to present intuitive space that will be required by policymakers and decisionmakers in unlocking Africa's current and future trade potential. It engages and grounds its readers in the issues to be confronted by showing how current trade policymakers and takers are innovatively linking instruments within and across different sectors towards fostering trade and growth.

It is our expectation that readers and the target audience will enjoy this book which is written by African practitioners and academics. It is written in a style that should interest anyone keen to learn about Africa's trade and business potential. The references that support every chapter will expand readers' horizons of understanding and applying workable policy instruments and lessons for fostering Africa's trade.

References

African Development Bank (AfDB) Group (2019) African Economic Outlook 2018, African Development Bank Group. Available online at https://www.afdb.org/fileadmin/uploads/afdb/Documents/Publications/African_Economic_Outlook_2018_-_EN.pdf

Odularu G, Alege P (ed) (2019) Trade facilitation capacity needs: policy directions for national and regional development in West Africa. Palgrave Macmillan, USA. Available online at https://www.palgrave.com/br/book/9783030059453

Africa and the WTO Trade Facilitation Agreement: State of Play, Implementation Challenges, and Policy Recommendations in the Digital Era

Mena Hassan

Introduction

Over the last decade, international trade flows and digital trade have dramatically increased. World merchandise and commercial service trade have increased by about 7% per year on average, reaching a peak of US$ 19.6 trillion and US$ 5.6 trillion, respectively, in 2018.[1] Global e-commerce totaled US$ 27.7 trillion in 2016, up from US$ 19.3 trillion in 2012. Many factors may have contributed to this remarkable expansion of trade and information technology, but the fact that this coincided with a significant reduction in trade barriers is inescapable. Although tariffs are still the most widely used policy instrument to restrict trade, their relative importance has been declining over the years. Conversely, the use of non-tariff measures (NTMs) has increased both in terms of the number of products covered and the number of countries utilizing them (WTO 2012).

Trade facilitation measures aim to lower transaction costs. Transaction costs fall under the category of NTMs and *behind the border* measures. These include domestic information costs, legal and regulatory costs, customs clearance procedures, and administrative red tape. In recent years, the case for undertaking such reforms and the trade benefits accruing from those reforms have been generally recognized by economists, trade negotiators, and experts from international organizations alike.

[1] World Trade Statistical Review, 2019. https://www.wto.org/english/res_e/statis_e/wts2019_e/wts2019_e.pdf.

[2] WTO Web site, available online at http://www.wto.org/english/tratop_e/tradfa_e/tradfa_intro_e.htm.

Disclaimer: This chapter represents the opinion of the author, and is the product of professional experience and research. It is not meant to represent the position or opinions of the WTO.

M. Hassan (✉)
Trade Policy Analyst, World Trade Organization (WTO), Geneva, Switzerland
e-mail: mena.hassan@gmail.com

G. O. A. Odularu et al. (eds.), *Fostering Trade in Africa*,
Advances in African Economic, Social and Political Development,
https://doi.org/10.1007/978-3-030-36632-2_2

Trade facilitation (TF) in the WTO is defined as "the simplification, harmonization, automation of the procedures applied to international trade, particularly the requirements and formalities related to importation and exportation as well as to international transit of merchandises."[2]

The African continent is remarkably rich with its natural resources, diverse cultures and is the second most-populous continent, behind Asia with the youngest average population among all continents. Agriculture remains the key driver of most economies in Africa but petroleum, minerals, and the services' sector are main contributors to the continent's overall GDP. In addition, African countries are Members of several regional economic groupings as well as the most recent African Continental Free Trade Agreement (AfCFTA), which entered in force in April 2019, in order to boost intra-African trade, enhance Africa's regional and continental integration, and further develop the industrial, manufacturing sector of their economies.

Nevertheless, Africa's share in world merchandise trade remains very low at 2.7% in 2018; and over the past ten years, Africa's share in world exports declined from 3.5% in 2008 to 2.5% in 2018, the lowest regional share.[3] Moreover, the African continent continues to suffer from very high trade costs and doing business is difficult. Cumbersome customs procedures, a myriad of fees and formalities, and a lack of transparency and awareness of trade rules and regulations by traders and officials continue to undermine the predictability of the continent's trade regime. According to the World Bank's Ease of Doing Business (2019a), it takes more days than in any other region to import and export goods in Africa, especially sub-Saharan due to the complex trade procedures and numerous documentation requirements. Similarly, the World Bank's Logistics Performance Index (2019b) shows that Africa is lagging (among other regions) in customs, infrastructure, competence in trade-related logistics and timeliness of exports and imports.

Furthermore, while in general, most of the world's least developed countries (LDCs), which include 34 African countries, are receiving duty-free and quota-free market access for almost all their exports in developed markets, their share in world trade remains a measly 1.02%.[4] In addition, it has been suggested that a country's geography or geographical disadvantage, such as being landlocked, can have a negative impact on a country's trade performance. On average, landlocked developing countries (LLDCs) trade 30% less than their coastal neighbors.[5] With the burgeoning trend of lowering tariff barriers, it is NTMs and *behind the border* barriers that are gaining ground in the trade policy debate.

Originally, African countries at large were staunchly against the trade facilitation agenda. Trade facilitation was first introduced in 1996 during the first WTO Ministerial Conference in Singapore, along with three other "Singapore issues."[6] It was only

---

[3]World Trade Statistical Review, 2019. https://www.wto.org/english/res_e/statis_e/wts2019_e/wts2019_e.pdf.

[4]WTO, International Trade Statistics 2019. https://www.wto.org/english/res_e/statis_e/wts2019_e/wts2019_e.pdf.

[5]Limão and Venables (2001).

[6]Trade and Investment; Trade and Competition, and Transparency in Government Procurement.

eight years later, in the summer of 2004, that WTO Members, including many African countries, had agreed to include trade facilitation in the work program of the Doha Development Agenda (DDA) and keep the other three issues outside its mandate.[7] African countries agreed to start WTO negotiations in the area of trade facilitation in 2004, with the view that any future multilateral commitments in trade facilitation would be tailor-made, based on the acquisition of TACB support, and linked to the implementation capacity of each country.[8] Unlike the contentious issues of agriculture, industrial goods and services liberalization in the WTO, trade facilitation is perceived as a "win-win" issue, i.e., "by reducing transaction costs for my traders, your traders benefit too." It took WTO Members close to ten years of negotiations until the WTO Agreement on Trade Facilitation was formally concluded at the Ninth Ministerial Conference of the WTO in Bali, Indonesia, in December 2013. The TFA entered into force in February 2017 after over two-thirds of the membership ratified the Agreement. On September 1, 2019, 35 African countries out of a total of 41 WTO African countries have ratified the TFA.

As opposed to other WTO Agreements, the TFA is considered unique in its flexibilities granted to developing countries and LDCs. Commitments are tailor-made so countries can choose which trade facilitation measures they can implement as soon as the Agreement enters into force (Category A); those measures they need time to implement (Category B); and those they need both time and the capacity to implement (Category C). Countries will only be required to implement, once they have attained the capacity to do so.

While WTO Members have successfully reached a deal on a multilateral TFA, the next challenge is implementation. Clearly, many African countries will require a great deal of TACB support in order to properly implement the TF measures in the Agreement. However, equally as important, the need for African policymakers is to recognize the political economy aspects of these challenges, which are intertwined in trade facilitation domestic reform. Prioritization of such reform initiatives may be particularly problematic, especially where policymakers fail to appreciate the complexity of conflicting stakeholder interests. This chapter will first outline some of the theoretical underpinnings of trade facilitation; second, it will address some of the key challenges facing African countries' trade potential and the benefits accruing from facilitating their trade. Then, a brief description of the TFA and its novel provisions will be outlined as well as the status of implementation of African countries. Finally, the constraints related to the implementation of trade facilitation measures are addressed and in conclusion, some policy recommendations.

---

[7] After the Decision Adopted by the General Council on 1 August 2004 (the July Package), WTO Members began negotiations in the area of trade facilitation.

[8] As set out in Annex D (Modalities for Negotiations on Trade Facilitation) of the Decision Adopted by the General Council on 1 August 2004, WTO document WT/L/579, 2 August 2004 (the July Package).

Theoretical Relevance

Trade facilitation regulates *behind the border* measures—those which aim to lower transaction costs or trade costs. While there are no existing theoretical foundations regarding trade facilitation per se, the theoretical and empirical literature regarding gains from trade in the context of NTMs, the importance of the "new new trade theory," and the political economy of NTMs will form the theoretical basis for this chapter.[9]

Trade barriers include all costs of getting a good to the final consumer other than the cost of producing the good itself: transportation costs (both freight costs and time costs); policy barriers (tariffs and non-tariff barriers); and internal trade and transaction costs (including domestic information costs, contract enforcement costs, legal and regulatory costs, local distribution, customs clearance procedures, administrative red tape).

Non-tariff Measures and the Gains from Trade

Policy barriers can be broadly divided into tariffs (*ad valorem* and specific) and NTMs. Although tariffs are still the most widely used policy instrument to restrict trade, their relative importance has been declining in recent years. On the contrary, the use of NTMs has been on the rise. The classification and quantification of NTMs are a long-standing area of research.[10] Following Staiger (2012), NTMs can be classified according to whether they are applied at the border, to exports (e.g., export taxes, quotas or bans) and imports (e.g., import quota, import ban), or behind the border. This latter category can be further subdivided according to whether the NTMs are domestic taxes, other charges and/or subsidies, or whether they are regulatory.

NTMs, such as technical barriers to trade (TBT) and sanitary and phytosanitary (SPS) measures, taxes, and subsidies, are often used by governments to achieve legitimate public policy objectives such as the protection of domestic consumers from injury or disease. On the other hand, NTMs may also be used by countries to manipulate the terms of trade or to protect domestic producers from foreign competition. The fact remains that NTMs used to pursue public policy objectives can also be misused for protectionist purposes (WTO 2012).

The theoretical and empirical literature documenting the positive impact of traditional trade liberalization is extensive. Nevertheless, other types of trade costs, such as domestic trade costs or transaction costs, still present significant barriers to trade. Anderson and van Wincoop (2004), for instance, show that for developed countries,

---

[9]For a comprehensive analysis of the theoretical underpinnings of trade facilitation, please refer to the WTO World Trade Report, 2015, Chapter C. "The theory and measurement of trade facilitation". Viewed at https://www.wto.org/english/res_e/booksp_e/wtr15-2c_e.pdf.

[10]A partial listing includes Baldwin (1970), Laird and Yeats (1990), Deardorff and Stern (1997) and Dee and Ferrantino (2005).

the overall impact of trade costs can be decomposed as follows: 21% transportation costs (including both directly measured freight costs and a 9% tax equivalent of the time value of goods in transit); 44% border-related trade barriers; and 55% retail and wholesale distribution costs. Hoekman and Nicita (2008) find that, while traditional trade policies continue to be important in developing countries, as well as for some sectors in high-income countries (agriculture in particular), NTMs and domestic trade costs are also of great importance.

Other empirical research shows that efficient infrastructure and a healthy business environment are positively linked to export performance (Portugal-Perez and Wilson 2012). Another study points out that economies with simpler processes for starting a business have higher international market integration on average (Norbäck et al. 2014).

The "New New" Trade Theory

The trade effects of NTMs can be vast in a world of deepening economic integration and shaped by complex cross-border production in the form of global supply chains. Over recent decades, one of the most important changes in the nature of international trade has been the growing interconnectedness of production processes across many countries on different continents, with each country specializing in particular stages of a good's production. In the trade literature, this phenomenon is referred to as "global supply chains," "global value chains," "international production networks," "vertical specialization," "offshore outsourcing," and "production fragmentation."

According to Paul Krugman, "international trade is no longer about trading *complete goods* amongst countries, as was the case during David Ricardo's time, but about producing and sourcing *highly specialized parts* ...in an attempt to reduce their costs, modern firms have refined their own comparative advantage" (Laniel 2009).

Various economic theories use fundamental economic factors to explain why countries trade and how trade patterns evolve. In David Ricardo's theory, for instance, technological differences between countries determine comparative advantage. In the Heckscher–Ohlin model, relative factor endowments (labor, capital, and natural resources) shape trade patterns. The "new new trade theory" predicts that countries with larger economies—as a result of growth in endowments and incomes—will develop an export edge in those goods consumed in greater quantities in the home market.

The "new new trade theory" identifies trade costs as a key impediment to entry into trade; hence, the importance of trade facilitation measures to lower domestic trade costs or transaction costs in an increasingly complex trading environment, based on the international fragmentation of production and on global value chains (GVCs). Moreover, World Bank research shows that trade flows in intermediate goods of the type traded within GVCs are more sensitive to improvements in trade facilitation than flows of final goods.[11]

In fact, a first attempt to formalize this phenomenon is attributed to Leontief in the 1960s (Leontief and Strout 1963). Yet, it is only recently that trade economists have looked into the theoretical implications of "trade in tasks." The seminal work of Grossman and Rossi-Hansberg (2008) referred to it as "the new paradigm." It is based on the idea that, in order to produce a final good, several tasks must be performed, some of which can be offshored.

On the empirical side, the estimation of GVCs has been a challenge for economists: statistics on international trade flows are collected in gross terms and therefore lead to a multiple-counting of trade in intermediate goods. This distorts the reality of international trade and influences public opinion and policy. For instance, the perceived comparative advantage of a country may be different if its trade is measured by the domestic content in exports rather than gross trade flows (Koopman et al. 2012). Similarly, bilateral global imbalances are influenced by the fact that countries engaged principally in completing tasks downstream have most of the value of the goods and services attributed to them.

The Political Economy of Non-tariff Measures

Non-tariff measures are attractive to governments and their beneficiaries. Political leaders may have other motivations beyond the welfare of citizens. Government officials can claim that the intent of an NTM is not for protectionism, but rather advancing a legitimate public policy objective. Also, since the effects of NTMs are often difficult to discern, the government may be able to assist even large, unpopular firms without incurring the same level of resentment. Private groups that believe they will encounter opposition in obtaining relief from foreign competition through tariffs may be able to obtain protectionism through NTMs (Lukaukas 2013). They may also depend on financial contributions from special interest groups who want a say in trade policy (Grossman and Helpman 1995). In these cases, trade protection is "for sale" to the highest bidder. If policies are being influenced by special interest groups, it should be apparent from the structure of the protection being offered and the nature of the lobbying behind it.

The distributional consequences of NTMs are similar to those of tariffs and quotas, but the identity of the winners and losers, as well as their general welfare effects, are often more difficult to determine. In the case of quantitative restrictions, such as import quotas, Bhagwati (1982), building on the seminal paper by Krueger (1974), first called it directly unproductive "rent-seeking." As import rights or licenses are valuable, private actors will expend considerable time and resources lobbying government officials to obtain them. Bhagwati (1980) pointed out that well-connected

[11]http://pubdocs.worldbank.org/en/124681548175938170/World-Development-Report-2020-Draft-Report.pdf.

actors are likely to prevail in these competitions (what the authors call the "brother-in-law theorem"), deterring other actors from expending resources to seek these rents. Against this background, in the context of trade facilitation, there will be winners and losers. Some specific domestic groups would potentially lose out, while others stand to gain, from implementing an Agreement on Trade Facilitation.

Another aspect of relevance to trade facilitation is the transparency of NTMs. Although there is no agreed definition of what constitutes a transparent NTM, information asymmetry generates uncertainty for the agents with less information. One of the main areas where WTO trade facilitation tries to regulate and promote the transparency of trade and customs-related information. It may be important to distinguish between different economic agents—the private sector and other governments—because each is likely to be concerned with different aspects of information. Governments are likely to want information that allows them to better evaluate whether their trade partners are abiding by international commitments, whereas the private sector is likely to be more concerned with information asymmetry that hampers its ability to take advantage of commercially profitable opportunities (WTO 2012).

Challenges Facing African Countries' Ability to Trade

Before we examine the benefits from undertaking trade facilitation reforms and implementation of the TFA, it is important to highlight the magnitude of the challenges facing African traders and businesses. First, red tape in Africa is insurmountable. Bureaucratic documentation requirements and lack of transparent rules and procedures are higher in African countries as a whole than in anywhere else in the world; the effective rate of protection is very high, at times 10%. The average customs transaction involves 40 paper documents and 200 data elements; with lots of duplication, as well as a myriad of fees and charges imposed by different agencies.

Second, customs delays in sub-Saharan Africa are the world's longest. Based on the World Bank's Doing Business Report for 2019,[12] average rankings for sub-Saharan Africa show great room for improvement in trading across borders (139). Completing border compliance procedures takes an exporter in the region 108 h and US$ 542 on average, compared with a global average of 64 h and US$ 389. In terms of imports, it takes 15 days on average to clear imports from customs in Africa.

Third, trade costs are a bigger challenge for landlocked countries; Africa has 15 landlocked countries, 12 of which are LDCs. These countries face numerous transit-related obstacles, border crossing delays, and high transport costs. On average, LLDCs trade 30% less than their coastal neighbors.[13] Border crossing points are a major source of trade costs, and any seaborne exports or imports of a landlocked

[12]Doing Business measures the time and cost (excluding tariffs) associated with three sets of procedures—documentary compliance, border compliance and domestic transport—within the overall process of exporting or importing a shipment of goods.

[13]Limão and Venables (2001).

country must pass through at least one extra set of border controls. For example, a one-day increase in transit time reduces exports by an average of 7% in sub-Saharan Africa (Freund and Rocha 2010). In the case of the East African Community's (EAC) landlocked countries, transport costs can be as high as 75% of the value of exports. According to Hummels and Schaur (2010), each day spent in transit is equivalent to charging an ad valorem tariff rate of 0.6–2.3%. Poor infrastructure accounted for 40% of predicted transport costs for coastal countries and up to 60% for landlocked countries. Another study found that a one-day delay in transport time for landlocked economies and for time-sensitive agricultural and manufacturing products reduces trade by more than 1% for each day of delay (Djankov et al. 2010).

Fourth, participation in GVCs for African countries is limited. According to a joint publication by the OECD and the WTO (2015), there is a clear association between lower trade costs and increased GVC participation. African countries may not be able to enter specific export markets or participate in global supply chains if there are lengthy delays in trade shipments and trade costs remain high. The Hummels and Schaur (2013) study estimated that a delay of three days can reduce the probability of export by 13%.

Fifth, African countries in general suffer from wider problems related to supply-side capacity constraints with poor quality of TF-related infrastructure such as ports, logistics, and transport systems. The high cost of transport constitutes an important obstacle, not just to development, but also to foreign trade investment flows to Africa. The transportation of goods by road within the region is more expensive relative to other parts of the world; this is likely to influence the regionalization of trade in the continent. Flying from one country to another is costly and railway infrastructure barely links African countries (Nkuepo 2012). Poor communications infrastructure continues to be regarded as another major impediment to trade within Africa (Mupela and Szirmai 2012).

Benefits from TFA Implementation for African Countries

According to the OECD (2014), implementation of the TFA could reduce worldwide trade costs by between 12.5 and 17.5%, with African countries expected to see the biggest average reduction in trade costs. Moreover, according to the WTO (2015), under the "conservative" scenario of partial implementation of the TFA, LDCs stand to increase the number of products exported by destination by 11.8–12.8%, on average. The gains become much larger under the full implementation scenario, with gains of 32.9–35.6%. Other African developing countries also stand to experience big gains, with an estimated increase in the number of products exported by destination ranging from 8.4 to 9.1% ("conservative" partial implementation scenario) to between 18.4 and 20% (full implementation scenario).

Trade facilitation implementation may benefit African countries in many ways. First, implementing the TFA should create significant export diversification gains for African countries as well as increase the opportunity to participate in GVCs as there are big potential opportunities to enhance their competitiveness in production processes and industrial specialization, with a view to attracting specific value-added shares in international trade transactions and boosting intra-African trade and regional integration efforts especially after the entry into force of the AfCFTA in 2019.

Second, implementing the TFA should also attract more foreign direct investment while improving the revenue collection and reducing the incidence of corruption. In this respect, African governments can also benefit directly from trade facilitation reforms by supporting easier ways to enforce tariff and duty payments and by making informal "facilitation payments" to certain customs officers more difficult.

Third, African traders, especially MSMEs can benefit from the availability of information under the transparency-related measures, such as publication of export and import procedures, required forms and documents for export and import, and fees and charges imposed on goods. In addition, traders can also take advantage of having a well-functioning enquiry point in place where they can easily access trade-related information. Moreover, traders who meet specific criteria can benefit from an authorized trader or operator scheme. Finally, improving the efficiency of customs procedures and addressing border bottlenecks are important components of trade facilitation measures by establishing a Single Window. Furthermore, according to the WTO (2015), there is statistical evidence to show that, with trade facilitation reform, micro-, small-, and medium-sized firms are more likely to export and to increase their export shares than large firms. Finally, TF implementation can help small cross-border traders, often women, enter the formal sector, make economic activities more transparent and accountable, promote good governance, generate better quality employment, strengthen information technology capabilities, and generally modernize societies by bringing about benefits related to administrative efficiency.

The WTO Trade Facilitation Agreement

The TFA entered into force on February 22, 2017, after obtaining two-thirds acceptance from its 164 Members.[14] Unlike in previous Uruguay Round Agreements, or even GATT Agreements, the TFA is a Multilateral Agreement that has been designed in a way that provides for the interests of all WTO Members, depending on their level of development. This is largely thanks to the 2004 Annex D of the July Package, which set an unprecedented and unique negotiating mandate. The fact that commitments are tailor-made for each developing country and LDC, coupled with the clear linkage between implementation and capacity, is a key premise for the success of this Agreement. WTO Director-General Roberto Azevêdo stated that: "the Trade Facilitation Agreement broke new ground for developing and least developed countries in the way it will be implemented. For the first time in WTO history, the requirement

[14]Agreement on Trade Facilitation, WTO document WT/L/931, 15 July 2014.

to implement the Agreement was directly linked to the capacity of the country to do so. In addition, the Agreement stated that assistance and support should be provided to help them achieve that capacity."

Section I of the TFA

The TFA is based on GATT Articles V, VIII, and X of 1994. Section I of the TFA comprises 12 Articles, with approximately 36 trade facilitation measures (Table 1). The three GATT Articles represent three different areas that combined, have formed the basis of the TFA. First, GATT Article X prescribes one of the GATT/WTO basic principles, namely transparency. It contains general commitments to assist in ensuring the timely publication of regulations regarding imports, including fees, customs valuation procedures, and other rules. It also provides general obligations for maintaining transparent administrative procedures for review of disputes relating to customs. Second, GATT Article VIII addresses fees and formalities connected with importation and exportation. The fees that fall under the ambit of this article exclude import and export duties, as well as internal taxes within the scope of Article III of the GATT 1994 (i.e., VAT, sales tax, etc.) It therefore applies to a residual category of fees and charges such as license fees, document fees, stamp fees, and inspection fees. Formalities include requirements relating to the documentation required for import and/or export and to the procedures to be followed for customs clearance. Article VIII includes specific legal obligations applicable to fees and charges and to the penalties that may be imposed for minor breaches of customs procedures, as well as hortatory statements recognizing the need to reduce the number and complexity of import- and export-related fees and formalities. Finally, GATT Article V prescribes freedom of transit and provides a basis for creating an environment in which the transit of goods is free from barriers to transport and discrimination between suppliers, firms, and traders from different countries.

As a result, TFA Articles 1–5 are transparency-related measures, which include measures related to publication of trade laws and regulations as well as through the Internet (Article 1); giving the opportunity for stakeholders to comment and consult on trade laws (Article 2); establish an advance ruling system (Article 3); having in place appeal procedures for traders (Article 4); and other measures to enhance transparency and non-discrimination such as detention and test procedures (Article 5).

TFA Articles 6–10 prescribe certain disciplines regarding fees and formalities connected to importation and exportation, as well as penalty disciplines (Article 6). In order to expedite the release and clearance of goods, Article 7 prescribes nine specific customs-related procedures (Articles 7.1–7.9). Other measures are cooperating between agencies at the border (Article 8) and the movement of goods intended for import under customs control (Article 9). Formalities connected with importation, exportation, and transit are covered under Article 10 with nine specific measures

Table 1 WTO Trade Facilitation Agreement (Section I)

Article 1: Publication and availability of information	
Article 1.1	Publication
Article 1.2	Information available through Internet
Article 1.3	Enquiry points
Article 1.4	Notification
Article 2: Opportunity to comment, information before entry into force, and consultations	
Article 2.1	Opportunity to comment and information before entry into force
Article 2.2	Consultations
Article 3: Advance rulings	
Article 4: Procedures for appeal or review	
Article 5: Other measures to enhance impartiality, non-discrimination, and transparency	
Article 5.1	Notifications for enhanced controls or inspections
Article 5.2	Detention
Article 5.3	Test procedures
Article 6: Disciplines on fees and charges imposed on or in connection with importation and exportation and penalties	
Article 6.1	General disciplines on fees and charges imposed on or in connection with importation and exportation
Article 6.2	Specific disciplines on fees and charges for customs processing imposed on or in connection with importation and exportation
Article 6.3	Penalty disciplines
Article 7: Release and clearance of goods	
Article 7.1	Pre-arrival processing
Article 7.2	Electronic payment
Article 7.3	Separation of release from final determination of customs duties, taxes, fees and charges
Article 7.4	Risk management
Article 7.5	Post-clearance audit
Article 7.6	Establishment and publication of average release times
Article 7.7	Trade facilitation measures for authorized operators
Article 7.8	Expedited shipments
Article 7.9	Perishable goods
Article 8: Border agency cooperation	
Article 9: Movement of goods intended for import under customs control	
Article 10: Formalities connected with importation, exportation, and transit	
Article 10.1	Formalities and documentation requirements
Article 10.2	Acceptance of copies
Article 10.3	Use of international standards

(continued)

Table 1 (continued)

Article 1: Publication and availability of information	
Article 10.4	Single Window
Article 10.5	Pre-shipment inspection
Article 10.6	Use of customs brokers
Article 10.7	Common border procedures and uniform documentation requirements
Article 10.8	Rejected goods
Article 10.9	Temporary admission of goods and inward and outward processing
Article 11: Freedom of transit	
Article 12: Customs cooperation	
Article 12.1	Measures promoting compliance and cooperation
Article 12.2	Exchange of information
Article 12.3	Verification
Article 12.4	Request
Article 12.5	Protection and confidentiality
Article 12.6	Provision of information
Article 12.7	Postponement or refusal of a request
Article 12.8	Reciprocity
Article 12.9	Administrative burden
Article 12.10	Limitations
Article 12.11	Unauthorized use or disclosure
Article 12.12	Bilateral and regional Agreements

Source Adapted from the WTO Trade Facilitation Agreement

with a view to minimize the incidence and complexity of such formalities (Articles 10.1–10.9).

TFA Article 11 focuses on freedom of transit in order not to discriminate against goods in transit which is especially important for traders from landlocked countries. Lastly, Article 12 has set out provisions for customs cooperation.[15]

Section II of the TFA

With respect to implementation, developed country Members shall implement the TFA upon its entry into force, while developing country Members and LDCs shall implement the Agreement in accordance with Section II of the TFA. Inspired by the

[15]This chapter is not intended to explain each of the 36 TF measures but rather to describe pertinent measures related to Africa's implementation status of the TFA. For an exhaustive description of the TF measures, please refer to the WTO's Trade Facilitation Agreement Facility website. Viewed at http://www.tfafacility.org/trade-facilitation-agreement-facility.

provisions in Annex D of the July Package, Section II of the TFA sets out the SDT provisions for developing countries and LDCs and most notably are the categories of commitments. Based on Article 14 of the TFA, not only will each developing and LDC member have their individual tailor-made implementation plans, but they will each have three categories of commitments, determined on an individual basis as follows:

(a) Category A commitments contain provisions that a developing country Member or an LDC Member has designated for implementation upon entry into force of the TFA; or in the case of a LDC Member within one year after entry into force of the TFA (Article 15).
(b) Category B commitments contain provisions that a developing country Member or an LDC Member has designated for implementation on a date after a transitional period of time following the entry into force of the TFA (Article 16).
(c) Category C commitments contain provisions that a developing country Member or a LDC Member has designated for implementation on a date after a transitional period of time following the entry into force of the TFA and upon the acquisition of implementation capacity through the provision of assistance and support for capacity building.

Other flexibilities for developing countries and LDCs include an "Early Warning Mechanism" and "Category Shifting" (Section II, Articles 17 and 19). An "Early Warning Mechanism" allows a Member to request an extension for the implementation of either a category B or category C commitment. "Category Shifting" allows a Member to shift a provision from category B to category C. Both types of flexibilities require prior notification to the WTO TF Committee. Moreover, developing countries and LDCs will benefit from different grace periods for the application of the dispute settlement mechanism (Section II, Article 20). The provision of TACB for developing countries and LDCs is set out in Articles 21 and 22 of Section II of the TFA.

It is important to highlight that most of the TF measures are binding, with the term "shall" used in the text of the Agreement. The fact that most of the commitments will not be on a "best endeavor" basis makes it a strong legally binding Agreement. Developed countries are satisfied that, by the end of all the transition periods and the provision of TACB, developing countries and LDCs will have implemented these measures. By the same token, developing countries and LDCs are comforted that, even though most of the TF measures are legally binding, implementation will only take place based on each country's tailor-made implementation plans and the receipt of the necessary TACB.

Section III of the TFA

Institutional arrangements and final provisions of the TFA are prescribed in Section III. The main provision relates to the establishment of a WTO Committee on Trade Facilitation (Article 23.1) and a National Committee on Trade Facilitation (NTFC) (Article 23.2). The NTFC is an obligation for each WTO Member to facilitate both domestic coordination and implementation of the provisions and measures of the TFA. According to the Agreement's final provisions (Article 24), all provisions of the TFA are binding on all WTO Members and that in addition to the exceptions, exemptions and/or waivers under GATT 1994, the WTO's Dispute Settlement Mechanism will be applied for any settlement of disputes under the TFA.

State of Play of TFA Implementation in African Countries

The WTO has 41 African Members: 17 developing[16] and 24 LDCs.[17] It is important to highlight this distinction within the context of the WTO since LDCs benefit from further flexibilities in the implementation of WTO Agreements than in developing countries. This is also the case for TFA implementation. On September 1, 2019, 35 out of 41 African countries (who are WTO Members) have ratified the TFA.[18]

Upon the entry into force of the TFA on February 22, 2017, and according to Section II of the TFA, developing countries were expected to: notify designations of categories A, B, and/or C; provide indicative implementation dates for category B and category C designations; and provide TACB requirements for category C designations. By February 22, 2018, developing countries were expected to: provide definitive dates for category B designations; and provide information on arrangements entered with Donors on TACB for category C designations. By August 22, 2019, developing countries needed to provide definitive implementation dates for category C designations and inform the TF Committee of progress in TACB provision for category C designations.

LDCs have more flexibilities than developing countries. One year after the TFA entered into force, i.e., by February 22, 2018, LDCs were expected to notify designations of categories A, B, and/or C and by February 22, 2019, provide TACB requirements for category C designations and could have notified indicative implementation dates for category B designations. By February 22, 2020, LDCs need to

---

[16]WTO African developing countries are Botswana, Cameroon, Congo, Cote d'Ivoire, Egypt, Gabon, Ghana, Kenya, Kingdom of Eswatini, Mauritius, Morocco, Namibia, Nigeria, Seychelles, South Africa, Tunisia, Zimbabwe.

[17]WTO African LDCs who benefit from the flexibilities prescribed for LDC Members are Angola, Benin, Burkina Faso, Burundi, Central African Republic, Chad, Democratic Republic of the Congo, Djibouti, The Gambia, Lesotho, Liberia, Madagascar, Malawi, Mali, Mauritania, Mozambique, Niger, Rwanda, Senegal, Sierra Leone, Tanzania, Togo, Uganda and Zambia.

[18]The six countries who are yet to ratify are Burundi, the Democratic Republic of the Congo, Liberia, Mauritania, Tanzania, and Tunisia.

provide definitive dates for category B designations and, by February 22, 2021, provide indicative dates for category C designations and information on arrangements entered with donors on TACB for category C designations. Finally, by August 22, 2022, LDCs need to provide definitive dates for category C designations and inform the TF Committee of progress in TACB provision for category C designations.

Reflections on Africa's Implementation Commitments

Overall, and on September 1, 2019, a total of 117 WTO Members have notified their category A commitments; 89 Members have notified their category B commitments; and 78 have notified their category C commitments.[19] Twenty-two African countries notified their categories A, B, and C commitments. In comparison with other developing countries, African countries, as a whole have notified the least in terms of coverage under their category A commitments, which is around 29.3%, whereas the coverage for Latin America and the Caribbean is 59.5% and Asia 53.2%, respectively.[20]

All 41 countries have notified their category A commitments to the WTO, except for Benin. For category A, the measures that a country can implement upon entry into force, the coverage of the commitments varies between African countries. Nine have notified over 50% of their commitments under category A. The countries are Namibia (51.3%), Mauritius and Seychelles (55.9%), Tunisia, (59.7%), Malawi (63%), Mali and Mozambique (65.5%), with the highest commitments undertaken under category A by South Africa (90.3%) and Morocco (91.2%). On the other side of the spectrum, ten African countries have notified less than 10% of their commitments under category A. The countries are Sierra Leone (0.8%), Cameroon and Djibouti (1.7%), Zambia (5.5%), Tanzania (5.9%), Kenya (7.1%), Uganda (8%), Ghana and Madagascar (8.8%), the Kingdom of Eswatini (9.7%) (Table 2).

Except for a few countries, there is no clear correlation between the level and coverage of commitments with the level of development of the country. For example, the coverage of category A commitments for some small African LDCs seems to be high in comparison with larger African developing economies. For example, the Gambia has 48.7% of its TF commitments as measures that can be implemented without any flexibilities related to either time or request for TACB. In the case of Mali and Mozambique, the coverage is even higher at 65.5% of all TF commitments. This is a large contrast with, for example, Cameroon which has only notified 1.7% of its commitments as category A, Kenya (7.1%) or Ghana (8.8%). Likewise, both Egypt and Nigeria's category A commitments are relatively low (20.2%) and (15.1%), respectively, considering their economic importance.

---

[19] WTO TFA Facility. http://www.tfafacility.org/notifications.

[20] WTO TFA Database. https://www.tfadatabase.org/notifications/global-analysis.

Table 2 WTO African Members and TFA implementation

	African member	Ratified Agreement	Notified Cat A	% A	Notified Cat B	% B	Notified Cat C	% C	% Not yet notified
1	Angola	√	A	22.7	B	47.1	C	30.3	0
2	Benin	√	–	–	– –	–	–	–	–
3	Botswana	√	A	28.2	B	67.2	C	4.6	0
4	Burkina Faso	√	A	12.2	–	0	–	0	87.8
5	Burundi	X	A	32.8	–	0	–	0	67.2
6	Cameroon	√	A	1.7	–	0	–	0	98.3
7	Central African Republic	√	A	26.9	–	0	–	0	73.1
8	Chad	√	A	34.5	B	30.3	C	35.3	0
9	Congo	√	A	12.2	–	0	–	0	87.8
10	Cote d'Ivoire	√	A	31.1	–	0	–	0	68.9
11	Democratic Republic of the Congo	X	A	42	–	0	–	0	58
12	Djibouti	√	A	1.7	B	23.5	C	0	74.8
13	Egypt	√	A	20.2	–	0	–	0	79.8
14	Eswatini, Kingdom of	√	A	9.7	B	41.2	C	49.2	0
15	Gabon	√	A	12.6	–	0	–	0	87.4
16	Gambia, The	√	A	48.7	B	38.2	C	13	0
17	Ghana	√	A	8.8	–	0	–	0	91.2
18	Kenya	√	A	7.1	–	0	–	0	92.9

(continued)

Table 2 (continued)

	African member	Ratified Agreement	Notified Cat A	% A	Notified Cat B	% B	Notified Cat C	% C	% Not yet notified
19	Lesotho	√	A	11.8	B	28.2	C	60.1	0
20	Liberia	X	A	35.7	B	31.9	C	32.4	0
21	Madagascar	√	A	8.8	B	2.5	C	88.7	0
22	Malawi	√	A	63	B	10.1	C	26.9	0
23	Mali	√	A	65.5	B	17.2	C	17.2	0
24	Mauritania	X	A	39.9	B	4.6	C	55.5	0
25	Mauritius	√	A	55.9	B	36.6	C	7.6	0
26	Morocco	√	A	91.2	B	0.8	C	8	0
27	Mozambique	√	A	65.5	B	11.3	C	23.1	0
28	Namibia	√	A	51.3	–	0	–	0	48.7
29	Niger	√	A	31.9	B	10.9	C	57.1	0
30	Nigeria	√	A	15.1	B	42.4	C	42.4	0
31	Rwanda	√	A	26.9	B	56.3	C	16.8	0
32	Senegal	√	A	45	–	0	–	0	55
33	Seychelles	√	A	55.9	B	12.2	C	31.9	0
34	Sierra Leone	√	A	0.8	B	19.7	C	79.4	0
35	South Africa	√	A	90.3	B	9.7	–	0	0
36	Tanzania	X	A	5.9	–	0	–	0	94.1
37	Togo	√	A	42.9	B	32.8	C	24.4	0
38	Tunisia	X	A	59.7	–	0	–	0	40.3
39	Uganda	√	A	8	–	0	–	0	92
40	Zambia	√	A	5.5	B	29.4	C	65.1	0
41	Zimbabwe	√	A	34.9	–	0	–	0	65.1

Source Author based on the WTO TFA database, September 1, 2019. Viewed at https://www.tfadatabase.org/

According to the WTO's TFA Database,[21] the top measures with the highest implementation rate for African countries are related to the movement of goods (75%); detention (68.2%); use of customs brokers (61.4%); rejected goods (60.2%); pre-shipment inspection (60.2%); and the temporary admission of goods and inward and outward processing (57.4%). These measures reflect actual TF measures that are already in place as a result of previous trade and customs reform policies. For example, most African countries no longer require the use of pre-shipment inspections in relation to tariff classification and customs valuation as stipulated in Article 10.5 of the TFA. Measures related to the detention of goods (Article 5.2), rejected goods (Article 10.8), and the temporary admission of goods and inward and outward processing (Article 10.9) are stipulated in the customs regulations of most African countries. With regard to the use of customs brokers, while many African countries still use customs brokers, the TFA prescribes that it should not be mandatory (Chart 1).

For those African Members who have notified all three categories of TF commitments, TF measures which require more time and TACB for the implementation for African countries include the Single Window, with an implementation rate of only 4.5%; border agency coordination (7.6%); authorized operators (11.4%); enquiry points (13.6%); risk management (15.3%); advance rulings (15.9%); publication (18.2%); and information available through Internet (18.2%).

First, during the negotiations phase of the TFA, it was common knowledge that the Single Window[22] (Article 10.4) was considered to be one of the most costly and difficult TF measures to implement; therefore, it is not a surprise that its implementation rate is so low among African countries. However, many case studies on the effect of the Single Window on trade have shown that there is a significant increase in time efficiency and a reduction in transaction costs for traders when dealing with the relevant authorities to obtain the relevant clearance and permits for moving cargo across borders. Blockchain and smart contracts could help administer border procedures and national Single Windows in a more efficient, transparent and secure manner and improve the accuracy of trade data (Ganne 2018). This is pertinent for Africa's regional trade integration efforts, and it is therefore crucial that it is implemented sooner rather than later. However, according to category C commitments of most African countries, once the TACB has been received, implementation of a Single Window is expected to range between the years 2020 and 2035.

Second, border agency cooperation (BAC) (Article 8) is an important prerequisite for the proper functioning of a Single Window. African traders have reasonable concerns on the number of border control formalities and their organization. Lengthy border crossing procedures cause delays and congestions and put a strain on the border post facilities, on land border posts, which are often not equipped with sufficient

[21] https://www.tfadatabase.org/implementation/progress-by-measure.

[22] A "Single Window" is a facility that allows traders to lodge standardized information and documents with a single-entry point to fulfill all import, export, and transit-related regulatory requirements. If information is electronic, then individual data elements need only be submitted once.

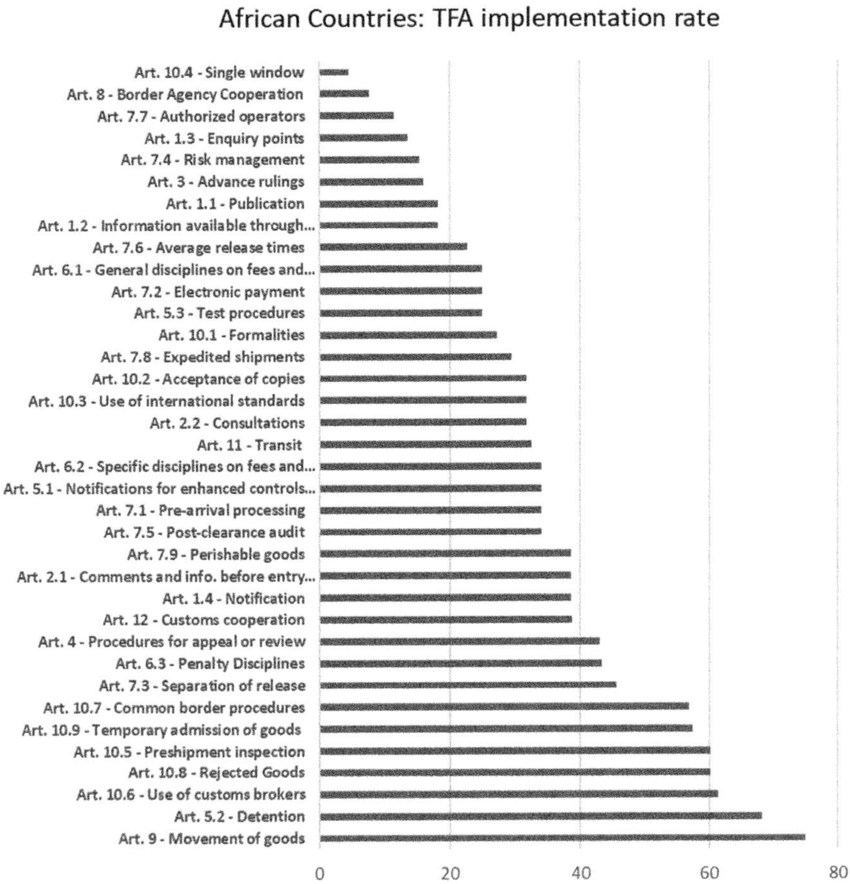

Chart 1 African countries: TFA implementation rate. *Source* Author based on the WTO TFA database, September 1, 2019. Viewed at https://www.tfadatabase.org/

parking lots for trucks and have only one access road. Unpredictable crossing times impact trade and the overall performance of the supply chain, which penalizes perishable goods in particular. According to UNCTAD,[23] coordination and cooperation of border agencies contribute to reducing compliance and enforcement costs and result in efficiency gains and lower operating costs. Benefits for the trading community include, for example, simplification of document preparation (lower compliance costs for the declarant); faster border crossing resulting from harmonization of physical inspections of crossing cargo, vehicles, and drivers and better flow management; reduced pressure on the infrastructure; cost savings in administration and streamlined procedures; improved working conditions for government officials due to the use of

[23]UNCTAD (2011) UNCTAD Trust Fund for Trade Facilitation Negotiations, Border agency coordination, available online at http://unctad.org/en/docs/TN14_BorderAgencyCoordination.pdf.

shared information, common premises, and services; and reduced staff needs owing to task sharing among different agencies, thus liberating skilled human resources for other activities.

Third, under the release and clearance of goods article (Article 7), with the exception of risk management (Article 7.4) than other measures under the same ambit of Article 7 such as pre-arrival processing and post-clearance audit which both have an implementation rate of 34.1%; and separation of release at 45.5%.

Fourth, transparency-related measures and the availability of information are considered as some of the important measures with the most impact on developing country exports, including African countries. Research conducted by the OECD (2012) has found that information availability has a high and robust impact across developing countries' trade volumes. Similarly, research conducted by Hassan (2015)[24] has found that out of the 36 TF measures, transparency-related measures, such as Internet publication (Article 1.2) and setting up enquiry points (Article 1.3) for traders, will have a significant impact on export performance of developing countries, including African countries. Another study conducted by Fontagné et al. (2015) finds that small firm's profit relatively more when trade facilitation improvements relate to information availability, advance ruling and appeal procedures. Large firms profit relatively more when the importing countries' facilitation reforms relate to formalities (documents, automation, and procedures).

The main reasons for this low level of implementation in African countries of Internet publication of trade laws and regulations can be the lack of IT-related infrastructure as well as trained IT professionals for setting up and maintaining the government Web sites for the timely dissemination of trade-related information. Similarly, enquiry points require trained personnel to reply to trade-related requests received by traders. While most WTO Members already have in place enquiry points in the context of the SPS and TBT Agreements, as well as services and intellectual property contact points, this measure goes beyond these requirements to include all-trade-related matters. According to category C commitments of most African countries, upon receipt of capacity-building support, implementation of Internet publication will range from 2019 to 2027 and enquiry points will range from 2020 to 2027.

Fifth, advance ruling (Article 3) is a customs-related procedure, which is a written decision provided by a Member to an applicant prior to the importation of a good, which covers the treatment of the good. The measure goes beyond the traditional advance ruling requests to include not only the good's tariff classification and its origin (already an obligation under the WTO Agreement on Rules of Origin) but also determination of customs value, as well as requirements for exemption from customs duties, etc. As a result, compliance is low, as African countries will either need more time to implement (20.5%) or time and capacity-building support (34.1%).

Sixth, risk management (Article 7.4) techniques are a useful means for simultaneously ensuring enforcement, security, and trade facilitation. By selectively categorizing goods and passengers for verification, a more rapid release and clearance can be achieved. Consignments and persons considered as "low-risk," based on their

---

[24]Hassan (2015).

risk profile, attract minimal attention and intervention from customs and can be processed quickly. Furthermore, it enables customs staff to concentrate their efforts and resources on fewer consignments. Risk assessment may mean significant infrastructural changes within a customs administration. For example, it will require a national and regional intelligence structure providing strategic and operational intelligence, respectively, less officers for physical and documentary examination and more auditors and investigators. Provided customs use automated systems in procedures and management, risk management requires access to an "intelligence" database and procurement of additional computer screens. In addition, the introduction of a new methodology requires additional training of staff involved. It is noteworthy to mention that the effective implementation of a risk management system is a prerequisite to most of the other customs-related measures for the expedited release and clearance of goods. As a result, trade facilitation measures for authorized operators (Article 7.7) also have a low compliance rate of 11.4%, since a proper system of risk management is needed to be able to select authorized operators. Risk management is therefore quite pertinent to implement sooner rather than later. However, according to category C commitments of most African countries, upon receipt of capacity-building support, implementation of risk management will range from 2019 to 2027.

Finally, regarding the kind of TACB that African countries have requested for TFA implementation under category C, human resources and training; and legislative and regulatory framework are the two areas with the most requests, at 43.8 and 41.3%, respectively. Other areas include information and communication technologies (ICT) with a share of 38.3%; infrastructure and equipment at 23.4%; followed by institutional procedures (22%); diagnostic and needs assessment (13.5); and awareness-raising (8.6%) (Chart 2).

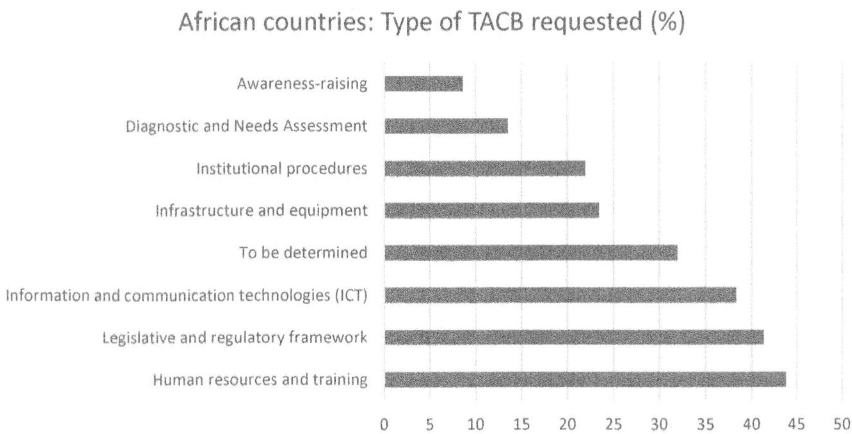

Chart 2 African countries type of TACB requested—Category C. *Source* WTO TFA database. Viewed at https://www.tfadatabase.org/

Implementation Challenges of the TFA in African Countries

While Members reached a breakthrough deal on a multilateral TFA in December 2013, making it the first Multilateral Agreement since the Uruguay Round, the next challenge facing Members is implementation. Clearly, many African countries will require a great deal of TACB support in order to properly implement the TF measures in the TFA. However, equally as important, the need for policymakers is to recognize the political economy aspects of these challenges, which are intertwined in trade facilitation domestic reform. Prioritization of such reform initiatives may be particularly problematic, especially where policymakers fail to appreciate the complexity of conflicting stakeholder interests.

In this context, according to a study conducted by the World Bank on TF implementation in developing countries,[25] "no country is starting from scratch—much donor support has already been provided and more is in the pipeline." However, many of the implementation challenges and barriers identified do not lend themselves to resolution by TACB, regardless of its quality or quantity. Some of the challenges identified are competition between government agencies; poor quality of public/private relationships; a focus on revenue maximization at the expense of all other priorities; restricted dissemination of information by some government bodies; low levels of voluntary compliance; underdeveloped private sector services (banking, information and communications technology (ICT), customs brokers); overly bureaucratic institutional structures; centralization of agencies in capital without proper dissemination mechanisms to other parts of the country; low levels of voluntary compliance; and a lack of sustained political will and/or commitment to change. It is important to highlight that many African countries already have customs modernization reform programs and infrastructural projects in place prior to the TFA.

With respect to the implementation costs of trade facilitation, it is generally agreed that the introduction and implementation of most TF measures would entail some start-up costs for the involved government agencies in the short term. However, once the measures are established, it is unlikely that significant financial burdens would be involved to maintain these measures. In fact, it is recognized that the introduction and implementation of TF would eventually reduce government expenditures through enhanced transaction efficiency and transparency, elimination of duplicative or bureaucratic functions, more economical allocation, and more reasonable and efficient use of administrative resources (Duval 2006). Both the World Bank and the OECD estimate that the likely costs of implementing the WTO TFA are much lower than the costs associated with upgrading transport infrastructure and are expected to be in the US$ 5–20 million range, depending on initial conditions (McLinden 2011; OECD 2012).

Trade facilitation, by its nature, requires cooperation and coordination for it to succeed. There are numerous stakeholders in TF, at the national, regional, and international level, and from both the public and private sector. The main stakeholders are

---

[25] World Bank (2006).

implementing agencies (customs, quarantine, standards board, port authority, and airport authority); policymaking agencies (Ministry of Trade, Foreign Affairs, Customs, Finance); private sector (importers and exporters, carriers, cargo forwarders, and cargo owners, Chamber of Commerce, customs brokers, shippers association, pre-shipment inspection (PSI) companies); border-control agencies (Ministry of Agriculture and Animals controls requests for SPS reasons; Ministry of Food and Drugs controls requests for human health reasons; Ministry of Environment controls requests for human health and wildlife conservation); Attorney General or Legal Department of Cabinet (legal matters, e.g., appeals); Ministry of Transport (physical control of goods flow); and the Central Bank (foreign currency controls).

Some of the problems identified as the main barriers for cooperation/coordination include restricted dissemination of information by some government bodies and lack of awareness; competition between government bodies; unclear/overlapping responsibilities of institutions; overly bureaucratic institutional structures; centralization of agencies/institutions in the capital without proper dissemination mechanisms for other parts of the country; and lack of political will/resistance to change/corruption, e.g., an abuse of discretionary power on the part of the implementing agencies.

Against this background, most TF measures will require cooperation and coordination for proper implementation. However, there are a few measures for which implementation is impossible without cooperation and coordination. These measures are national and cross-border agency coordination; establishment of a national and/or regional Single Window; a national and/or regional enquiry point; a NTFC; and the opportunity to comment on newly amended rules and consultations. For a successful trade facilitation implementation process to materialize, major coordination and cooperation initiatives will be a prerequisite on the national and regional levels.

(i) National Level

At the national level, the main actors in trade facilitation are officials from the trade ministry, the customs authority, border agencies, and traders (Fig. 1).

Customs and Trade Authorities

At the national level, the relationship between the customs authority and the trade ministry, specifically in the context of the WTO trade facilitation agenda, may be challenging. While WTO issues mainly fall under the ambit of the trade ministry, some trade ministries believe that TF is a customs-related issue, that customs authorities are the ones equipped with the technical know-how. This idea is also reinforced by many customs administrations themselves, who feel that TF is purely a customs-related area. Yet TF within the WTO framework encompasses different aspects, not only customs-specific, but also trade policy and transparency-related provisions.

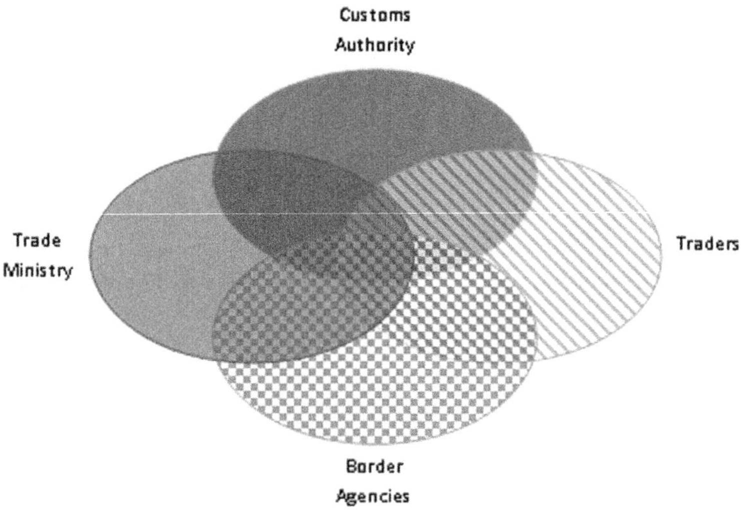

Fig. 1 Main national trade facilitation actors *Source* Author

Coordination and cooperation between the trade ministry and customs and also all other government agencies will be vital during the implementation phase of the TFA. The establishment of the NTFC (Article 23.2) is an obligation for all WTO Members. There may be some rivalry as to whether the trade ministry or customs will be in charge of this committee. As previously mentioned, since the TFA is WTO-related and given that customs is one of the many stakeholder agencies, albeit a very crucial one, the trade ministry should be the one to formalize a national committee on TF and to act as the focal point in the implementation of a TFA.

The challenges for a proper functioning of the NTFC may be twofold: First, there is already a plethora of different trade-related national committees that government administrations must grapple with, whether WTO-related or bilateral/regional. A new committee on trade facilitation will be an additional burden to the overwhelmingly high number of committees and relatively limited number of government officials. Second, many government officials from small African countries believe that such committees are beyond their job functions and that participation in them should come with financial rewards. This aspect may have future consequences for the proper functioning of the NTFC.

Customs and Border Agencies

In addition to the interplay between customs and trade, there are the other regulatory agencies, including those at the border, without which goods could not be released. These agencies include quarantine and veterinary services, agriculture and health ministries, port and airport authorities. In most cases, customs are far more advanced in its TF reform implementation than these other agencies. This is largely due to three reasons: first, customs are the forefront authority of revenue collection, making it a "rich" government body; and, second, customs authorities have been receiving a myriad of TACB and donor funding over the years through, for example, the WCO and the World Bank. When establishing the average release and clearance of goods by using the WCO's average time and release study (TRS), most of the studies show that goods are cleared quickly by customs but are delayed by other border-related agencies. These delays can be due to for example different laboratory tests of the same shipment or a missing veterinary certification.

Traders have reasonable concerns over the number of border-control formalities and their organization. Lengthy border–crossing procedures cause delays and congestions and put a strain on the border–post facilities, in particular, on land border posts, which are often not equipped with sufficient parking lots for trucks and have only one access road. Unpredictable crossing times impact trade and the overall performance of the supply chain, which penalizes perishable goods in particular.

Another problem is the distance between the border and capital. While policy may be guided by top-down international recommendations/Agreements, their implications at the operational level may not be fully understood. Similarly, operational frustrations experienced at the border may not necessarily be effectively communicated back to the capital (Grainger 2012: 137).

Likewise, the TF measure to establish a Single Window is a case in point. The main premise of the Single Window is that, first, one single entity is set up where traders can lodge all of their documentation at once; and, second, this single entity would then coordinate with the other border agencies for the release and clearance of goods. While, in most cases, a national Single Window is established within the custom's authority, many experts believe that a separate standalone entity should be created for the functioning of the Single Window to give it more autonomy. For example, one of the best functioning electronic Single Windows is Singapore's TradeNet. TradeNet is a separate public–private entity that is not under the ambit of just one government agency.[26] One of the key challenges for the functioning of TradeNet was not in its establishment per se, but rather to promote coordination and participation of various border agencies.

In order to reap any benefits from putting in place TF measures related to the release and clearance of goods, such as pre-arrival clearance, separating release from clearance, and/or expedited shipments, customs and all of the other border-related agencies must be able to coordinate and cooperate with each other. Border agency cooperation, as a TF measure, calls for the coordination of activities and requirements of all border agencies by ensuring that a country's authorities and agencies involved at the border and other import and export controls cooperate and coordinate their procedures in order to facilitate trade.

---

[26]For information on Singapore's TradeNet Single Window, refer online at: http://www.customs.gov.sg/leftNav/trad/TradeNet/An+Overview+of+TradeNet.htm.

Government Bodies and the Business Community

Trade facilitation is essentially a public (government)/private (traders) partnership where both parties can reap significant benefits. The active participation and commitment of the business community in the development of TF initiatives are paramount to their success. Further, the business community can be a major source of funding for implementing TF initiatives as in the case of Singapore and Mauritius, for example (Butterly 2003: 48).

In addition to the complexities of coordination among government bodies, coordination with the private sector is also a prerequisite for a successful TF implementation agenda. As the main group to benefit from TF reform, the private sector needs to be represented in the NTFC and be on board during the implementation process of the TF measures. Some TF measures are particularly important for consultations with traders, such as providing them with the opportunities and a reasonable time period to comment on the proposed introduction or amendment of trade-related and/or customs laws and regulations. In addition, regular consultations between border agencies and traders or other stakeholders within the country are also a TF requirement (Article 2.2).

(ii) Regional Level

While the interplay between the different actors at the national level may be challenging, the dynamics taking place cross-border or at the regional level can be more daunting. Many of the TF measures require coordination and cooperation with non-domestic actors. These measures include, *inter alia*, the creation of cross-border posts, customs cooperation, and transit-related issues.

Cross-Border Posts

In order to facilitate trade, many TF measures go beyond borders. Customs procedures at border crossings are called for but on a "best endeavor" basis (Article 8.2). This cooperation and coordination may include the alignment of procedures and formalities, such as working days and hours; the development and sharing of common facilities; the provision of joint controls; and the establishment of one-stop border post-control.

The establishment of a one-stop border post-control can be a big challenge for African countries, not only in terms of the high level of cooperation and coordination required, but also because the classic case of "winners and losers" is at play. Instead of having two border posts, one for each country, there will only be one post serving both countries. Obviously, enforcement officers on both sides of the border will lose their jobs or may be transferred to capital. Efforts to establish one-stop border posts have been frustrating in spite of the demonstrable benefits that they bring. One example in Africa is the Chirundu border post between Zambia and Zimbabwe [Box 1]. Implementation is normally supported by a bilateral Agreement between bordering countries. There is a further need to ensure that national legislation allows extra-territorial exercising of powers by officials to enable them to perform their functions in a foreign country. Common procedures have to be developed and agreed upon for managing the "Common Control Zone," clearance processes, traffic flows, and other operational issues at the border post. Donors, in particular, have expressed frustration at the lack of progress in removing barriers to trade in this area, despite their increased levels of investment. Weighed alongside the benefits of trade facilitation reform is an increasing realization among stakeholders of its complexities, which are not limited to questions of technical knowledge or capacity building but extend also to issues of governance and the political economy of particular reform processes (TradeMark Southern Africa 2010).

Box 1 Chirundu One-Stop Border Post

The Chirundu one-stop border post between Zambia and Zimbabwe was officially inaugurated in December 2009. It was hailed as the first African one-stop border post. The establishment of the one-stop border post has provided some significant improvements. For example, passengers and commercial traffic stop only once to complete border formalities for both countries, and waiting times for commercial traffic have been reduced from about four to five days to a maximum of two days and, in some cases, just a few hours. However, the process of transforming the border crossing and complete integration of all procedures is a long-term project that has shown that trade facilitation is not only about bricks-and-mortar investment but requires commitment, negotiations, and harmonization of procedures and policies. The initial results also indicate that it is very important to start the discussion on the reform of rules and procedures early in the process.

Source TradeMark Southern Africa (2010)

Transit

Transit-related measures form the third pillar of the TF measures under the TFA, after the transparency and fees and formalities-related measures. Transit issues are a subset of the overall TF agenda, as such issues matter most to landlocked countries and their neighbors. The basic premise of transit-related measures is neither to discriminate against goods in transit nor to hinder traffic in transit by imposing unnecessary delays or restrictions or by imposing unreasonable charges (Article 11).

Landlocked countries are believed to suffer from particularly high trade costs, as emphasized by Arvis et al. (2007). Border crossing points are a major location of trade costs, and any seaborne exports or imports of a landlocked country must pass through at least one extra set of border controls. For example, for the EAC landlocked countries, transport costs can be as high as 75% of the value of exports.[27]

For the smooth operation and flow of goods in transit, cooperation and coordination with the authorities of landlocked countries and the authorities of their neighbors will be an important prerequisite. In Africa where the continent has 15 landlocked countries, the main concern raised by transiting countries pertains to the damage caused by the trucks that transit through them, harming the domestic infrastructure. In addition, the different checks that take place for traffic in transit often lead to an opportunity for local officials to demand unofficial favors rather than undergo serious tests of roadworthiness (Sourdin and Pomfret 2012: 128).

For example, in the EAC, traders from the landlocked countries of Burundi, Rwanda, and Uganda use the transit transport corridors through either Tanzania (Central Corridor) or Kenya (Northern Corridor) to reach the ports of Darussalam and Mombasa, respectively. As a result, both Tanzania and Kenya have raised concerns about the negative impact that this transiting traffic has on their road infrastructures.

Regional Organizations

There have been many initiatives to implement TF measures on the regional level, where cooperation and coordination are paramount. In Africa, there are several initiatives for TF reform taking place regionally. In East Africa, the customs formalities in the five member states of the EAC should be based on standardized and harmonized documentation and procedures. However, in practice, customs procedures and documentation requirements have not been fully harmonized, in part because of the difficulties of coordination among the five African countries. For example, under the EAC framework, an initiative is underway to establish a fully integrated and interconnected customs system for the whole region, yet EAC countries continue to use different customs systems: ASYCUDA World is in place in Rwanda, Uganda, and Burundi. In 2017, Kenya replaced its Simba system with the Integrated Customs Management System (iCMS). Tanzania also replaced ASYCUDA++ with the Tanzania Customs Integrated System (TANCIS). The use of these different systems is potentially a source of delays in cargo clearance, mainly for transit goods (WTO 2019).

[27]Information on East African Corridors, available online at http://www.eastafricancorridors.org/cds.

Policy Recommendations

Given the benefits from trade facilitation reforms for African countries, the successful implementation of a WTO Agreement on Trade Facilitation would eventually encounter considerable challenges as discussed in previous sections. Lack of good governance, vested interests of domestic groups, and lack of cooperation and coordination among the relevant TF stakeholders are some of the key issues reinforcing the challenges for implementation. Some policy recommendations for African countries to maximize the benefits from facilitating trade and implementation of the TFA as follows:

1. *African ownership is paramount*: African countries need to embrace the TFA as part of a pro-trade development agenda which tackles trade costs through simplifying customs procedures, increasing transparency and improving regulatory frameworks. In order to promote good governance and attenuate resistance to change, a TF reform agenda needs to be placed in an economy-wide setting within a framework of sound domestic economic management and good governance. Each African country and its region need to establish a strategic agenda for TF development that has broad support from both the government and the business community and is based on an overall international TF agenda. This will require the restructuring and strengthening of various institutions to focus on TF; receive appropriate backing and support from senior management; and strengthen and recruit additional staff. Each county needs to identify a lead agency to act as the focal point for the TF reform agenda and help achieve ownership of reforms. The trade ministry can play this role as it will lead the NTFC, based on the assessment made earlier, and will have direct links with the Geneva trade negotiators (delegates), regional and international organizations, and donors (Fig. 2).
2. *Setup a NTFC*: While this is required under the TFA (Article 23.2), this committee will be indispensable for the proper coordination and implementation of the TFA's numerous TF measures. Committee membership needs to be inclusive. There are numerous stakeholders in TF and from both the public and private sector. The main prerequisites for a well-functioning NTFC are a clear mandate with agreed leadership, participation, and governance model; as well as administrative and legislative provisions to ensure internal coordination and cooperation among the different agencies, including those at the border. In addition, the NTFC will need to sensitize key stakeholders on trade facilitation matters; consult widely prior to adoption of policies; and develop a strategic vision which is translated into a comprehensive implementation plan.
3. *Engage the business community in the process*: As the main beneficiary, an engaged private sector is a crucial factor in TF reform and must drive the agenda, as well as play an active role in the NTFC. A strong public–private partnership will help accelerate TFA implementation. More attention should be given to the public–private exchange, consultation, and coordination. Such interface should take place before the regulatory reform initiation and throughout its implementation

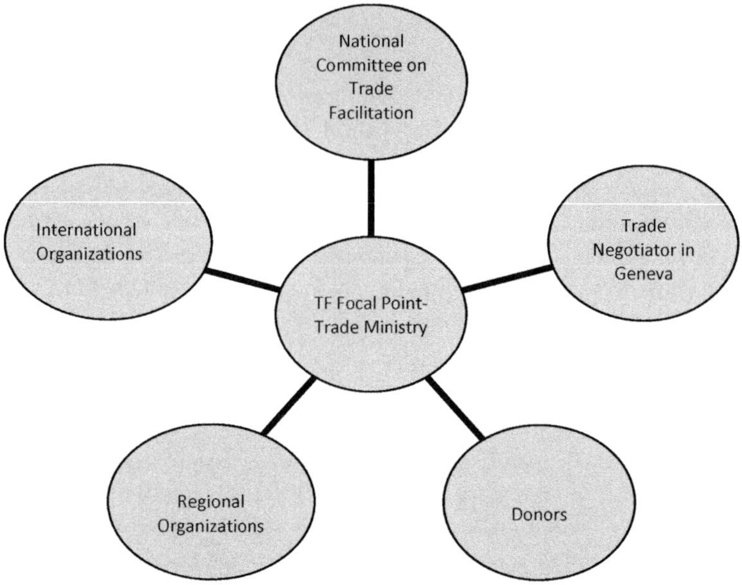

Fig. 2 Trade facilitation coordination network. *Source* Author

process. Private sector partnership should involve all-trade-related functions having an interest in cross-border business transactions for goods and services. Such private interest groups should comprise traders (exporters and importers), producers, transporters, shippers, brokers, bankers, and insurers. These professions and services should be represented through associations, chambers, federations, syndicates, as well as other civil society representations.

4. *Donor support needs to be carefully targeted*: Donor commitments directed to simplifying and modernizing border rules and procedures have expanded in recent years, with the largest beneficiary being Africa. African countries must coordinate such funding based on an agreed comprehensive implementation plan and not on "piecemeal cherry-picking" of individual TF measures. Moreover, TF projects should be centrally managed in order to avoid duplication and overlapping of implementation.
5. *Sequence implementation*: An important factor in TF is the sequencing of implementation. The implementation process needs to be managed holistically as many measures are interdependent. For example, a country needs to establish a proper risk management system at customs before setting up expedited procedures for the release and clearance of goods; and border agencies should coordinate among each other prior to establishing a Single Window.
6. *Acknowledge that in any kind of trade reform, there are winners and losers*: The losers from TF implementation and reform will require assistance to target those specifically affected. In the case of the domestic groups with vested interests, for example, pre-shipment inspection companies, customs brokers and ministries of

finance affected by loss of revenue or loss of jobs, will require support that is time-bound, with a clear exit strategy, and incentives to adjust and innovate; aimed at redeploying displaced workers; compatible with general safety net arrangements that are transparent and accountable.

7. *Count on the numerous regional and international organizations whose mandate is to help in the implementation phase of the TFA*: In addition to the WTO and its Trade Facilitation Agreement Facility (TFAF), several intergovernmental organizations are directly involved in work related to trade facilitation. They develop and administer relevant international conventions and Agreements; conduct TF-related research; provide TACB to developing countries and LDCs; and provide a forum for the discussion of TF matters. Some of these include the World Customs Organization (WCO), the World Bank, the Organization for Economic Cooperation and Development (OECD), the United Nations Committee on Trade and Development (UNCTAD), the United Nations Economic Commission for Europe (UNECE), the International Trade Center (ITC), and more recently the World Economic Forum (WEF) with the Global Alliance for Trade Facilitation. In Africa, the United Nations Economic Commission for Africa (UNECA) and the African Development Bank (AfDB), as well as a number of regional African organizations, have been assisting African countries in this area.
8. *Finally, Coordinate…Coordinate…Coordinate*: Trade facilitation by its very nature requires cooperation and coordination for it to succeed. This is crucial on three main levels: national, regional, and international. On the national level, some of the possible challenges are lack of coordination and cooperation between customs and trade ministries, customs and border agencies, and government bodies and traders. At the regional level, coordination challenges may arise related to cross-border posts, transit systems, customs authorities among regional blocs, and regional organizations. At the international level, coordination between donors and beneficiaries; and countries and international organizations will be paramount.

Conclusion

Trade facilitation as a new issue in the WTO has come a long way over the course of its 20-year adventure. From its introduction in 1996 with the three other "Singapore issues," to the launching of its negotiations in 2004, to reaching consensus on a new Multilateral Agreement on Trade Facilitation almost ten years later, in 2013.

From the outset, the case for the positive direct relationship between trade facilitation reforms and economic development has been brought forward due to numerous researchers, academics, and international organizations working in this area. Trade facilitation reforms aim to lower transaction costs for traders and increase their trade flows. As a result, African countries in general became convinced that trade facilitation in the WTO brings a "good news" agenda to their economic reform initiatives and has been perceived a "win-win" issue.

Since the entry into force of the TFA in 2017, 35 African Members out of a total of 41 ratified the Agreement (as at 1 September 2019). In addition, all but one African country has not notified its category A commitments to the WTO and 22 African Members have notified all the three designations for categories A, B, and C. While this highlights African countries' positive engagement in the ratification and implementation phase of the TFA, it is important to also recognize that most trade facilitation measures that are not yet implemented (category B and category C designations) are the ones with the greatest economic impact for African countries. TF measures such as publication through the internet, enquiry points, advance rulings, risk management, border agency coordination, and Single Window are some of those which can improve transparency and the availability of information to traders but also help expedite the release and clearance of their goods. While a few African countries are able to implement some of these measures soon, most countries have requested TACB and more time, ranging from 2020 to 2027.

With a full implementation of the TFA, African countries can better reap the potential opportunities to enhance their economic diversification efforts; integrate into GVCs; and develop digital trade and e-commerce in order to boost regional and continental economic integration. Moreover, given the many benefits from trade facilitation reforms, the need for African policymakers to recognize the political economy aspects of the implementation challenges, which are intertwined in trade facilitation domestic reform, ise paramount. One can conclude that there is no "one size fits all" solution to implementation of trade facilitation measures. In fact, a range of possible approaches to the implementation, both in terms of resources and in pace, may be adopted by individual African countries depending upon their specific circumstances and the relative priorities they accord to specific areas within their trade and customs reforms and modernization programs.

References

Anderson JE, van Wincoop E (2004) Trade costs. J Econ Lit 42:691–751

Arvis J-F, Raballand G, Marteau J-F (2007) The cost of being landlocked: logistics costs and supply chain reliability. World Bank Policy Research

Baldwin RE (1970) Nontariff distortions of international trade. Brookings Institution Washington

Bhagwati JN (1980) Revenue seeking: a generalization of the theory of tariffs. J Polit Econ 88:1069–1087

Bhagwati JN (1982) Directly unproductive, profit-seeking (DUP) activities. J Polit Econ 90:988

Butterly T (2003) Trade facilitation in a global trade environment. In: Trade facilitation: the challenges of growth and development. United Nations, New York and Geneva

Deardorff AV, Stern RM (1997) Measurement of nontariff barriers A1.159 WP 395. Available at SSRN: https://ssrn.com/abstract=54045 or https://doi.org/10.2139/ssrn.54045

Dee P, Ferrantino M (2005) Quantitative methods for assessing the effects of non-tariff measures and trade facilitation. APEC Secretariat and World Scientific, Singapore

Djankov S, Freund C, Pham CS (2010) Trading on time. Rev Econ Stat 92(1):166–173
Duval Y (2006) Cost and benefits of implementing trade facilitation measures under negotiations at the WTO: an exploratory survey. Asia-Pacific Research and Training Network on Trade Working Paper Series, No. 3 (January)
Fontagné L, Fouré J, Beverelli C, Keck A (2015) Medium-run impacts of a multilateral Trade Facilitation Agreement. WTO Working Paper, Geneva
Freund C, Rocha N (2010) What constrains Africa's exports? Policy Research Working Paper No. 5184. World Bank, Washington, DC
Ganne E (2018) Can Blockchain revolutionize international trade? World Trade Organization, Geneva
Grainger A (2012) Trade facilitation. In: Heydon K, Woolcock S (eds) The Ashgate research companion to international trade policy. Ashgate, UK, pp 127–142
Grossman GM, Elhanan H (1995) Trade wars and trade talks. J Polit Econ 103(4):675–708
Grossman GM, Rossi-Hansberg E (2008) Trading tasks: a simple theory of offshoring. Am Econ Rev 98(5):1978–1997
Hassan M (2015) A WTO agreement on trade facilitation: can it really facilitate trade? PhD thesis, University of St. Gallen. Viewed at http://verdi.unisg.ch/www/edis.nsf/SysLkpByIdentifier/4279/$FILE/dis4279.pdf
Hoekman B, Nicita A (2008) Trade policy, trade costs, and developing country trade. World Bank Policy Research Paper 4797, The World Bank, Washington, DC
Hummels DL, Schaur G (2010) Hedging price volatility using fast transport. J Int Econ 82(1):15–25
Hummels DL, Schaur G (2013) Time as a trade barrier. Am Econ Rev 103(2): 2935
Koopman R, Wang Z, Wei S-J (2012) Estimating domestic content in exports when processing trade is pervasive. J Dev Econ Elsevier 99(1):178–189
Krueger A (1974) The political economy of the rent seeking society. Am Econ Rev 64:291–303
Laird S, Yeats A (1990) Policy issues involving nontariff trade barriers. In: Quantitative methods for trade-barrier analysis. Palgrave Macmillan, London
Laniel DJ (2009) Trade in intermediary goods and industrial development. The Broker: Connecting World of Knowledge, October 7
Leontief W, Strout A (1963) Multi-regional input-output analysis. In: Barna T (ed) Structural interdependence and economic development. St Martins Press, London, pp 243–259
Limão N, Venables AJ (2001) Infrastructure, geographical disadvantage, transport costs and trade. World Bank Econ Rev 15:451–479
Lukaukas A (2013) The political economy of protectionism. In: Laukaukas A, Stern R, Zanini G (eds) Handbook of trade policy for development. Oxford University Press, UK
McLinden G (2011) World Bank gap assessment study. In: Symposium on practical experience of implementing trade facilitation reforms, including their costs and benefits, Geneva. Available online at http://www.wto.org/english/tratop_e/tradfa_e/case_studies_e/wb_pres_e.ppt
Mupela E, Szirmai A (2012) Communication costs and trade in Sub-Saharan Africa. UNU MERIT Working Paper Series No. 2012-060
Nkuepo HJ (2012) Reducing non-tariff barriers to trade in Africa. Bridges Afr Rev 1(3):260–278
Norbäck J-P, Persson L, Douhan R (2014) Entrepreneurship policy and globalization. J Dev Econ Elsevier 110(C):22–38
OECD (2012) The costs and challenges of trade facilitation measures. OECD, Paris
OECD (2014) OECD trade facilitation indicators: calculating the potential impact of the WTO Trade Facilitation Agreement on trade costs. OECD, Paris
Portugal-Perez A, Wilson JS (2012) Export performance and trade facilitation reform: hard and soft infrastructure. World Dev Elsevier 40(7):1295–1307
Sourdin P, Pomfret R (2012) Trade facilitation: defining, measuring, explaining and reducing the cost of international trade. Edward Elgar Publishing, UK and USA
Staiger RW (2012) Non-tariff measures and the WTO. Geneva, World Trade Organization, Working Paper ERSD 2012-01

TradeMark Southern Africa (2010) Chirundu one stop border post: progress report and lessons learned, November

World Bank (2006) Needs, priorities and costs associated with technical assistance and capacity building for implementation of a WTO Trade Facilitation Agreement: a comparative study based on six developing countries. International Trade Department Working Paper, November, The World Bank, Washington, DC

World Bank (2019a) Doing business 2019: going beyond efficiency. World Bank, Washington, DC

World Bank (2019b) Logistics performance index. World Bank, Washington, DC

WTO (2012) World trade report 2012: trade and public policies: a closer look at non-tariff measures in the 21st century. WTO, Geneva

WTO (2015) World trade report 2015: speeding up trade: benefits and challenges of implementing the WTO Trade Facilitation Agreement. WTO, Geneva

WTO (2019) Trade policy review: east African community. WTO document, WT/TPR/S/384, WTO, Geneva

Correlating Nuances of Trade Facilitation and SPS from an Africa Perspective

Tsotetsi Makong

Introduction

The effects of non-tariff measures (NTBs) on export growth have been well documented and the most challenging of these measures include sanitary and phytosanitary (SPS) measures. According to IFPRI, Sub-Saharan Africa imposes least NTBs, these being below 100 marks, relative to the rest of the world of which some countries impose as many as close to 2000 SPS measures.[1] Of a number of categories of non-tariff measures (NTMs), SPS measures are the main culprit that negatively affects export growth in Africa. In this context, a 10% increase in the number of products affected by SPS measures is said to reduce trade by about 3%.[2] This supports a finding by Didier et al., namely that SPS measures penalize less developed countries more strongly than other countries.[3] It is therefore not surprising that the significant impact of non-tariff barriers (NTBs) on trade and their growth over time present significant challenges to policy makers and more importantly the exporters. On one hand, key to addressing these challenges is finding solutions to minimize the adverse effects of SPS measures at intergovernmental level, particularly where SPS

[1]Figure 5.9 on frequency of NTBs on agricultural products (2012–2015 IFPRI (2018) African Agriculture Trade Monitor http://ebrary.ifpri.org/utils/getfile/collection/p15738coll2/id/132819/filename/133030.pdf at 102.

[2]IFPRI (2018) African Agriculture Trade Monitor http://ebrary.ifpri.org/utils/getfile/collection/p15738coll2/id/132819/filename/133030.pdf at 102, Fig. 5.10 on Effects of NTBs on export growth in Africa 2013.

[3]Disdier, A.-C., L. Fontagne, and M. Mimouni. 2008. "The Impact of Regulations on Agricultural Trade: Evidence from SPS and TBT Agreements." American Journal of Agricultural Economics 90 (2): 336–350.

T. Makong (✉)
Trade Policy Training Centre in Africa—(TRAPCA), Trapca House, ESAMI Road, Njiro Hill, 3030 Arusha, Tanzania
e-mail: makongt@gmail.com; makongt@yahoo.com; tsotetsi.makong@trapca.org

G. O. A. Odularu et al. (eds.), *Fostering Trade in Africa*,
Advances in African Economic, Social and Political Development,
https://doi.org/10.1007/978-3-030-36632-2_3

measures manifest themselves as non-tariff barriers (NTBs). On the other hand, the paradox of choice arises whereby the corollary to minimizing these effects must be reconciled with public concerns that justify the introduction or maintenance of SPS measures.

Given relatively high trade responsiveness to NTBs relative to tariffs, SPS measures that manifest themselves as NTBs inevitably undercut expected benefits from trade in agriculture in Africa.[4] From an export orientation, third markets of interest to African countries are reportedly in the lead with respect to SPS measures imposed on the imports of agricultural products. The illogicality regarding the SPS measures is that despite having a greater impact on trade than any other measures, their requirements are politically and environmentally acceptable because they relate to health, safety, and hygiene.[5] This, however, does not mean there are no tools that can be employed to minimize adverse effects arising from SPS measures, in a manner that fosters beneficial trade in agricultural products, in particular with respect to African countries. Consequently, the relationship between SPS measures and other measures, and in this context, with trade facilitation cannot be overemphasized.

The nexus between trade facilitation (TF) and SPS measures is as important as the expected benefits from trade in agriculture among African countries as well as their trade with third countries. Some trade facilitation measures have an important synergetic relationship with SPS measures in a manner that their confluence may result in enhanced trade in agriculture products. This is an important issue in the context of Africa's bid to increase intra-Africa trade of which currently, the share of intra-Africa trade grew from 8% for agricultural products to 20% between 1998 and 2013. During the same time, the value of agricultural trade grew from $2.2 billion to $12.8 billion during the same period.[6]

Objective

In view of the foregoing, the objective of this paper is to explore the interface of SPS and trade facilitation measures from an African perspective. In the first instance, it provides an in-depth exploration of the links between trade facilitation and SPS measures and reviews Pro-SPS TF measures in the context of WTO's Trade Facilitation Agreement (TFA) and the AfCFTA. In the second and third instances, it considers specific issues relevant to trade facilitation and SPS in regional trade agreements,

[4] IFPRI (2018) African Agriculture Trade Monitor http://ebrary.ifpri.org/utils/getfile/collection/p15738coll2/id/132819/filename/133030.pdf at 101.

[5] IFPRI (2018) African Agriculture Trade Monitor http://ebrary.ifpri.org/utils/getfile/collection/p15738coll2/id/132819/filename/133030.pdf at 102.

[6] IFPRI (2018) African Agriculture Trade Monitor http://ebrary.ifpri.org/utils/getfile/collection/p15738coll2/id/132819/filename/133030.pdf at 28–29.

focusing on the AfCFTA and ongoing implementation issues from selected country-specific case studies, respectively. Last but not least, it provides conclusions and recommendations.

Links Between Trade Facilitation and SPS Measures

The links between trade facilitation and SPS measures are undeniable particularly following the pronounced recognition of this fact in the lead up to and subsequent to the adoption of WTO TFA. This section discusses various ways in which SPS and trade facilitation measures are linked to each other. Therefore, the discussion analyzes the convergence of SPS and TF measures. It recognizes and considers the inseparability of TF and SPS measures, particularly in respect of value addition of TF measures under both WTO's TFA and AU's AfCFTA Annexes covering TF.

In a nutshell, TF measures seek to reduce and/or eliminate trade-related transaction costs. On the contrary, SPS measures may have the legitimate effect of increasing trade-related transaction costs, necessitated by a need to protect human, animal, and plant health. Transaction costs can manifest directly in the form of fees for applications, certificates, or inspections as well as costs for preparation and submission of documents. Indirectly, further costs may manifest in a form of delays in handling, uncertainty about procedures, contradictory requirements, or difficulties to access information. Given that fundamental rationale for SPS measures is justified, the key is to ensure that transactions costs arising therefrom are not more onerous than necessary.

In the context of the WTO's TFA, Article 24 (6) recognizes the uncontestable rationale of the SPS measures by noting that nothing in TFA shall be construed as diminishing the rights and obligations of Members under SPS Agreement. This implies that there are areas in which TFA goes beyond SPS Agreement. It is in these areas that rights of Members to enforce their rights arising from the SPS Agreement are preserved. Nevertheless, there are specific measures under the TFA that are intricately related to the SPS Agreement, hence SPS measures. These measures have a positive relationship with the SPS measures and may enhance trade in agriculture if they are effectively and efficiently implemented. These are considered below in Table 1.

Table 1 highlights TF measures that correspond to or may enhance implementation of their counterpart SPS measures. These measures range from use of international standards, border agency cooperation, fees and charges, release and clearance of goods, rejection of goods, pre-shipment inspection to formalities and documentary requirements. These measures represent the confluence of TF and SPS measures and affirm an inextricable link between trade facilitation and SPS measures. There is therefore no shred of doubt that WTO's TFA measures have the positive effect on SPS Agreement and brings about some value addition. Nonetheless, the challenge is whether at the implementation level, the above Pro-SPS TF measures will be streamlined in SPS-related measures and processes. In this context, implementation

Table 1 Analysis of the links between trade facilitation and SPS measures[a]

SPS Agreement	Measure	Relevant TFA measure
1. Article 3	Use of international standards	Articles 5 and 10.3
2. Article 7, Annex B, G/SPS/7/Rev.3[b],	Committee recommendations Border agencies, traders and other stakeholders consultations, Border agency cooperation	Article 1, Article 2, Article 8
3. Article 8 and Annex C	Control, inspection and approval procedures	Article 6, Article 4.1
4. New obligations	Advanced Ruling—on additional matters (may include SPS)	Article 3(9)
5. Annex C Article 1(i)	Appeals procedures	Article 4
6. New obligation	Impartiality, non-discrimination and transparency, detention of goods, Scientific justification	Article 5
7. Annex C	Fees and charges—this ***may cover fees phyto-sanitary inspections*** which are border measures as per Annex A defining SPS measures	Article 6
8.New obligations[c]	Release and clearance of goods Prior submission of import and ***other required information*** (pre-arrival processing) Electronic payment of duties, taxes, fees and charges (***may include fees for SPS control***) Risk based border controls (7.4): central to SPS Agreement and ISPMs hence, TFA largely borrowed this principle from the SPS Authorized operator schemes 7(7): covers trade in AG hence products subject to SPS regulations Expedited release of goods 7(8): Perishable products 7(9)—adds to SPS Agreement (new obligation)	Article 7(1), (2), (4) and (7–9)

(continued)

Table 1 (continued)

SPS Agreement	Measure	Relevant TFA measure
9. New obligation	Border agency cooperation	Article 8
10. New obligation	Formalities and documentary requirements 10(2): —simplifies border procedures, e.g., acceptance of paper and electronic copies Use of international standards 10(3): already part of SPS Agreement Single window 10(4): Pre-shipment inspection 10(5): outlawed for the purposes of tariff classification or customs valuation but preserved for the purposes of SPS related inspection thus implies acceptance of pre-clearance inspection for SPS-related reasons. Uniform and consistent application of procedures and document requirements 10(7): clarifies SPS Agreement in that without scientific justification procedures cannot be varied in ports of entry. Rejected goods 10(8): SPS Agreement does not deal with how to deal with rejected goods (i.e., rejected on the basis of SPS considerations) hence this provides some additionally	Article 10

[a]The table is based of TFA measures, SPS Agreement measures and documents adopted by the WTO Members some of which are non-binding
[b]World Trade Organization (WTO) (2013) "Recommended procedures for implementing the transparency obligations; G/SPS/7/Rev.3"
[c]New obligations except for risk based border controls

of the TFA implies that domestication of the TFA measures must cut across border agencies that deal with SPS matters.

This notwithstanding, the subsection hereunder considers Pro-SPS TF measures currently notified under the TFA by African countries and juxtaposes them against their implications on SPS measures identified in Table 1.

Assessment of SPS-Related Measures Notified Under TFA

The inextricable relationship between trade facilitation measures lies in the fact that a good number of SPS controls are implemented at the border. There are a number of Pro-TF measures from the TFA that intersect with existing SPS Agreement measures. The net effects of all these measures may be best understood in the context of five pillars of trade facilitation, namely transparency, harmonization, standardization, simplification, and coordination.[7] The confluence of the two agreements enhances these pillars as highlighted below. In this context, Table 2 highlights specific Pro-SPS TF measures so far notified by Sub-Saharan African countries with respect to WTO's Agreement on trade facilitation. It categorizes Pro-SPS TF measures notified under WTO's TFA by Sub-Saharan African Members of the WTO in accordance with specific TF pillars they represent.

From Table 1, it is notable that most Pro-SPS measures notified by Sub-Saharan African countries fall under transparency and simplification pillars of trade facilitation. This implies that if implemented accordingly, the measures as currently notified will importantly enhance transparency and simplify border procedures that relate to SPS-related processes and goods. Regarding coordination and harmonization pillars, they are expected to positively impact on SPS-related processes and goods. In view of Table 1, specific ways in which distinct trade facilitation measures positively relate to SPS measures are considered in the subsection below, which explores confluence of TFA's measures and general measures from the WTO's SPS Agreement.

---

[7]Specific Pro-SPS TF measures covered under the TF pillars are as follows: **Transparency**: This entails description of procedures; advance rulings on border based SPS measures; appeals and review procedures that may apply of border based SPS procedures; inspection and detention of goods and; fees and charges. Transparency measures will be a treasure drove to the business operators who will benefit from knowing border requirements in advance. They will avert unnecessary costs associated with vague requirements; **Harmonization**: This covers risk assessment measures at the border; basing measures on international standards (TFA principle derived from SPS Agreement). This will importantly create a predictable system thus reduce cost of compliance associated with fragmented application of regulations; **Standardization**: review and streamlining of formalities and documentary requirements; consistent and unvaried application of requirements at ports of entry; and review of fees and charges; **Simplification**: Pre-arrival processing; electronic payment acceptability; authorized operators; expedited shipment; perishable goods inspections, storage facilities and ease of release; acceptance of electronic and paper copies of required documents; single window; and SPS targeted pre-shipment inspection. This will inject a sense of predictability to the business operators and further spare them from incurring cost resulting from measures that may be much burdensome than necessary; **Coordination**: border agencies and operators; border agencies; and cross-border coordination with other countries.

Table 2 SSA's measures notified under WTO's agreement on trade facilitation[a]

TF pillars	**Pro-SPS TF measure TFA notification by SSA**
Transparency	Article 5: other measures to enhance impartiality, non-discrimination and transparency
	Article 10.3: use of international standards
	Article 1(1): publication
	Article 1(2): information available through internet
	Article 1(3): enquiry points
	Article 2(1): opportunity to comment & info. Before entry into force
	Article 2(2): consultations
	Article 3: advance rulings
	Article 4: procedures for appeal or review
	Article 5(1): notification for enhanced controls or inspections
	Article 5(2): detention
	Article 5(3): test procedures
	Article 6(1): general disciplines on fees and charges imposed on or in connection with importation and exportation
	Article 6(2): specific disciplines on fees and charges for customs processing imposed on or in connection with importation and exportation
	Article 6(3): penalty disciplines
	Article 7(1): pre-arrival processing
	Article 7(2): electronic payment
Simplification	Article 7(8): expedited shipments
	Article 7(9): perishable goods
	Article 10(2): acceptance of copies
	Article 10(4): single window
	Article 10(5): pre-shipment inspection
	Article 10(8): rejected goods
	Article 10(2): acceptance of copies
Coordination	Article 8: consultations
	Article 8: border agency cooperation
Harmonization	Article 7(4): risk management
	Article 10(3): use of international standards
Standardization	Article 10(7): common border procedures

[a]The measures were drawn from the WTO website
Source WTO Web site on Members TFA notification

The Relationship Between WTO's TFA Measures, AfCFTA TF Measures, and SPS Measures

This section considers the relationship between WTO's and AfCFTA's Pro-SPS TF measures and relevant measures under WTO's SPS Agreement. It is followed by a commentary on the prospects for implementation viability of these Pro-SPS TF measures under WTO's TFA and AfCFTA.

TFA Article 2: Opportunity to Comment, Information Before Entry into Force and Consultations

The SPS Agreement requires publication of a notice at an early stage of proposal to introduce regulation/s so as to bring such to the awareness of WTO Members and this must be done through an agreed format[8] of notification. Coupled with this notification is a requirement for provision of a reasonable time[9] for comments, which may be discussed upon request and taken into account in the process of finalizing the regulation.[10] This is not an absolute requirement by virtue of SPS Agreement's Annex B.6, which addresses circumstances that pertain to urgent health problems. In consideration of this Annex, such problems may compel finalization of regulations without having provided Members with an opportunity to comment, albeit they can still do so after the measure has been introduced. At the publication stage, the regulation and its entry into force, a reasonable interval not less than six months should be granted with the exception of situations deemed urgent.[11] The provisions of the SPS Agreement and the Doha decision are much more elaborate relative to the TFA's Article 2 in as far as opportunity to comment and entry into force are concerned. Notably, these provisions are highly customized to the SPS-related circumstances as opposed to TFA Article 2.1, which is limited to measures of general application. This implies that the transparency measures under the SPS Agreement are much more advanced relative to those under the TFA, at least in as far as an opportunity to comment and entry into force of regulations are concerned. However, value addition brought by TFA resides in Article 2(2), which requires Members to provide for regular consultations between their border agencies and traders or other stakeholders located within its territory. The implementation of this Article is, however, discretional. It is notable that AfCFTA's Annex 4 does not provide for provisions on the opportunity to comment.

---

[8]The format can be found on the following link: http://www.wto.org/english/tratop_e/sps_e/transparency_toolkit_e.htm.

[9]See document G/SPS/7/Rev.4, paragraph 2.8, which defines reasonable time as a minimum of sixty calendar days.

[10]SPS Agreement Annex B.5.

[11]The Doha Decision on Implementation-Related Issues and Concerns, WT/MIN(01)/17, paragraph 3.2.

TFA Article 3: Advance Rulings

TFA Article 3.1 sets out important obligations for the WTO Members, namely to issue advanced rulings in reasonable, time-bound manner. If a Member declines to issue one, it must promptly notify the applicant in writing and most importantly setting out the facts and basis for such denial.[12] Read in the context of paragraph 9(a), the scope of facts and basis for denial will be limited to two distinct technical areas, namely good's tariff classification and origin of the good. Consequently, the scope of application of denials is extremely limited and seeks to ensure that advance rulings are transparent and non-arbitrary. Bearing this in mind, Article 3(9)(b)(iv) encourages Members to open up the overall scope of application by issuing advance rulings to additional matters for which they consider appropriate. Given that the SPS Agreement does not provide for issuance of advance rulings, this provision is SPS Agreement plus albeit it is expressed in discretionary language. However, the AfCFTA provides much certainty regarding the validity period of the advance rulings wherein it sets a period of 6 months.[13]

TFA Article 4: Procedures for Appeal or Review

TFA Article 4.1 obliges Members to provide a right to a person to whom customs issues an administrative decision to administrative and/or judicial appeal of such decisions. The scope of the Article under paragraph 6 extends to other non-customs boarder agencies, albeit on best endeavor basis. It therefore means border entities handling SPS measures in this context are covered. This notwithstanding, SPS Annex C paragraph 1(i) extensively obliges Members to adopt a complaints review procedure with respect to the operation of control, inspection, and approval procedures, and to further take remedial action regarding justified complaints. In this area, TFA does not add much to the SPS Agreement except for some modicum of specificity such as in Article 4(2), which recognizes the concept of exhaustion of review processes and procedures. However, elaborations in Annex C can benefit the TFA.

AfCFTA generally maintains TFA standard and improves it by refraining from opening a possibility for the review to be subject to hierarchical reviews whereby administrative appeal or review must be initiated prior to a judicial appeal or review. It is, therefore, less cumbersome and TFA plus.

[12]There are two limited circumstances under which the denials may be made, namely: is already pending in the applicant's case before any governmental agency, appellate tribunal, or court; or has already been decided by any appellate tribunal or court.

[13]AFCFTA, Annex 4 Article 6.6.

TFA Article 5: Other Measures to Enhance Impartiality, Non-discrimination and Transparency

TFA Article 5 covers a number of measures such as controls of imports where violations are detected as well as import-rapid alert systems; inspections; detention of goods; and test procedures. The overarching aim of the provision is to enhance impartiality, non-discrimination, and transparency. Paragraph 1 of the Article introduces measures for enhanced controls, which are not covered by the SPS Agreement. Similarly, paragraph 2 on detention obliges Members to inform the carrier or importer about detention of imported goods for inspection while paragraph 3 on test procedures deals with opportunity for second tests. This is particularly in cases where a sample taken upon the arrival of goods for importation shows an adverse finding. The SPS Agreement does not cover these issues thus rendering these TFA measures providing value to the SPS Agreement since they equally apply on SPS related cases. With respect to inspection, this is covered in sub-paragraph 1 which requires notification with respect to the systems of issuing notifications or guidance.

While the AfCFTA Article 10 on import or export inspections and fees does not provide for notification obligations, it takes obligations on inspection further by obliging Members to charge inspection fees that are proportional to the service rendered. The inspection notification obligations under the Agreement arise only where they concern non-compliant consignment. Where such a scenario arises, AfCFTA State Parties are obliged to notify both the importer and the competent authority of the exporting State Party. This provision further enhances notification provisions that relate to goods subject to SPS measures.

TFA Article 6: Disciplines on Fees and Charges Imposed on or in Connection with Importation and Exportation and Penalties

Article 6 of the TFA is on fees and charges other than import and export duties and certain internal taxes. In this context, the SPS Agreement's Annex C, paragraph 1(f) regulates a category of fees and charges referred to by TFA Article 6. These are fees levied for control, inspection, and approval procedures. Annex C1 (f) must be interpreted in the context of SPS Agreement's Article 8 which provides that control, inspection, and approval procedures must not be inconsistent with the provision of the SPS Agreement. This is important to note because the scope of coverage of TFA Article 6 seems to encompass SPS control, inspection, and approval procedures-related fees and charges. Consequently, to the extent of a potential conflict, the SPS Agreement will prevail. This is key taking into account Article 24(6) which when interpreted in this context provides that nothing in TFA "... shall be construed as diminishing the rights and obligations of Members under the ... the Agreement on the Application of Sanitary and Phyto-sanitary Measures." Nevertheless, to the extent that it is inferred from practice that measures under TFA may positively enhance SPS Agreement transparency measures, a cross-fertilization of best practices can be considered at the regional level.

An outright additionally of the TFA Article 6 to the SPS regulatory framework is that it enhances transparency by virtue of obliging Members to periodically review fees and charges thereby going beyond Annex C and Article of SPS Agreement, which do not require such a review. Similarly, AfCFTA Article 21 on Fees, Charges, and Penalties pursues the same objective.

TFA Article 7: Release and Clearance of Goods

Article 7 is one of the most extensive TFA provisions setting out procedures pertaining to release and clearance of goods for import, export, and transit measures that Members must maintain or establish. These include pre-arrival processing, expediting the release and clearance of goods, electronic payment, risk management, post-clearance audit, average release times, expedited shipments, perishable goods, etc. Article 7 TFA provides much more specific requirements in these areas. Consequently, it enhances the scope of coverage of the SPS Agreement by virtue of applicability of these measures on SPS issues. Of the above-listed procedures, commitment on expedited shipments is qualified in Article 7 by a subordinate clause, which preserves the right of Members to examine, detain, seize, or confiscate or deal with in any manner not otherwise inconsistent with the Member's rights and obligations.[14] By the same token, a specific preservation of Members rights and obligations under SPS agreement is provided for under TFA Article 24.6 stating that, nothing in the TFA diminishes Member's rights and obligations under the SPS Agreement.

TFA Article 8: Border Agency Cooperation

Article 8(1) obliges Members to ensure that border authorities and agencies in charge of importation, exportation, and transit of goods border controls and procedures cooperate with each other and coordinate their activities with a view to facilitating trade. This Article is inward looking in respect coordination and cooperation of individual WTO Member's agencies and authorities. This applies to border authorities and agencies involved in SPS matters thus the provision brings in trade facilitative measures as new addition to the SPS Agreement. Last but not least, Article 8(2) provides for an avenue for Members mutual cooperation for the purposes of trade facilitative border procedures which among others include joint controls, one-stop border post control, etc. While the provision is couched in best endeavor language, there is no doubt that it is a positive obligation that may enhance trade facilitation aspects of

[14]TFA Article 7.3.6 and TFA Article 7.8.3.

SPS measures between and among WTO Members. AfCFTA Article 25 on customs cooperation adopts the similar approach as TFA Article 8.

TFA Article 9: Movement of Goods Intended for Import Under Customs Control

Article 9 obliges Members allow goods intended for import to be moved under customs control from the point of entry to another customs office. This amounts to a new obligation albeit qualified by preservation of Members right to ensure that all regulatory requirements are met. This is because movement of goods in a territory of a Member may amount to SPS-related risks, such as spread of diseases and pests. What is key though is a fact that Article 9 represents new provision that gives member states to apply a necessity test system when it comes to allowing movement of goods intended for import in their territory.

TFA Article 10: Formalities Connected with Importation, Exportation, and Transit

The thrust of Article 10 is minimization of the incidence and complexity of import, export, and transit formalities and associated simplification of documentary requirements. A host of measures covered by the article include perishable goods, acceptance of paper and electronic copies, use of international standards, establishment of single window, pre-shipment inspection, common border procedures and uniform documentation requirements, rejection of goods, etc. Generally, these provisions are additional to the SPS Agreement's provisions. Nevertheless, there are a few issues worth noting. In the case of common border procedures and uniform documentation requirements, exemption from the requirements of the Article applies where this concerns SPS measures. In this regard, Article 10.7.2(e) allows for differentiation of these requirements in line with SPS Agreement. By the same token, the rejection of goods is allowed on account of incompliance with SPS agreement albeit re-consigning or returning of goods to the exporter as well as an entity designated by the importer is allowable. Noting that SPS Agreement makes reference to Codex, OIE, and IPPC international standards, guidelines and recommendations, TFA opens up for a possibility for consideration of additional international standards with respect to import, export, or transit formalities and procedures. In a nutshell, TFA Article 10 minimizes formalities connected with importation, exportation, and transit although this is contingent on consistency of such measures with the SPS Agreement. This is further under the general auspices of TFA Article 24(6), which maintains pre-eminence of Members rights and obligations under the SPS Agreement *vis a vis* any

TFA measures that may undermine the same. It worth noting AfCFTAs Annex 8 covers transit matters in a much extensive manner.

TFA Article 11: Freedom of Transit

This is a novel provision, which in the first instance prohibits maintenance of regulations or formalities where circumstances or objectives giving rise to their adoption no longer exist or where changes in circumstances or objectives can be addressed in a less trade restrictive manner. The reference to application of less trade restrictive standards where there are changes in circumstance and regulations giving rise to maintenance of regulations and formalities introduces a concept of necessity test in determining applicability of measures on transit trade. It further subjects application of regulations or formalities applicable to transit trade with a view to ensuring that they do not constitute disguised restriction of traffic in transit. This part of the provision is clearly positive in respect of overall treatment of agricultural products and may be understood to complement other TFA provisions that have a bearing of SPS issues, such as those on expedited shipment. Therefore, Article 11's elaborate measures applicable to transit procedures will have the effect of facilitating transit of goods, including those that are subject to SPS controls. This is due to Article 11(6) and Article 11(9), which, respectively, limit formalities and documentation requirements and allow advance filing and processing of documental and data.

The AfCFTA has a whole Annex 3 to the Protocol on Trade in Goods devoted to the subject matter of transit. Part of the general provisions create an obligation on State Parties to grant all transit traffic freedom to traverse their territories without restrictions on the means of transport. It further creates a national treatment obligation with respect to treatment of goods, persons and means of transport coming from, or bound to State Parties and rates and tariffs for use of their facilities. It creates also obligations on transit documents, exemption from customs examination and charges, transit procedures, obligations of State Parties, and liabilities of sureties. These provisions provide new measures that are not covered in FTA or SPS Agreement. They are importantly peculiar to African continent given the fact that Africa has a number of countries that are land locked. Moreover, market liberalization under the AfCFTA will inevitably lead to an increased volume of SPS-related goods crossing borders.

TFA Article 12: Customs Cooperation

As its title suggests, Article 12 is about customs cooperation. The thrust of this Article is sharing of information between customs authorities for the purposes of among others, verifying import and exporter declarations. Therefore, this exchange of information covers limited areas, which are specified in Article 12(6) (b–c). While the provision does not provide for any specific SPS measures, Article 12(1) (1.2) opens a window for WTO Members to share information on best practices and to cooperate on technical guidance and support for capacity building for the purposes of administering compliance measures and enhancing their effectiveness. This can be extended to SPS specific measures.

Annex 3 of the Protocol on Trade in Goods of the AfCFTA provides extensive measures on customs cooperation. The scope of cooperation includes improvement of the regulation of trade flows and enforcement of applicable laws; mutual administrative assistance; and simplification and harmonization of customs procedures. In view of the expected deepening of economic integration among African countries, there is no doubt that this provision will improve regulation of trade flows, enforcement of applicable laws and facilitation as well as simplification and harmonization of customs procedures. Article 5 of the Annex commits State Parties to use international standards, practices and practices as a basis for designing and standardizing their trade documents and the information contained in such documents.

The reviewed Articles of the TFA and AfCFTA highlight the fact that both Agreements provide for measures that are intricately related to SPS measures. The confluence of the two measures implies that, at implementation level, trade facilitation has an important role to play in SPS-related processes and products. Both the WTO's TFA and AU's AfCFTA trade facilitation measures, if fully implemented by African countries, will enhance and improve key pillars of trade facilitation, namely transparency, harmonization, simplification, standardization, and coordination. The following subsection discusses identified Pro-SPS TF measures notified under WTO's TFA by Sub-Saharan African Members of the WTO. The notification of the measures is positively linked SPS-related measures wherein the earlier the implementation of the measures the sooner SPS process in the African continent and the SPS-related products will receive a positive treatment.

Trade Facilitation Pillars and Pro-SPS TF Measures Notified WTO's TFA

Sub-Saharan African countries have made their notification across 28 TF measures provided for under the TFA. The measures are notified under three distinct categories.[15] On the whole, measures notified by Sub-Saharan African countries under the WTO's TFA in respect of 5 TF pillars,[16] proportionally compared to each other as follows: A. 26.9%, B 16.7%, and C 27.4%.[17] Out of these measures, an exclusive look at *Pro-SPS measures* highlighted in Table 2 reveals that in the context

[15]WTO TFA Agreement provides for notification modality under which measures that Members are ready to implement immediately are scheduled under category A, those they wish to implement subject to self designated timeframe under Category B and lastly those they can only implement upon receipt of assistance in Category C.

[16]These are namely transparency, harmonization, simplification, standardization and coordination.

[17]WTO TF Facility.

of categories A, B, and C, notifications by Sub-Saharan African countries are proportionally apportioned as follows: Category A: 40.85%, Category B: 26.74%, and Category C: 32.4%.[18] In respect of the representativeness of the Pro-SPS TF measures in the respective 5 TF pillars, Sub-Saharan African countries' notification under WTO's TFA were proportionally notified as follows: transparency—58.76%; simplification—24.88%; coordination—6.91%; harmonization—3.56%; and standardization—3.68%. Table 3 provides an overview of Pro-SPS TF measures notified under the TFA pillar by pillar and category by category.

In view of Table 3, African countries have notified more of transparency and simplification Pro-SPS TF measures relative to other pillars. This should be understood in the context of the TFA, which qualitatively has more of transparency and simplification measures relative the number of measures falling under other TFA pillars.

It is worth noting that according to the WTO, of all measures covered by the TFA the Sub-Saharan African Members of the WTO fell short of notifying 28% of these measures.[19] This means these measures are unaccounted for in their notifications. As a general point, the statistics above cannot alone provide a decisive determination of the qualitative nature of Pro-SPS measures notified by Sub-Saharan African Members of the WTO under TFA.

A review of Pro-SPS measures in the context of trade facilitation pillars provides a much better insight into pillar representativeness of categories A, B, and C notifications of the Sub-Saharan African Members of the WTO under the TFA. This is considered hereunder.

Transparency Pillar Pro-SPS Notifications

Under the transparency pillar, the notification of notified Pro-SPS measures under TFA by Sub-Saharan African Members of the WTO was as follows: A—39.35%; B—25.67%; and C—34.95%. Transparency measures with highest share of category C notifications are as follows: Article 1 (1–3) covering publication, information available through Internet and enquiry points 51.8%; Article 10.3 on the use of international standards 40.02%; Article 3 on advanced rulings 51.7%; Article 5(3) on test procedures 66.66%; Article 7(1) on pre-arrival processing 41% and electronic payment 53.58%. While this publication is not about passing judgment on the quality of these notifications, the longer it takes to implement these measures the more delayed the potential benefits on SPS processes and products will be. Noting that resources will be needed, consideration could, therefore, be given to by AfCFTA State Parties on ways to fast track implementation of these measures under the auspices of the Agreement.

---

[18] Authors computation based on WTO data on percentage share of each measure of each measures by Sub-Sahara African Members of the WTO.

[19] Author's own computation from the WTO TFA Dataset.

Table 3 Proportions of category A, B, and C notifications

TF Pillars	**SSA Pro-SPS TF measure notified under WTO's TFA**
Transparency	Article 5: A 34.4% B. 24.4%, C 12.2% other measures to enhance impartiality, non-discrimination and transparency
	Article 10.3: A 26.8%, B 17.1%, C 29.3% use of international standards
	Article 1(1): A 12.2%, B 26.8%, C 26.8% publication
	Article 1(2): A 12.2%, B 19.5%, C 34.1% information available through internet
	Article 1(3): A 7.3%, B 17.1%, C 41.5% enquiry points
	Article 2(1): A 31.7%, B 26.8%, C 12.2% opportunity to comment & info. Before entry into force
	Article 2(2): A 29.3%, B 26.8%, C 14.6%: consultations
	Article 3: A 12.3%, B 19.5%, C 34.1% advance rulings
	Article 4: A 34.4%, B 24.4%, C 12.2% procedures for appeal or review
	Article 5(1): A 36.6%, B 36.6%, C 24.4% notification for enhanced controls or inspections
	Article 5(2): A 69.9%, B 12.2%, C 9.8% detention
	Article 5(3): A 19.5%, B 4.9%, C 48.8% test procedures
	Article 6(1): A 22%, B 24.4%, C 22% general disciplines on fees and charges imposed on or in connection with importation and exportation
	Article 6(2): A 29.3%, B 22%, C 19.5% specific disciplines on fees and charges for customs processing imposed on or in connection with importation and exportation
	Article 6(3): A 38.7%, B 17.4%, C 14.6% penalty disciplines
	Article 7(1): A 34.1%, B 7.3%, C 29.3% pre-arrival processing
	Article 7(2) electronic payment: A 24.4%, B 7.3%, C 36.6%
Simplification	Article 7(8) expedited shipments: A 26.8%, B 14.6%, C 29.3%
	Article 7(9) perishable goods: A 41.55%, B 17.1%, 17.1%
	Article 10(2) acceptance of copies: A 24.4%, B 28.5%. C 17.1%
	Article 10(4) single window: A 4.9%, B 9.8%, C 51.2%
	Article 10(5) pre-shipment inspection: A 57.3%, B 9.8%, C 14.6%
	Article 10(8) rejected goods: A 54.9%, B 17.1%, C 7.3%
	Article 10(2) acceptance of copies: A 24.4%, B 28.5%. C 17.1%
Coordination	Article 8: consultations A 5.8%, B 12.6%, C 48.4%
	Article 8 border agency cooperation: A 41.1%, B 17.1%, C 17.1%
Harmonization	Article 7(4) risk management: A 16.5%, B 2.4%, C 47%
	Article 10(3) use of international standards: A 26.8%, B 17.1%, C 29.3%
Standardization	Article 10(7) common border procedures: A 53.7%, B 9.8%, C 12.2%

Other Pro-SPS TF measures notified by the African Members of the WTO have high incidence of notifications under categories A and B. These are: Article 2(1–2) on opportunity to comment & info. Before entry into force and consultations; Article 4 on procedures for appeal or review; General Article 5 on other measures to enhance impartiality, non-discrimination and transparency; Article 5(1–2) on notification for enhanced controls or inspections and detention; Article 6(1–3) on general disciplines on fees and charges imposed on or in connection with importation and exportation and on specific disciplines on fees and charges for customs processing imposed on or in connection with importation and exportation as well as penalty disciplines; and Article 7(2) on electronic payments.

Simplification Pillar Pro-SPS Notifications

Under the simplification pillar, Sub-Saharan African Members of the WTO notified Pro-SPS TF measures as follows: A—41.76%; B—30.82%; and C—27.40%. Pro-SPS TF measures that have high incidence of notification under category C of the TFA are as follows: Article 7(8) on expedited shipments at 41.61%; and Article 10(4) on single window at 77.69%. The rest of the Pro-SPS measures are notified under categories A and B. These are Articles 7(9) on perishable goods; 10(2) on acceptance of copies; 10(5) on pre-shipment inspection; and 10(8) on rejected goods. Category C measures will have the effect of delaying realization of Pro-SPS TF benefits hence delayed simplification of relevant procedures.

Coordination Pillar Pro-SPS Notifications

Under the coordination pillar, Sub-Saharan African Members of the WTO notified Pro-SPS TF measures as follows: A—33%; B—20.9%; and C—46.09%. In this context, one Pro-SPS TF measure, namely "consultations" is mostly notified under category C of the TFA at 66.8%. Consultations represent important measures that at their core represent regional integration. Delayed implementation of measures under consultations will inevitably delay potential benefits that may further enhance continental integration under the AfCFTA. Categories A and B notification in this pillar was made with respect to TFA Article 8.

Harmonization Pillar Pro-SPS Notifications

Under the harmonization pillar, Sub-Saharan African Members of the WTO notified Pro-SPS TF measures as follows: A—36.61%; B—23.36%; and C—40.02%. All Pro-SPS TF notifications under this pillar have been scheduled under category C of the TFA, with Article 8 on risk management notifications standing at 71.3% and Article 10 (3) on use of international standards at 40%. Clearly, this implies that harmonization will take much longer to be realized given that implementation category C notified measures is subject to receipt of development partners support. Depending on when each of the AfCFTA State Parties secures support, this may in effect result in heterogeneous implementation of the harmonization measures.

Standardization Pillar Pro-SPS Notifications

Last but not least, under the standardization pillar, Sub-Saharan African Members of the WTO notified Pro-SPS measures thereunder as follows: A—70.93%; B—12.94%; and C—16.11%. This represents a positive inclination toward standardization and highlights the fact that most African countries are already implementing most of these measures.

In view of the above Pro-SPS TF notifications by Sub-Saharan African countries, Table 3 provides detailed measure by measure levels of notifications across categories A, B, and C of the WTO's TFA. The highlighted measures are classified under respective TF pillars.

Issues Relevant to Trade Facilitation and SPS in Regional Trade Agreements, CFTA

The above sections highlight the confluence of the trade facilitation and SPS measures, the extent to which Pro-SPS TF measures have been notified under WTO TFA as well as classification of Pro-SPS trade facilitation measures under the five key trade facilitation pillars. In this context, a number of issues with respect to recently ratified AfCFTA are worth considering as discussed below.

TFA notifications by Sub-Saharan African Members of the WTO are intricately related to Annex 4 of the AfCFTA Protocol on Trade in Goods, on trade facilitation. This notwithstanding, the effectiveness of measures notified is contingent upon the effectiveness and timeliness of their implementation.[20] It is notable that under the WTO TFA Agreement, most Pro-SPS TF measures are couched in best endeavor language. Implementation of the measures may be automatic if measures are notified under category A of the TFA, subject to self-designated timeframes if notified under category B or implementable subject to receipt of implementation support from development partners for measures notified under category C. In light of this

[20] WTO TFA Agreement provides for notification modality under which measures that Members are ready to implement immediately are scheduled under category A, those they wish to implement subject to self designated timeframe under Category B and lastly those they can only implement upon receipt of assistance in Category C.

description of the nature of WTO's TFA category of measures, a number of issues are key to note in the context of the AfCFTA. These are considered hereunder.

The AfCFTA's Protocol on Trade in Goods Annex 4 bears an "*effect and cause*" relationship with WTO's TFA agreement in as far as Pro-SPS TF measures are concerned. In this context, Article 29 of the AfCFTA Protocol on Trade in Goods' Annex 4 titled, "Implementation" provides that, the extent and the timing of implementation of the provisions of the Annex shall be related to the implementation capacities of State Parties, among others, as notified under the WTO Agreement on Trade Facilitation. Simply put, implementation of Annex 4's Pro-SPS TF measures is coterminous with notifications of AfCFTA State Parties as scheduled under categories A, B, and C of the WTO's TFA. Given an overview of the extent of notifications under categories A, B, and C in Table 3, a number of issues are worth considering. These issues arise from the implications of Article 29 in relation to implementation of Pro-SPS TF measures.

Regarding the Pro-SPS TF measures scheduled under category A of the WTO's TFA, these will be implemented immediately. This will bring about immense benefits to the State Parties, in particular with respect to SPS-related processes and goods. However, for those measures scheduled under category B, their implementation shall be subject to self-designated timeframe for their implementation under TFA. These measures will not be binding on the State Parties until such a time that self-designated timeframes expire. There is therefore a possibility of heterogeneous implementation of specific measures which will result from differing self designated timeframes for the implementation of the measures in Sub-Saharan African Members of the WTO notifications. Given that WTO's TFA allows for shifting of measures, there is also a possibility that these measures may be re-notified under category C. In the final analysis, this will delay strengthening of the five TF pillars in the context of the AfCFTA and implementation of Pro-SPS TF measures.

Pro-SPS TF measures scheduled under TFA category C present a special case. Implementation of these measures is dependent of receipt of support from development partners. This implies that where AfCFTA State Parties do not secure such assistance, the implementation of these measures will remain pending. Article 29 as currently drafted does not capture situations where State Parties acquire capacity to implement measures that are scheduled under category C outside of the WTO system. This lacuna may imply that as long as measures are scheduled under category C and no assistance is forth coming implementation of Pro-SPS TF obligations under TFA even in cases where State Parties have the capacity to do so will remain suspended. Nevertheless, in consideration of the concept of shifting of measures provided for in TFA, this may present an opportunity for the State Parties to critically review their WTO notifications with a view to either rescheduling them under category A or B. This will add value to TF-related SPS processes and goods. Moreover, given the importance of measures notified under category C, in particular their SPS dimension, AfCFTA State Parties should own the whole Agreement including through collectively raising of resources for the purposes of implementation of category C measures. Ownership of the Agreement will ensure that AfCFTA becomes truly WTO plus and further the integration of the continent in SPS related processes and traded products.

Seen from a systemic viewpoint, it is also notable that most measures under category C as notified are best endeavor. To add value to the AfCFTA, consideration should be given in the future to assess the importance of these measures in agricultural trade, with a view to making them binding in the FTA context. This will ensure that the positive discriminatory effect of the FTA adds more benefits to the AfCFTA State Parties relative to third parties particularly with respect to the Pro-SPS TF provisions highlighted.

The implementation of AfCFTA Protocol on Trade in Goods' Annex 4 would largely depend on external circumstances in as far as categories B and C Pro-SPS TF measures are concerned. This may have unintended effect of multispeed implementation of Pro-SPS TF measures thus resulting in heterogeneous implementation of measures across the continent. Harmonization of measures and coordination may therefore present implementation challenges.

One further systemic issue is that the Annex does not provide clarity on the position of non-WTO Members State Parties. It is not clear whether for these parties they should implement the whole agreement with no caveats similar to AfCFTA State Parties that are Members of the WTO. The Agreement seems not to provide a notification template for these parties. This presents an opportunity for the AfCFTA State Parties to further clarify the provisions and this can immensely benefit State Parties in the context of Pro-SPS TF measures.

As noted in the statistics provided above, Sub-Saharan African Members of the WTO have not notified all measures covered by the WTO TF Agreement. This is a major systemic concern as it does not come out clear how such measures will be treated under the AfCFTA. It may therefore be useful that State Parties take a full audit of notifications submitted to the WTO with a view to determining those pro-SPS measures that have been omitted and determine their subsequent treatment.

Ongoing Issues in Implementation

This section highlights the country examples on the interface of trade facilitation and agriculture. Trade in agriculture is said to be remarkably low in most African economies compared to the sector's contribution to their GDP.[21] Numerous factors are said to contribute to the low levels of intra-African agricultural trade and trade barriers are part of the challenges.[22] Burdensome import and export procedures characterize the underdeveloped and complex agricultural supply chains in the region.

---

[21] Ahmad Mukhtar (2017) Enhancing Food Security in Africa Through Implementing the Trade Facilitation Agreement https://www.ictsd.org/bridges-news/bridges-africa/news/enhancing-food-security-in-africa-through-implementing-the-trade.

[22] tralac (2018) Intra-Africa agricultural trade—an overview https://www.tralac.org/documents/events/tralac/1845-willemien-viljoen-intra-africa-agricultural-trade-tralac-poster-presentation-2018/file.html.

This exacerbates food insecurity in Africa. Various regions in Africa, in particular, EAC, SADC, and COMESSA have put in place trade facilitation measures to address some of these burdens.

One of the key areas that have emerged in Africa is the development of a simplified trade regime (STR). At the core of STR is trade facilitation that targets unregistered traders. While it is useful to reflect on SPS and trade facilitation measures as discussed in the subsequent sections, the makeup of Africa's market structure involves unregistered traders. Some studies suggest that the value of unregistered trade, also known as informal cross-border trade (ICBT) may exceed that of formal trade.[23] Moreover, informal cross-border trade provides a source of income for approximately 43% of Africa's population.[24] The further importance of female traders is synonymous with unregistered trade. In the SADC region, female traders account for approximately 70%[25] of informal cross-border traders and in west and central Africa, nearly 60%.[26] This highlights the importance of STR in African trade and unregistered trade defines the market structure of many African countries.

In order to facilitate ICBT, the East African Community (EAC) and the Common Market for East and Southern Africa (COMESA) have adopted simplified trade regimes (STRs) for small-scale cross-border traders. These STRs importantly simplify customs documents and certificates of origin. They ensure that products, mostly agricultural, that originate from REC Members whose value does not exceed US$1000 (COMESA) or US$2000 (EAC) per consignment qualify automatically for duty-free entry in the respective markets. Part of the simplification procedures includes issuing of certificates at the border posts that enables remotely located traders to benefit from STR.

Under COMESA, STR has yielded benefits. According to Fundira, due to STR, experienced informal cross-border traders who have been in the business for a long time increased their incomes and, through government support measures, have been able to transform their informal businesses to become formal traders.[27]

In EAC, goods eligible for clearance through the simplified certificate of origin are covered in a list of originating goods commonly traded by small-scale cross-border traders. 370 products include agricultural commodities composing of products such as maize and beans, fish products. The simplified certificate of origin under the STR has allowed traders to clear their consignments quickly, safely, and with less bureaucracy.

The STR mechanism is in a process of being worked on in SADC. Work is underway to develop STR that will be compliant with WTO provisions. Based on a research conducted in 8 SADC countries and data collected from 146 cross-border

---

[23] Ama et al. (2014).

[24] Afrika and Ajumbo (2012).

[25] United Nations Development Fund for Women (2009).

[26] Afrika and Ajumbo (2012).

[27] Tuka Fundira (2018) A Look at the Simplified Trade Regimes in East and Southern Africa http://www.ictsd.org/bridges-news/bridges-africa/news/a-look-at-the-simplified-trade-regimes-in-east-and-southern-africa.

traders, it was established that traders lack formal protection due to the informal nature of their operations. Borrowing from experiences of other regions there is no doubt that STR will importantly improve trade in agricultural products in the African continent, particularly because simplifying of TF regulations would have a big impact.

Conclusions

The relationship between trade facilitation and SPS is as important as achievement of effective regional integration. The above account has shown that specific trade facilitation measures are intricately linked to SPS measures. This implies that it is important to consider trade facilitation from a sectoral perspective, in this case, agriculture. This will ensure that trade facilitation and SPS measures in the context of this paper are based on actual sector realities. It will also ensure that measures are or not introduced devoid of consideration of their actual practical effects.

The account above further situates Pro-TF SPS measures within the context of TF's five main pillars. This showed that most measures are on transparency. It further highlighted the proportions of measures notified across three key categories of WTO's TFA in which measures are scheduled. For measures notified under category B and C, consideration should be made with respect to their implication of eventual implementation of the AfCFTA. The contiguous relationship between TFA and AfCFTA as explored in detail highlights challenges that must be addressed and opportunities these challenges present. Central to these opportunities is ensuring that AfCFTA becomes TFA plus with a view to enhancing SPS processes as well as trade in SPS related products.

The relevance of market structure of most African countries as represented by ICBTs is considered a key piece of the puzzle in trade in agricultural products, which inevitably involves SPS issues. Concrete regional initiatives have been introduced in COMESA and EAC while SADC is still on its maiden efforts to create a formal regime ICBT regime.

References

Afrika J-GK, Ajumbo G (2012) Informal cross-border trade in Africa: implications and policy recommendations. AfDB Afr Econ Brief 3(10):1–13

Ama NO, Mangadi KT, Ama H (2014) Characterization of informal cross-border traders across selected Botswana borders. Int J Manage Mark Res 7(1):85–101

Disdier AC, Fontagne L, Mimouni M (2008) The Impact of regulations on agricultural trade: evidence from SPS and TBT agreements. Am J Agric Econ 90(2):336–350

IFPRI (2018) African agriculture trade monitor. http://ebrary.ifpri.org/utils/getfile/collection/p15738coll2/id/132819/filename/133030.pdf

Mukhtar A (2017) Enhancing food security in Africa through implementing the Trade Facilitation Agreement. https://www.ictsd.org/bridges-news/bridges-africa/news/enhancing-food-security-in-africa-through-implementing-the-trade

tralac (2018) Intra-Africa agricultural trade—an overview. https://www.tralac.org/documents/events/tralac/1845-willemien-viljoen-intra-africa-agricultural-trade-tralac-poster-presentation-2018/file.html

Tuka Fundira (2018) A look at the simplified trade regimes in East and Southern Africa. http://www.ictsd.org/bridges-news/bridges-africa/news/a-look-at-the-simplified-trade-regimes-in-east-and-southern-africa. WTO Sanitary and Phyto-Sanitary Agreement

World Trade Organization (WTO) (n.d.) The Doha decision on implementation-related issues and concerns. WT/MIN(01)/17

WTO (1995) Sanitary and Phyto Sanitary Agreement. https://www.wto.org/english/docs_e/legal_e/15-sps.pdf

WTO (2013) Recommended procedures for implementing the transparency obligations. G/SPS/7/Rev.3. http://www.wto.org/english/tratop_e/sps_e/transparency_toolkit_e.htm

WTO (2014) Trade Facilitation Agreement. https://www.wto.org/english/thewto_e/20y_e/wto_tradefacilitation_e.pdf

United Nations Development Fund for Women (2009) Findings of the baseline findings studies on women in informal cross-border trade in Africa. United Nations Development Fund for Women, Brussels

Does Trade Facilitation Promote Bilateral Trade in Sub-Saharan Africa? Policy and Issues

Festus Ebo Turkson, Robert Mensah Adjei and Alfred Barimah

Introduction

Regional integration has been fundamental to the African continent's principal strategy for economic transformation for an extensive period of time. The formation of Regional Economic Communities (henceforth RECs) and subsequently, signing of Regional Trade Agreements (henceforth RTAs) among members of RECs was perceived to be the solution for a wide array of socioeconomic, developmental and political challenges. These include the promotion of intra-regional trade, policy harmonization and the management or improvement of pooled physical infrastructure. The fundamental challenge, however, has been the means to develop the procedures for trade across national borders, in addition to the establishment and running of proficient border posts and custom procedures accompanied by well-functioning institutions and business.

Trade is extensively recognized as a fundamental component of economic growth. Many regions and countries of the world have used trade as a catalyst toward reducing the poverty levels of their countries or region and as an engine for achieving development. Notwithstanding the fact that the SSA economy is viewed as a comparatively, one with a high degree of openness and recording a robust growth of 5% in 2014, due to strong investment in mining and infrastructure, trade has not been able to serve as a powerful tool for achieving fast and sustainable economic growth

F. E. Turkson (✉)
Department of Economics, School of Social Sciences and College of Humanities, University of Ghana, LG57, Accra, Ghana
e-mail: feturkson@ug.edu.gh; feturkson@yahoo.com; feturkson@post.harvard.edu

R. M. Adjei
Research Department, Bank of Ghana, Accra, Ghana

A. Barimah
Department of Economics, School of Social Sciences and College of Humanities, University of Ghana, Accra, Ghana

G. O. A. Odularu et al. (eds.), *Fostering Trade in Africa*,
Advances in African Economic, Social and Political Development,
https://doi.org/10.1007/978-3-030-36632-2_4

and development for most member countries. Africa's GDP growth was expected to drop to 4.5 in 2015 and subsequently improve meagerly to 5.1% thereon in 2016 after a fairly considerable expansion of 5.2 and 5.0% recorded in 2013 and 2014, respectively. In view of this, African countries stand to be the most aid-dependent due to member countries inability to fully capitalize on the gains from trade.

The WTO defines trade facilitation as "the simplification and harmonization of international trade procedures, covering the activities, practices and formalities involved in collecting, presenting, communicating and processing data required for the movement of goods in global trade." African countries inability to trade much with each other implies that member countries have been incapable of completely harnessing the interactions, in addition to the complementarities of their economies to fully enjoy the benefits arising from greater market integration, such as economies of scale, increased employment opportunities and increased income. Moving goods from the point of production to market overseas often encompasses bureaucratic and complex supply chain, coupled with the risk of a solitary bottleneck posing a threat to the entire trade process. Creating an efficient network to facilitate the connection of markets is therefore crucial for emerging economies, whose industries and labor naturally enjoy less margin of international competitiveness making it difficult for them to cope with high transaction cost.

Trade facilitation has thus become a predominant attribute in unilateral and bilateral trade agreements following the liberalization of trade through lower tariffs and quotas in the past years. Policymakers have shifted attention to other bottlenecks that impede cross-border movement of goods and service notably those related to administrative and logistics to enhance business competitiveness and improve the trade environment.

In addition, the international trade landscape is characterized by global value chains that span national boundaries. A study by (Draper 2013) revealed that intermediate inputs comprised more than fifty percent of products imported by OECD countries and almost three quarters of such imports come from emerging economies such as China and Brazil. The implementation of trade facilitation policies bodes well for emerging markets and developing economies in global value chains, trade in manufactured products and regional integration.

Most African countries have resorted to negotiations with national organizations in an attempt to better integrate into the global trading system and improve trade performance, notably among these negotiations include the World Trade Organization (henceforth WTO) Doha Round and the economic partnership agreement (henceforth EPA) negotiations with the European Union (EU). These negotiations created a sense of optimism within Africa with the anticipation that conclusions arrived at would be welfare enhancing while addressing the concerns and interest of the entire region in international trade. The concept of trade facilitation has therefore received unparalleled attention and it is against this backdrop that discussions on trade facilitation were included in the WTO's negotiating agenda in 2004. An agreement on trade facilitation was finalized in November 2014 to guide policymakers on the reforms and policies to implement to fully benefit from the trade facilitation reforms. The concept of trade facilitations focuses on the operational aspects of international trade contrary to the traditional deliberations on trade tariffs and quotas. Specifically, trade facilitation concentrates on the quality of the trade environment and how policies affect the efficiency of trade operations.

There has been growing interest in identifying factors other than tariffs and quotas that deter the free movement of goods and services within the SSA region and subsequently developing policies that will address these problems. Obviously, increasing tariffs and non-tariff restraints decreases a nation's capacity to wholly export, however, self-imposed restrictions, high transaction and production costs similarly affect a country's trade volume.

This chapter seeks to answer two research questions':

1. Do trade facilitation policies promote bilateral exports?
2. To what extent do trade facilitation measures impact trade flows controlling for zero-valued trade flows?

To answer these questions this study seeks to

1. To estimate the impact of trade facilitation on the bilateral exports between countries in SSA over an 11 year period (2004–2014).
2. To estimate the extent to which trade facilitation impacts on zero-valued trade flows between two countries within a particular year.

The rationale behind this study is to understand and recognize the economic significance of trade facilitation so as to provide a foundation for governments' prioritization of trade facilitation measures and mobilization of technical support and capacity building efforts for developing economies in a more targeted way.

Literature Review

Global trade has evolved primarily in two forms in recent years and this has influenced opportunities as well as challenges facing developing and emerging economies in leveraging for sustainable growth. First of all, trade between developing countries and advanced economies has dwindled following the emergence of south–south trade (trade between developing economies). In addition, the proportion of trade in intermediate goods and services organized along regional and global value chains with multiple cross-border activities has also increased within the global trading system. The change in the global trade landscape highlights the need for policymakers to reassess and re-examine trade policies to capitalize on new developments in the international trade market.

Reforms on trade facilitation are not limited to simplification and standardization of customs and administrative procedures related to global trade but also includes policies to improve the business climate, infrastructure quality and regulations. The scope of literatures on trade facilitation includes *econometric analysis of one area of trade facilitation for a set of countries*, *econometric modeling of multiple areas of trade facilitation* and *multiple countries and case studies of trade facilitation in a single-country setting*.

Empirical research to determine the extent to which trade facilitation impacts bilateral exports has been to address three vital subject matters. This includes the definition and measurement of trade facilitation variables, choice of model backed by economic theory to assess how trade facilitation affects bilateral exports and consequently developing a model to estimate the effect of improved trade facilitation on trade flows. The draft consolidated negotiating text (DCNT) on trade facilitation has provided a basis for some empirical research with the focus on policies likely to impact measures specified under each article of the draft agreement.

Some studies have considered a narrow view on trade facilitation by focusing on analyzing the effect of one specific aspect of trade facilitation on trade flows. An example of such studies includes Hummels in 2006 and 2007, MacKeller et al. (2002), Hummel and Skiba (2004) and Limao and Venables (2001).

Hummels and Lugovskyy (2006) exhibits this by analyzing the cost of freight for both large and small exporters. In his study, he compared transport costs from Cote d'Ivoire and Japan who are equally distant from the east and west coast of the USA, respectively. His results found the cost of shipping from Cote d'Ivoire to be two times more than the cost of shipping from Japan. This he found to be still evident even after controlling for heterogeneity in the structure of commodities being traded. In 2004, Hummels and Skiba found the scale of economies to be relevant in global trade. Their findings showed that expanding trade volumes causes a 12% decrease in costs of shipping.

In 2007, Hummels further examined transport cost along with global trade over time. Three forms by which Hummels categorized the economic significance of transportation expenditures was with respect to

- Transport cost contingent upon the worth of products being transported.
- Cost relative to other acknowledged trade barriers such as tariffs and quotas.
- The extent to which these transport cost changed relative prices.

He employed a regression analysis in order to sort out the contribution of cost shocks, composition and technological changes in modeling the time series with regards to costs associated with transportation. Going forward, he mapped out implications of these trends for the fluctuating nature of global integration and trade.

He was of the view that transport costs were the usual suspects in undermining global trade levels but with little systematic evidence documenting its decline. His work showed that the ad valorem effect of ocean shipping costs had not experienced any significant reduction as compared to the 1950's with technological advances largely boasted by adverse cost shocks. Contrary to findings was air shipping costs that experienced a decline, transmitting into a rapid growth in airborne trade and leading to a significant rise in the speed of international trade.

Geography can as well play an important role in determining overall transport cost and transit cost. Studies show that being geographically landlocked greatly increases the costs of transporting goods. The cost of being a landlocked country has been highlighted via the nexus between trade, geographical location and economic growth in new trade theories, neoclassical and endogenous growth models. MacKellar et al. (2002) highlight the excessive transaction bill for border crossing as a result of dealing with customs and charges. Therefore, being landlocked is associated with unfavorable terms of trade. For landlocked countries that depended on transit countries, they were likely to face higher cost of transactions. Their study also found the cost of shipment for a landlocked country to be double that of other countries and that being landlocked lowered economic growth by 1.5% year on average.

From the above, one can conclude there is an expensive trade cost for most landlocked African countries due to high transportation costs. To better integrate into the global market, the African continent has to therefore rely on its logistics capacity, level of infrastructure, administrative practices and a sound political atmosphere in transit nations.

Limao and Venables (2001) also made evident the importance of infrastructure in determining transport costs. Using the basic gravity model in analyzing SSA's bilateral trade, their study finds the median landlocked country's transportation cost to be about 46% greater than those of a median coastal economy. Lima and Venables also found the distance between two trading countries to account for only 10% of the difference. Their study associated transport cost to road infrastructure with depleted road infrastructure accounting for 40 and 60% of the transport costs of coastal and landlocked countries, respectively.

Some researchers have also studied the impact of improved customs procedures on trade flows. Yang's (2008) study of developing countries that have employed private firms to conduct pre-shipment inspections of imports established that countries who implemented such programs experienced large increases in import duty collections. These programs were found to be most at times cost effective, with improvements in imports duty collections in the first five years of a typical inspection program worth almost three times the program cost. Djankov et al. (2010) employed a difference gravity equation to determine the cost of trade impact on trade. Results showed that a one-day delay at customs was equal to adding 85 km between two trading countries. This then highlights the economic importance of keeping a prudent but comprehensive customs procedures to save time and money.

On the other hand, some studies similar to this paper also take a broader definition of trade facilitation and build other variables such as institutional quality into their frameworks. Portugal-Perez and Wilson (2012) examined the relationship between export performance and trade facilitation. With a sample size of 101 countries between 2004–2007, their study employed an augmented gravity model approach together with a Helpman–Melitz–Rubestein (HMR) framework to combine both "hard" and "soft" infrastructure as trade cost between two trading countries in other to ascertain the extent to which trade facilitation affects the performance of exports. From their finding, there was evidence of a marginal decreasing outcome of transport efficacy and business environment on export in terms of income per capita. However, physical infrastructure and ICT's impact on exports appeared to be progressively significant as a country became wealthier. They made use of an international trade model developed by (Helpman et al. 2008) that included sector heterogeneity which enabled them to incorporate sectors that had a different level of output and observed that only productive sectors found it profitable to export.

The first approach to examine the effect of trade facilitation on trade flows employing the gravity approach was by Wilson, Mann, and Otsuki (WMO 2003). The authors concentrated on four aspects of trade facilitation namely infrastructure of ports, customs setting, regulatory environment and infrastructure of e-business. Modeling four indicators for the Asia Pacific Economic Cooperation (APEC) countries on yearly basis via the World Economic Forum, their study revealed a possible rise in intra-APEC trade flow by $254 billion once its members recording below-average indicators improved their capacity halfway to the average of all members. This half rise was expected to come from enhanced port efficiency. Wilson et al. (2005) further expanded their sample to a larger set of countries. Their findings using simulation based on their gravity model estimate the gains from trading in manufacturing products to increase international trade by $377 billion for "below-average" nations engaged in trade facilitation midway to global average stages.

Ackah et al. (2012) analyzed the impact of improvements in trade logistics, institutions and facilitation on the costs and volume of bilateral trade among sub-Saharan African countries. Using a logistics augmented gravity model their study identified that a percentage increase in score of the aggregate LPI will increase a country's exports by approximately 18% and also an improvement in transport infrastructure increases a country's export by approximately 19% over time. They concluded that improvements in the performance both aggregate and individual components of the LPI, especially customs efficiency and procedures at borders, trade transport-related infrastructure, and the access and affordability of international shipping have a positive impact on bilateral trade as they lowered the costs of trading.

The traditional approach to estimate the gravity model is to take logarithms and estimate its log-linear form. However, this approach can be problematic given log of zero is not defined therefore zero trade flows will be dropped out of the estimation. This paper would therefore analyze the impact of some selected trade facilitation variables of bilateral trade while accounting for zero-valued trade flows. An example of zero-valued trade flow information could be a prohibitive transport costs arising from being landlocked or small economic size and therefore to incorporate such cost into the model these zeros needed no to be dropped else results will be inconsistent and bias.

Methodology, Data and Estimation Technique

Researchers have mostly used the gravity model as an econometric model to determine the volume of bilateral trade between two country pairs and having being empirically justified given its strong fit to the data (Kien 2009). The gravity equation for trade simply states that "the trade flow from country i to country j denoted by X_{ij} is proportional to the product of the two countries' GDPs denoted by GDP_{it} and GDP_{jt} and inversely proportional to their distance d_{ij}."

In its general formulation, the gravity equation can be of the multiplicative form:

$$X_{ij} = GS_i M_j \phi_{ij} \tag{1}$$

where X_{ij} denotes the monetary value of exports from country i to country j, S_i denotes exporter-specific factors that influence an exporter's total supply such as the exporting country's GDP and M_j denotes all importer-specific features such as the importer's GDP that represent the total amount importers are willing to demand. The variable G represents autonomous factors such as the level of world liberalization not dependent on country i or country j and $\emptyset_{ij}$ representing the ease to which the exporting country can get market access in the importing country (that is the inverse costs of bilateral trade).

Current studies have created more support with regards to the theoretical foundation of the gravity equation by demonstrating the need to include crucial variables capable of leading to proper inferences from estimations using the gravity equation.

Notable among these studies has been the work of Anderson and Van Wincoop's (2003), their findings show that for a well-specified gravity model there is the need to control for relative trade cost and not absolute trade cost.

Theoretically, their findings demonstrate that bilateral trade is determined by the tendency of country j to import from country i, dependent on country j's trade cost toward country i relative to its overall "resistance" to imports (weighted average trade costs) and to the average "resistance" facing exporters in country i. The underlying principle for including these "multilateral trade-resistance" (MTR) terms is based on the assumption that all other things being equal, two countries bordered by other large trading economies, will trade less between themselves than if they were surrounded by oceans or by vast stretches of deserts and mountains.

In particular, the authors demonstrate that to set up a world with N number of countries producing commodities differentiated by country of origin a well-defined funded gravity equation is given as:

$$X_{ij} = \frac{Y_i Y_j}{Y^w}\left(\frac{v_{ij}}{\prod_i P_j}\right)^{1-\sigma} \tag{2}$$

$$v_{ij} = \sum_{m=1}^{M}\left(Z_{ij}^m\right)^{m\gamma} \tag{3}$$

where Y represents world gross domestic product, Y_i and Y_j representing the gross domestic product of countries i and j, respectively; v_{ij} (one plus tariff equivalent cost of trade) denotes the cost in country j when importing a product from country i; Z_{ij}^m represents the set of observables to which bilateral trade restrictions are interrelated and impose trade cost; and $\sigma > 1$ is the elasticity of substitution.

Country i and j's outward and inward resistance terms, respectively, are denoted by $\prod_i$ and P_j, respectively. These variables will capture the ease at which an exporter can easily get access to a market of an importing country and resistance terms are expected to be low if a country is far distant from the world market. The remoteness of a country from the world market will also be determined by employing physical factors such as physical distance from large markets including policy dynamics such as high tariff barriers or other trade costs. Studies that estimate the gravity model without controlling for multilateral resistance terms are prone to biased estimated coefficients. A typical gravity equation can be of the form:

$$\ln X_{ij} = \beta_0 + \beta_1 \ln Y_i + \beta_2 \ln Y_j + \beta_3 \ln \upsilon_{ij} + \beta_4 \ln \prod_i + \beta_5 \ln P_j + \varepsilon_{ij} \quad (4)$$

where $\beta_3 = 1 - \sigma$ and φ_{ij} captures variables that generally capture trade costs.

Generally, most studies proxy cost associated with trade to bilateral distance. Nonetheless, other variables are traditionally included examples of which are dummies for landlocked nations, common borders and islands. Researchers most often employ such dummies in gravity models to reflect the hypotheses that cost of transportation rise with distance and therefore landlocked countries and islands face higher cost while neighboring countries incur lower cost.

To capture information costs, dummies for common language, adjacency and other important cultural characteristics will be used.

Tariff barriers are usually incorporated in the form of dummies for the existence of regional trade agreements. Due to issues of data availability, few studies use information on bilateral tariffs.

Trade cost (υ_{ij}) within the gravity model can be expressed as

$$\begin{aligned} \upsilon_{ij} = d_{ij}^{\alpha_1}.\exp\big(&\alpha_2 \text{contig}_{ij} + \alpha_3 \text{comcol}_{ij} + \alpha_4 \text{lang}_{ij} + \alpha_5 \text{col45}_{ij} \\ &+ \alpha_6 \text{landlock}_{ij} + \alpha_7 \text{RTA}_{ij} + \alpha_8 \text{remote}_{ij} \\ &+ \alpha_9 \text{comcur}_{ij} + \alpha_{10} \text{pop}_{it} + \alpha_{11} \text{pop}_{jt}\big) \end{aligned} \quad (5)$$

where d_{ij} denotes distance between the two trading countries and contig_{ij}, lang_{ij}, comcol_{ij}, col45_{ij}, landlock_{ij}, comcur_{ij} and RTA_{ij} are dummy variables equal to 1, when country pairs i and j share a common border and common official language have a common colonizer, when two trading countries had colonial pairs post 1945, when country i or j is landlocked (or both are landlocked), when country pairs share a common currency and when the two trading countries are members of a RTA, respectively.

In an attempt to control for multilateral resistance, some studies employ iterative methods to build estimates of the price raising effects of barriers to multilateral trade (Anderson and Van Wincoop 2003).

Nonetheless, this approach is not regularly used as it needs a nonlinear least square (NLS) program to find an estimate. An alternative and widely employed approach includes the use of a proxy for these indices called "remote" variable and the use of "country fixed effects for importers and exporters" (Rose and Van Wincoop 2001; Baldwin and Taglioni 2006). Using the remote variable in this study will serve as a proxy to control for multilateral resistance terms for importing and exporting nations given as:

$$\text{remote}_{ij} = \sum\nolimits_j \frac{\text{dist}_{ij}}{\text{GDP}_j / \text{GDP}_w} \tag{6}$$

(Head 2003) defines this formula as "a formula that measures a country's average weighted distance from its trading partners, where weights are the partner countries' shares of world GDP denoted by (GDP_w)."

Model for Empirical Estimation

In studying the relationship between trade facilitation and bilateral exports, this paper estimates a logarithm-transformed augmented gravity equation. It estimates the impact of trade facilitation on bilateral exports over a time period (2004–2014).

This study follows that of Kien (2009), who used an augmented gravity model approach to examine the determinants of export flows of countries in the Asian Free Trade Area (AFTA). Portugal-Perez and Wilson (2012) also employed the gravity model approach to determine the relationship between trade facilitation and export performance among developing countries while (Turkson 2011) employed the same technique to assess the impact of logistics quality on bilateral exports.

Transforming Eq. (4) to a logarithm-transformed augmented gravity equation yields the model to be estimated as:

$$\begin{aligned} \ln X_{ijt} = {} & \gamma_0 + \gamma_1 \ln Y_{it} + \gamma_2 \ln Y_{jt} + \gamma_3 \text{pop}_{it} + \gamma_4 \text{pop}_{jt} \\ & + \gamma_5 \ln d_{ijt} + \gamma_6 \text{Int}_{ij} + \gamma_7 \text{contig}_{ijt} + \gamma_8 \text{comcol}_{ijt} + \gamma_9 \text{lang}_{ijt} \\ & + \gamma_{10} \text{col45}_{ijt} + \gamma_{11} \text{landlock}_{ijt} + \gamma_{12} \text{RTA}_{ijt} + \gamma_{13} \text{Inremote}_{ij} \\ & + \gamma_{14} \text{comcur}_{ij} + \varepsilon_{ij} \end{aligned} \tag{7}$$

Including variables that measure trade facilitation (Eq. 5) transforms to:

$$\begin{aligned} \ln X_{ijt} = {} & \gamma_0 + \gamma_1 \ln Y_{it} + \gamma_2 \ln Y_{jt} + \gamma_3 \text{pop}_{it} + \gamma_4 \text{pop}_{jt} \\ & + \gamma_5 \ln d_{ijt} + \gamma_6 t_{ii} + \gamma_7 \text{contig}_{ijt} + \gamma_8 \text{comcol}_{ijt} + \gamma_9 \text{lang}_{ijt} \\ & + \gamma_{10} \text{col45}_{ijt} + \gamma_{11} \text{landlock}_{ijt} + \gamma_{12} \text{RTA}_{ijt} + \gamma_{13} \ln \text{remote}_{ijt} \\ & + \gamma_{14} \text{comcur}_{ijt} + \gamma_{15} \ln x \cos t\text{exp}_{it} + \gamma_{16} \ln m \cos imp_{it} \\ & + \gamma_{17} docimp_{it} + \gamma_{18} doc\text{exp}_{it} + \gamma_{19} \ln \text{int ernetusers}_{it} + \gamma_{20} \ln \text{IITPS}_{it} \\ & + \gamma_{21} \text{AIRTRANSP}_{it} + \gamma_{22} \text{CCOR}_{it} + \gamma_{23} \text{REGQUA}_{it} + \gamma_{24} \text{EFFCUS}_{jt} \\ & + \gamma_{25} \text{EACPS}_{jt} + \varepsilon_{ijt} \end{aligned} \tag{8}$$

Description of Variables

Bilateral Exports (X_{ij} and X_{ji}) Data on bilateral exports was obtained from the International Monetary Fund's Direction of Trade Statistics (DOTS). Bilateral trade flow reported in the data is goods, value of exports measured in US dollars (free on board) with zero values recorded for countries that did not report or reported no exports to a particular destination.

Gross Domestic Product Y_i and Y_j will represent the importer-specific factors that make up the total importer's demand and exporter-specific factors that represent the total amount exporters are willing to supply, respectively. GDP provides a guide to measuring the economic size of the two trading countries and the larger the country size economically under the computation of GDP we expect that country to export and import more as compared to economically small size countries. Data used was obtained from the World Development Indicators (WDI).

Distance The "distance effect" measuring the elasticity of trade flows to distance has been on the ascendancy since the early 1970s in a series of works with the gravity model as the main framework, this has led to most observers naming it as the "distance puzzle." Bilateral distance is at the bedrock, of the gravity equation with Tinbergen (1962) empirically demonstrating the negative relationship between bilateral distance and trade flows. Data employed in the study was sourced from CEPII.

Common Border Countries that share common borders can be described as neighboring countries. With trade, related costs such as transport considerably less among neighboring countries, countries that share common border are expected to trade more than countries that do not share a common border. Data used for the study was obtained from CEPII.

Landlocked Countries To start with being a landlocked country implies a high transport cost burden. The economic definition of a landlocked country is much more complex than the geographic one. "Countries are economically landlocked in the sense that their economic development is constrained when several factors (geographical, economic and even political) are present like remoteness from major markets, poor infrastructure, border crossing difficulties or high transportation costs." According to Limao and Venables (2001), being a landlocked country reduces trade by 70% among the large used country sample and thus it is expected that countries that are landlocked trade less comparatively to countries that are not landlocked.

Exporter and Importer Ease to Access Market The business environment prevailing in two trading country is key for bilateral trade. Countries have various different systems controlling the import of products. Often authorization from certification bodies and/or international product certification is required. Simultaneously, both importers and exporters need to have smooth access to the market with one failing to do so being crucial to the volume of trade. With the study focusing on export performance and trade facilitation, African countries are likely to export more to the developed world as a result of importer ease to access market. On the contrary, where there is a poor business environment hampering the opportunities of importers to receive consignments of goods and services, trading partners will face difficulties landing their products at the shores of the importers' country, and thereby increasing the cost of trading among such countries. Trade therefore will be expected to be low between countries whose exporters or importers face difficulties in accessing markets.

Regional Trade Agreements, Common Language and Colonization Ties

Dummy variables were used to denote the above variables for trading partners that had the following characteristics:

- 1 for countries that have a common RTA and 0 if otherwise.
- 1 for country pairs who share a common language and 0 if otherwise.
- 1 for country pairs with one partner having been colonized or colonized the other trading partner and 0 if otherwise.

Trade Intensity Index (t_{ij}) The trade intensity index (T_{ij}) is used in most trade literature to determine the intimacy of the trading relationship between two countries based on their importance in world trade. As a method of trade research, it helps determine the right market for a particular product and is based on an actual observation of bilateral trade flow. It is defined as the share of one country's exports going to a partner divided by the share of world exports to the partner. The trade intensity index (t_{ij}) of a country i's export with a country j is calculated as:

$$t_{ij} = \frac{X_{ij} / X_{it}}{X_{wj} / X_{wt}} \tag{9}$$

X_{ij}, X_{wj} represent country i's exports value and value of world exports to country j and X_{it}, X_{wt} represents country i's total export and that of the world.

t_{ij} takes the value of unity in a simplest gravity model. When t_{ij} exceeds one, trade is very intensive between country pairs and becomes less than one, where trade is less intensive between the two.

Trade Facilitation Variables The combination of both hard and soft trade-related infrastructure is expected to promote trade among two economies. The essence of this paper is to examine the contribution of policies aimed at strengthening institutions and the business environment in promoting bilateral trade beyond controlling for artificial barriers such as tariffs and quotas.

Trade Facilitation Policies

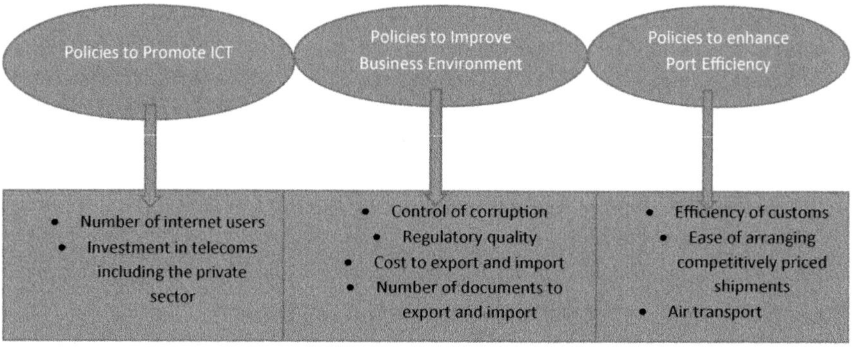

Recently, more advanced studies have raised issues of handling zero trade flows for a given year between two country pairs. Not only being an estimation issue, but it is also an issue about measurement and as a result affects all exercises related to gravity estimations.

Alternative ways primarily used to handle the issue of zero trade flows is to truncate the sample where observations of zero trade are dropped, or by estimating the model in levels. Also, some studies add a small constant (say a dollar) to the trade value before taking the logarithmic form.

Most trade literatures have therefore adopted different approaches to analyze zero trade flows notably the Tobit estimator and the (Pseudo) Poisson maximum likelihood (ML) estimator.

Estimation Technique A panel estimation technique using the gravity model will be used to quantify the impact of the trade facilitation variables on bilateral exports. Using panel data to analyze bilateral trade helps mitigate the bias created due to differences across individual observational units (countries). The estimation of gravity equation within a panel framework is generally centered on the estimation of stochastic version of the Anderson's model with the only difference is that we assume the estimation in a time frame (t). A panel-based approach is, therefore, more desirable as it has the merit of moderating the bias generated by heterogeneity across countries.

A panel equation of the form

$$y_{it} = \beta_0 + \beta_1 x_{it} + e_{it},$$
$$\text{with } i = 1{,}2 \cdots\cdots\cdots\cdots, N \text{ and } t = 1, 2 \cdots\cdots\cdots\cdots, T \quad (10)$$

where i denotes households, individuals, firms, countries among others and t representing the time period. The i subscript represents the cross-section dimension, t represents the time-series dimension, β_0 is a scalar, β_1 is $P \times 1$ and x_{it} is the i'th observation on P explanatory variables. Assuming we have T observations on N individuals, the indices i and t are such that $i = 1, 2 \cdots\cdots\cdots\cdots, N$ and $t = 1, 2 \cdots\cdots\cdots\cdots T$, implying a total of NT observations.

Frequently used is a one-way error component model in panel data applications the disturbance term, with

$$e_{it} = f_{it} + v_{it}, \tag{11}$$

where f_{it} represents the unobservable individual-specific effect and v_{it} denotes the remainder disturbance which varies across time and individual. With respect to this paper, v_{it} are specific factors that affect trade but are not related to GDP, distance, language or other variables included in the model.

This paper similar to studies such as (Turkson 2012) will employ either the fixed effects model, the random effects model or the Hausman–Taylor model based on the assumptions about the individual effects.

Zero Trade Flows

To retain a zero-valued trade flow in the sample requires the use of an appropriate estimation technique. Most trade literatures have therefore adopted different approaches to analyze zero trade flows notably the Tobit estimator and the (Pseudo) Poisson maximum likelihood (ML) estimator.

The use of the Tobit estimator in handling issues of zero trade flows has been subject to many criticisms. Firstly, using the Tobit estimator depicts the case where unobserved observations are recorded as zero. Also, in cases, where values of trade are small in figure, using the Tobit estimator rounds it zero and actually zero trade might mirror "desired" negative trade. A more prudent approach has thus been the (Pseudo) Poisson maximum likelihood (ML) estimator which is applicable to the various levels of trade. It estimates directly the nonlinear form of the gravity equation and prevents the dropping of zero trade flows. Westerlund and Wilhelmsson (2006) adopted this approach in estimating gravity equations while Silva and Tenreyro (2006) demonstrated that this approach is the most robust in the absence of homoscedasticity.

Results and Discussions

Summary Statistics

Table 1 provides a descriptive statistic on the mean, standard deviation and the maximum and minimum of variables that apply to the twenty-nine (29) countries within the SSA between the periods of 2004–2014.

As observed from Table 1, the average of bilateral trade among sub-Saharan African countries is US$35 million with a high standard deviation of US$220 million.

Table 1 Summary statistics

Variable	Mean	Std. Deviation	Minimum	Maximum
Export (USD millions)	35	220	0	5120
GDP *i* (USD billions)	34.9	83.4	0.513	569
GDP *j* (USD billions)	34.9	83.4	0.270	569
Population *i* (millions)	21.1	30.8	468985	177
Population *j*(millions)	21.1	30.8	468,985	177
Trade intensity index	2.245959	12.56823	0	513.0278
Distance (weighted)	3162.277	1839.505	162.1818	8744.852
Cost to export (per container USD) *i*	1880.49	1046.926	463	5491
Cost to import (per container USD) *j*	2463.696	1466.931	682	7709
Number of docs to export	7.758621	1.630738	5	13
Number of docs to import	9.517241	2.745958	6	21
Number of Internet users *i*	6.920803	9.250874	0.1553345	49
Private sector investment in telecoms *i*(USD millions)	271	554	0	3060
Air transport (freight in millions) *i*	100.4938	249.4124	0	1232.995
Control of corruption estimate *i*	−0.6224483	0.5157411	−1.512267	0.903527
Regulatory quality estimate *i*	−0.5971455	0.4538369	−1.879218	0.7083526
Efficiency of custom clearance process index *j*	2.272072	0.3248497	1.5	3.35
Ease of arranging competitively priced shipments index *j*	2.537066	0.3496974	1.57	3.56

Source Authors' Estimation Using Stata

Such wide disparity gives an indication of the huge gap present in the volume of export traded among countries in the SSA.

The GDPs of both the exporting and importing countries record the same mean and standard deviation of US$34.9 billion and US$84.3 billion, respectively. However, among the exporting countries, the country with the lowest GDP records a value of US$531 million compared to the importing country that records a value of US$270. Importing countries with such low levels of GDP symbolize a country of low economic strength and consequently will import less from its trading partners. The average population size of both importing and exporting countries stands at about 21 million with population ranging from 468,985 to 177 million people. A huge country size in terms of residents has the ability to increase a country's demand for import since most SSA countries production are not able to meet domestic demand.

Average GDP per capita of SSA countries is US$1575.829 and US$1575.759 for exporting and importing countries, respectively, between 2004 and 2014. There appears to be some evidence of inequality with some countries GDP per capita as low as US$119.4601 while a few of the SSA countries have a higher value of US$11530.15.

One striking feature of Table 1 is the correlation between trade intensity and the value of exports with such low index of 2.25. This confirms African countries trade most with the rest of the world than with its fellow members.

Exporters having to face an average cost of US$1880.49 per container to export could be detrimental to trade volumes. Even if they manage to overcome such prohibitive trade cost, an importing price of US$2463.70 per container could significantly affect a country's ability to import. Exporters would thus find trading outside the region comparatively cheaper with importers as well preferring to import from outside the region, consequently reducing the level of intra-regional trade. The highest cost to export and import per container are US$5491 and US$7709, respectively, with exporters requiring a maximum of 13 documents to export while importers require a maximum of 21 documents to import.

The average number of Internet users per 100 people is about seven with private sector in investing in telecommunication about US$271 million. It is believed that private sector involvement in developing ICT complemented with an increase in the number of Internet users would improve communication within the region and consequently provide simpler means of trading in goods and services. Private sector participation is, however, low given the poor level of regulatory quality and corrupt practices of political leaders in the various countries.

The average estimate to which corruption is controlled is −0.62 with that of regulatory quality being −0.60 and the maximum for both at 0.90 and 0.70, respectively. With the highest rank being 2.5, it appears most governments within the region have not exercised much power to control corruption and have also not strengthened institutions as much as required to provide the necessary platform for to facilitate private sector development. Perceptions of such nature affect the level of investment and with indexes as low as −1.5 and −1.9 for control of corruption and regulatory quality, private sector participation in enhancing trade will be very low.

The average LPI index for efficient custom procedures and ease of arranging competitively priced shipments record a value of 2.3 and 2.5, respectively. With maximum index value of 3.4 for efficient custom procedures and 3.6 for ease of arranging competitively priced shipments, countries within the region can still improve to enjoy full gains from intra-regional trade given the highest possible rank is 5.

Diagnostic Tests

Correlation Matrix The correlation matrix reported in appendix (Table 7) does not indicate the presence of severe multicollinearity among the trade facilitation variables. The correlation matrix clearly shows that the pair-wise correlation is almost non-existent for most of the variables. The only two variables for which there appears to be the presence of some negative correlation are air transport infrastructure index and regulatory quality index. But even for these variables, the correlation coefficient does not exceed 0.8 and thus not pose a serious multicollinearity problem. For a multicollinearity to cause a serious problem, the rule of thumb is that the correlation coefficient between two regressors must exceed 0.8.

Hausman Test for Fixed Effects Versus Random Effects Model The decision as to which model is appropriate depends on assumptions made with regards to the possible correlation between the individual, or cross-section specific, error component f_i and the x_{it} regressors. If it is assumed that f_i and the X's are uncorrelated, random effect model may be appropriate, whereas if f_i and the X's are correlated, fixed effect model might be appropriate.

This decision to determine the choice between the FE and the RE model will be made based on a test developed by Hausman (1978). The test statistic has an asymptotic χ^2 distribution with degrees of freedom equal to the number of regressors.

Under the null hypothesis of zero correlation, the RE model is more efficient. Conversely, if the null is rejected, the inference is that RE model is not appropriate and hence only the FE model provides consistent estimators, in which case statistical inferences will be conditional on ε_i in the sample.

Discussion of Results

The results as shown in Table 2 are obtained from estimating the gravity Eq. (8) using the random effect, fixed effect and Hausman–Taylor estimators. The Hausman test shown below confirms the appropriateness of the random effects model by accepting the null hypothesis that the regressors and individual effects (heterogeneity) are not correlated at 5% level of significance.

The Hausman–Taylor model is a hybrid that combines the consistency of a fixed effects model with the efficiency and applicability of a random effects model. "The choice of the Hausman–Taylor over the REM and FEM is to allow for controlling the variations across countries, while at the same time incorporating time-invariant variables that are correlated with bilateral specific effects in the estimation. By making use of instrumental variables that are uncorrelated to unobservable characteristics, the Hausman–Taylor panel technique has proven to be more efficient than the REM and FEM techniques. The Hausman–Taylor panel technique also allows for the control of the endogeneity bias from the trade agreement dummy within the gravity framework (Turkson 2012)". Table 7 in the appendix confirms the presence of endogeneity within the RTA dummy using the Durbin–Wu–Hausman test as countries could self-select themselves into a particular trade agreement based on the magnitude of trade that takes place between these trading nations justifying the rationale to prefer the Hausman–Taylor panel technique over the REM and FEM.

Table 2 Hausman test for fixed effect versus random effect

	(b)	(B)	(b−B)	sqrt(diag(V_b−V_B))
	FE	RE	Difference	S.E.
Log of GDP*it*	1.934023	0.908474	1.02555	0.2694316
Log of GDP*jt*	1.225618	0.613293	0.612325	0.2312199
Log of POP*it*	1.514827	0.058447	1.45638	1.427178
Log of POP*jt*	0.366095	0.275633	0.090462	1.181817
Trade intensity index	0.909911	0.891194	0.018717	0.0051076
Log of remoteness	−5.20746	−0.56668	−4.640784	1.348467
Log of cost to export	−2.17993	−0.74531	−1.434624	0.2441096
Log of cost to import	−0.03895	−0.06434	0.025391	0.0824781
Number of docs to import	−0.00716	−0.04535	0.038196	0.0153673
Number of docs to export	−0.0071	0.046524	−0.053627	0.0102141
Log of Internet users (per 100)	−0.40924	−0.1116	−0.297641	0.0812594
Log of invest in telecoms	0.167376	0.120796	0.04658	0.0148669
Air transport	0.002574	0.000945	0.001629	0.0006989
Control of corruption	−0.13049	−0.44751	0.317015	0.0895111
Regulatory quality	−0.8019	−0.52482	−0.277079	0.1839734
Efficiency of customs	0.2032	0.568662	−0.365462	0.0275249
Ease of arranging comp. shipments	0.191833	0.349198	−0.157365	

Test: Ho: difference in coefficients not systematic
$\chi^2(17) = (b - B)' [(V\_b - V\_B)\hat{}(-1)] (b - B)$
$= 20.51$
Prob > χ^2 $= 0.2492$
Source Author's Computation Using Stata

Summary of Findings

The results from Table 3 depict the estimated coefficients for fixed effect, random effect and Hausman–Taylor estimation techniques combining trade facilitation variables for both exporting and importing countries within the sub-Saharan African region. Column 1 shows estimated coefficients for fixed effect while that in column 2 represent estimated coefficients from random effects approach. The third column shows estimated results from the Hausman–Taylor estimation controls for both country pair effects and time effects incorporating an RTA dummy. Discussions are based on results from Hausman–Taylor estimations as it is preferred over the random and fixed effect models.

The results support the theory that trade facilitation impacts bilateral exports and policies aimed at improving trade facilitation variables within importer and exporter countries has the potential to increase trade flows among countries within the SSA

Table 3 Results for regression of trade flows on trade facilitation indicators

	(1)	(2)	(3)
Lnexports	FE	RE	HT
Log of GDP_*it*	1.934***	0.908***	1.447***
	(0.292)	(0.112)	(0.169)
Log of GDP_*jt*	1.226***	0.613***	1.001***
	(0.245)	(0.0811)	(0.120)
Log of Pop_*it*	1.515	0.0584	0.00546
	(1.431)	(0.0991)	(0.173)
Log of Pop_*jt*	0.366	0.276***	0.241*
	(1.184)	(0.0723)	(0.133)
Trade intensity index	0.910***	0.891***	0.906***
	(0.0158)	(0.0150)	(0.0127)
Remoteness_*ij*	−5.207***	−0.567	−2.855***
	(1.413)	(0.421)	(0.665)
Log of cost to export	−2.180***	−0.745***	−1.396***
	(0.300)	(0.174)	(0.191)
Log of cost to import	−0.0390	−0.0643	−0.0796
	(0.122)	(0.0897)	(0.0909)
Number of doc to import	−0.00716	−0.0454**	−0.0155
	(0.0256)	(0.0205)	(0.0204)
Number of doc to export	−0.00710	0.0465**	−0.000274
	(0.0213)	(0.0187)	(0.0159)
Log of Internet users_*i*	−0.409***	−0.112**	−0.246***
	(0.0973)	(0.0535)	(0.0590)
Log of telecom_Invst_*i*	0.167***	0.121***	0.122***
	(0.0329)	(0.0294)	(0.0245)
Air transport_*i*	0.00257***	0.000945***	0.00145***
	(0.000759)	(0.000297)	(0.000334)
Control of corruption_*i*	0.130	0.448***	−0.296**
	(0.170)	(0.144)	(0.126)
Regulatory quality_*i*	0.802***	0.525***	−0.646***
	(0.271)	(0.198)	(0.194)
Efficiency of custom procedures_*j*	0.203*	0.569***	0.365***
	(0.116)	(0.113)	(0.0875)
Arranging comp. priced shipments_*j*	0.192***	0.349***	0.231***
	(0.0733)	(0.0754)	(0.0580)
Log of bilateral distance_*ij*		0.0352	0.260

(continued)

Table 3 (continued)

	(1)	(2)	(3)
Lnexports	FE	RE	HT
		(0.124)	(0.416)
Common border_*ij*		0.330	0.290
		(0.208)	(0.427)
Common colonies_*ij*		−0.0447	−0.0853
		(0.220)	(0.502)
Common language_*ij*		−0.269	−0.360
		(0.177)	(0.421)
Col_45_*ij*		1.840	1.771
		(1.187)	(2.394)
Landlocked_*ij*		0.0688	0.550
		(0.223)	(0.338)
Rta*ij*		0.599***	0.884
		(0.166)	(0.980)
Common currency_*ij*		0.473**	0.385
		(0.213)	(0.412)
Constant	−72.02***	−24.59***	−38.16***
	(16.83)	(3.547)	(6.105)
Observations	878	878	878
R^2	0.888	0.873	
Number of bilateral trade id	391	391	391

Standard errors in parentheses ***$p < 0.01$, **$p < 0.05$, *$p < 0.1$. Country *i* and *j* represent exporter and importer, respectively

region. Results obtained are similar to studies by (Wilson et al. 2003; Akinkugbe 2009; Portugal-Perez and Wilson 2012; Turkson 2012).

In line with theory, the results support the gravity equation which posits that exports between countries are directly related to the proportion of their GDPs. Export and import elasticities to GDP obtained were 1.447 and 1.001 implying a 10% increase in the GDP of and exporting country will raise exports up to about 14.47%. Similarly, a 10% increase in the GDP of an importing country can increase exports by 10.01% implying countries will trade more with each other as GDP increase. These results are similar to (Akinkugbe 2009; Portugal-Perez and Wilson 2012) including other literatures support the view that GDPs of two trading countries affect bilateral trade patterns.

The population of the importing country is significant as a large country size can influence a country's decision to import more due to huge demand which might not be met by domestic production. Indeed, sub-Saharan African countries can capitalize on labor endowments to increase their level of productivity and consequently export more to other countries within the region. Similar to studies by (Portugal-Perez and Wilson 2012), this study shows a 10% increase in the population of the importing country will increase trade flows by 2.4%.

A trade intensity index of 0.9 indicates there is still more room for African countries to trade more among themselves than with the rest of the world. As a means for controlling for multilateral resistance terms, the remoteness variable is significant at 1% with an estimated coefficient of (−2.855). This implies that a 10% increase in the average weighted distance of a country from its trading partners will reduce trade flows by 28.55%. This supports claims of Anderson and Wincoop (2003) on the need to control for multilateral resistance terms in a well-defined gravity model.

Increasing cost of export also has a negative impact on bilateral trade flows. It is estimated that a 10% increase in the cost to export per container measured in US dollars would reduce trade flows by 13.96%. This is in conformity with findings of similar literature (Wilson et al. 2003) also showing the decreasing effects of increasing cost to export on trade flows. Also similar to the findings of the other trade literature is the impact of increasing number of documents required to export and import on trade flows. Lengthy and bureaucratic procedures resulting from delays and the need to satisfy the necessary conditions that would guarantee the movement of goods across borders at ports are likely to impede the smooth flow of transactions. Increase in the number of documents required to export and import has a decreasing marginal impact on trade flows although values obtained were insignificant at 10%.

Most studies have found increase in number of Internet users to positively affect trade flows. However, considering the fact that the use of Internet in developing economies is predominantly for social purposes and to keep up to date with modern technology, they compete with private investors who decide to invest in the area of ICT for bandwidth. The general public having more access can invariably reduce how much bandwidth will be available for business purposes, and hence the study estimates a 10% increase in the number of Internet users per 100 of the population to reduce trade flows by 2.46%. On the contrary, a 10% increase in telecommunication investment by businesses will increase trade flows by 1.22%. These results are consistent with the findings in Wilson et al. (2003) that good telecommunications could increase bilateral trade flows supporting efforts within the SSA region to enhance e-commerce usage in trade transaction.

Developing air transport and restraining from using ports only as a means of exporting goods and services has the potential to increase trade flows. Although the effect of such transport means is marginal, with time further developments can increase trade flows more than the estimated 0.00145 obtained from the findings. These results are consistent with the findings in Wilson et al. (2003) that trade facilitation involves more than reducing transport costs, despite it being an important factor. The results indicate that measuring the benefits of trade facilitation using improvements in air transport as a proxy is likely to underestimate trade elasticity with regards to broad trade facilitation efforts.

With regards to port infrastructure in an importing country, improvement in custom clearance procedures and the ease at with importers can arrange competitively priced shipments also has the potential to increase trade flows within the sub-Saharan

African region. The coefficients for individual measures of logistics in importing countries within the SSA show that an improvement is likely to increase trade flows 0.37 and 0.23%, respectively. This result strongly aligns with past literatures that have studied the relationship between infrastructure and trade (Wilson et al. 2003; Limao and Venables 2001; Lisinge 2004; Djankov et al. 2010). With Ghana currently implementing the "paperless" port system which seeks to minimize the bureaucratic processes associated with port transaction, it is expected that this strategy might improve ports efficiency, increased revenue mobilization and smooth trade flows.

Institutional strength and quality play a prominent role in a country's productivity level. Studies by Akinkugbe (2009) used the corruption perception index as a proxy to determine the extent to which trade flows can be affected by perception of the level of corruption people hold about a particular economy. Similar to his studies, policies to improve the control of corruption and the reduction of extent to which people with political influence within an economy can exercise public power for private gain is expected to increase trade flows. A well-regulated economy with good institutional strength can also increase trade flows on condition of implementing good and sound policies that promote private sector development. In cases, where such controls are abused (over exercised), regulations act as border barriers which will be welfare reducing. Coefficient signs of −0.30 and −0.65 for control of corruption and regulatory quality align to findings of (Wilson et al. 2003) which point out to the fact that tightening regulations can offset improvements in other trade facilitation measures.

Zero Trade Flows

Summary of Findings Comparing results obtained in Table 3 column 3 to Table 4 column 3, most variables have the same expected sign notably (GDP_i, GDP_j, cost to export, number of documents to import and LPI variables), however, there is a change in the coefficient sign of Internet users per 100 people indicating a good telecommunication complemented with greater access to Internet could increase bilateral trade flows supporting efforts within the SSA region to develop ICT.

Also, it turns out controlling for corruption can be vital in Africa's championing course for regional integration and development. A well-regulated economy devoid of corrupt practices as well as an increase in number of Internet users as shown from Table 4 can increase trade flows marginally by 0.11 and 0.03%, respectively. Excluding the zero-valued export flows to some extent neglect the importance of some variables in determining trade flows. Also, the results show a much lower level of trade intensity of 0.06 compared to a 0.9 obtained in the Hausman–Taylor estimations indicating the level of intra-regional trade is far lower than as shown by the Hausman–Taylor estimation. With the RTA dummy significant at 1%, these results strongly align with past literature (Turkson 2012) that the regional trade agreements also impact bilateral trade flows. Similar to the Hausman–Taylor, the results from

Table 4 Results in the case of zero trade flows

	(Tobit)	(Poisson)	(PPML)
	Log of exports+1	Log of exports+1	Log of exports
Log of GDP_*it*	0.980***	0.0229	0.0229***
	(0.119)	(0.0225)	(0.00618)
Log of GDP_*jt*	0.683***	0.0333**	0.0332***
	(0.0865)	(0.0134)	(0.00393)
Log of Pop_*it*	0.0786	−0.00190	−0.00192
	(0.105)	(0.0195)	(0.00572)
Log of Pop_*jt*	0.259***	0.0266**	0.0266***
	(0.0776)	(0.0120)	(0.00452)
Log of bilateral distance_*ij*	0.0678	−0.00322	−0.00318
	(0.134)	(0.0208)	(0.00604)
Trade intensity index	0.897***	0.0658***	0.0658***
	(0.0142)	(0.00442)	(0.00176)
Common border_*ij*	0.315	0.00297	0.00297
	(0.227)	(0.0314)	(0.0101)
Common colonies_*ij*	−0.0621	0.0298	0.0299***
	(0.241)	(0.0363)	(0.0114)
Common language_*ij*	0.303	0.0430	0.0431***
	(0.193)	(0.0285)	(0.00966)
Col_45_*ij*	1.822	0.0692	0.0693***
	(1.298)	(0.161)	(0.0200)
Landlocked_*ij*	0.0205	−0.00740	−0.00742
	(0.224)	(0.0471)	(0.0152)
Rta*ij*	0.622***	0.0338	0.0338***
	(0.181)	(0.0258)	(0.00811)
Remoteness_*ij*	−0.981**	0.0167	0.0168
	(0.453)	(0.0746)	(0.0218)
Common currency_*ij*	0.462**	0.0469	0.0469***
	(0.234)	(0.0351)	(0.00975)
Log of cost to export	−0.727***	−0.0561	−0.0561***
	(0.169)	(0.0413)	(0.0125)
Log of cost to import	−0.0829	0.00956	0.00959
	(0.0885)	(0.0194)	(0.00615)
Number of doc to Import	−0.0376*	−0.00817*	−0.00817***
	(0.0201)	(0.00450)	(0.00124)
Number of doc to export	−0.0107***	−0.000225	−0.000227

(continued)

Table 4 (continued)

	(Tobit)	(Poisson)	(PPML)
	(0.00303)	(0.000941)	(0.000291)
Log of Internet users_*i*	−0.146***	0.0262	0.0262***
	(0.0530)	(0.0172)	(0.00539)
Log of telecomm_Invst_*i*	0.114***	0.0277**	0.0277***
	(0.0272)	(0.0135)	(0.00411)
Air transport_*i*	0.00110***	3.03e-05	3.02e-05
	(0.000291)	(8.55e-05)	(2.70e-05)
Control of corruption_*i*	0.0354**	0.0111*	0.0111***
	(0.0174)	(0.00636)	(0.00203)
Regulatory quality_*i*	−0.0145***	−0.00231*	−0.00231***
	(0.00484)	(0.00138)	(0.000385)
Efficiency of custom procedures_*j*	0.493***	0.0632	0.0632***
	(0.104)	(0.0538)	(0.0177)
Arranging comp. priced shipments_*j*	0.317***	0.0718*	0.0719***
	(0.0691)	(0.0386)	(0.0118)
Constant log of exports +1		0.505	
		(0.711)	
Constant log of alpha		−18.49	
		(97.55)	
Constant	−25.89***		0.505**
	(3.732)		(0.210)
Observations	874	874	874
R^2			0.886
Number of bilateral id	389	389	

***$p < 0.01$, **$p < 0.05$, *$p < 0.1$. Country *i* and *j* represent exporter and importer, respectively

the *ppml* estimates show the extent to which regulations used can act as border barriers and as such appropriate enforcement of these regulations can positively impact trade flows. To appropriately enforce such regulations, requires institutional quality and this makes it imperative for governments to channel resources to strengthening institutions within their respective countries.

Summary and Conclusions

One fundamental innovation from this study centers on considering varieties of indicators of trade facilitation suited to policymaking. Trade between countries is thus not dependent on endowments and economic size of countries but as well other factors that impose further trade costs. Increasing trade costs has been a major barrier to trade among African countries despite significant reductions in tariff and non-tariff barriers. Government policies, including restrictive trade policies, poor customs administration and regulations all of which are trade facilitation-related issues continue to discourage export growth.

For sub-Saharan, African countries to effectively compete in global trade there is the need to develop both "hard" and "soft" infrastructure. The study analyzed the effect of trade facilitation on trade flows using country-specific data for 29 selected African countries. Results prove that over the eleven years under review, major improvements in infrastructure, well-functioning institutions and development in ICT can expand trade.

One highlight of this study is as to whether governments are doing "too much" or "less" in controlling corruption as shown from the results. Too much control will adversely affect export growth as exporters would be frustrated by overburdensome procedures while too little would adversely affect the business environment. There is a need for policymaker to design and implement appropriate policies to check corruption.

Policies geared toward investment in infrastructure and technology can help support economic recovery and minimize costs associated with trade in the long term. Results are consistent with findings of (Buys et al. 2006) which show that developing transport infrastructure can have a positive impact on trade flows despite the marginal effect. Nonetheless, an overall development in the entire transport network within the subregion can potentially lead to higher volumes of trade flows than estimated in the long term.

Appendix

See Tables 5, 6, 7, 8 and 9.

Table 5 List of the twenty-nine (29) sub-Saharan African countries in the study by region *(United Nation's Classification of countries)*

West Africa	East Africa	Central Africa	Southern Africa
Benin	Burundi	Angola	Namibia
Burkina Faso	Ethiopia	Cameroon	South
Cape Verde	Kenya	Congo Republic	Africa
Cote D'Ivoire	Madagascar	Gabon	Zambia
The Gambia	Malawi	Central Africa Republic	
Ghana	Mozambique		
Guinea	Rwanda		
Guinea-Bissau			
Liberia Mali			
Niger			
Nigeria			
Senegal			
Togo			

Table 6 Correlation matrix

	Inxcostexp	Inmcostimp	docimp	docexp	Inintusr	Iniit	airtransp	ccor	rq	ec	eac
Inxcostexp	1.0000										
Inmcostimp	−0.0832	1.0000									
docimp	0.1125	−0.4815	1.0000								
docexp	−0.1359	0.1155	−0.0030	1.0000							
Inintusr	−0.0033	−0.0940	0.0063	0.0097	1.0000						
Iniit	0.1837	0.0178	−0.0188	−0.3137	−0.2807	1.0000					
airtransp	−0.4335	−0.0027	−0.0891	0.0748	−0.2818	−0.1956	1.0000				
ccor	−0.0166	−0.1371	0.1021	0.0640	0.3643	0.0873	0.0726	1.0000			
rq	0.0984	0.1358	−0.0172	0.2816	−0.2648	−0.2457	−0.2179	−0.6859	1.0000		
ec	0.4263	0.0793	−0.0220	−0.0178	0.2215	0.0893	−0.7310	−0.1172	0.0357	1.0000	
eac	0.0259	−0.0789	0.1287	−0.1329	−0.0912	−0.0291	−0.2900	−0.1422	−0.0015	−0.0832	1.0000

Table 7 Test for endogeneity of RTA dummy using Durbin–Wu–Hausman test instrumental variables (2SLS) regression

Variables	lnexports
rta	1.482***
	(0.151)
rq	−1.886***
	(0.157)
ec	0.852***
	(0.228)
eac	0.950***
	(0.151)
lnintusr	0.547***
	(0.0619)
lniit	0.545***
	(0.0467)
airtransp	0.00122***
	(0.000360)
landlocked	−0.0110
	(0.193)
lnremoteness	0.707**
	(0.275)
comcur	0.489***
	(0.121)
lnxcostexp	−0.757***
	(0.174)
lnmcostimp	−0.00562
	(0.0772)
lnmgdp	0.612***
	(0.0478)
lntii	0.813***
	(0.0171)
Constant	−11.52***
	(2.278)
Observations	878
R^2	0.879

Standard errors in parentheses ***$p < 0.01$, **$p < 0.05$, *$p < 0.1$
Tests of endogeneity
Ho: variables are exogenous
Durbin (score) $\chi^2(1) = 21.4459$ ($p = 0.0000$)
Wu-Hausman F (1862) = 21.5823 ($p = 0.0000$)

Table 8 Summary of *Doing Business* indicators for sub-Saharan Africa (SSA)

Indicator	Lowest regional performance	Best regional performance	Regional average	Best global performance
Starting a business (rank)	189 (Central African Republic)	19 (Burundi)	128	1 (New Zealand)
Starting a business (DTF score)	31.36 (Central African Republic)	94.51 (Burundi)	74.42	99.96 (New Zealand)
Procedures (number)	18.0 (Equatorial Guinea)	3.0 (3 Economies[a])	8.0	1.0 (New Zealand[a])
Time (days)	135.0 (Equatorial Guinea)	4.0 (Burundi)	26.8	0.5 (New Zealand)
Cost (% of income per capita)	330.1 (South Sudan)	0.3 (South Africa)	53.4	0.0 (Slovenia)
Paid-in min. capital (% of income per capita)	540.1 (Central African Republic)	0.0 (25 Economies[a])	45.1	0.0 (105 Economies[a])
Dealing with construction permits (rank)	189 (Eritrea)	31 (Mozambique)	130	1 (Singapore)
Dealing with construction permits (DTF score)	0.00 (Eritrea)	77.58 (Mozambique)	58.77	92.97 (Singapore)
Procedures (number)	27.0 (Guinea)	10.0 (8 Economies[a])	14.3	7.0 (5 Economies[a])
Time (days)	448.0 (Zimbabwe)	74.0 (Liberia)	162.2	26.0 (Singapore)
Cost (% of warehouse value)	30.8 (Madagascar)	0.3 (Botswana)	6.6	0.0 (Qatar)
Building quality control index (0–15)	1.0 (Equatorial Guinea)	13.0 (Mauritius)	6.9	15.0 (New Zealand)
Getting electricity (rank)	188 (Madagascar)	41 (Mauritius)	149	1 (Korea, Rep.)
Getting electricity (DTF score)	18.27 (Madagascar)	81.93 (Mauritius)	46.97	99.88 (Korea, Rep.)
Procedures (number)	9.0 (Nigeria)	3.0 (Togo[a])	5.4	3.0 (14 Economies[a])

(continued)

Table 8 (continued)

Indicator	Lowest regional performance	Best regional performance	Regional average	Best global performance
Time (days)	465.0 (Liberia)	34.0 (Rwanda)	130.1	18.0 (Korea, Rep.[a])
Cost (% of income per capita)	16,315.4 (Burundi)	260.0 (Mauritius)	4075.6	0.0 (Japan)
Reliability of supply and transparency of tariff index (0–8)	0.0 (33 Economies[a])	6.0 (Mauritius)	0.9	8.0 (18 Economies[a])
Registering property (rank)	182 (Togo)	12 (Rwanda)	132	1 (New Zealand)
Registering property (DTF score)	30.93 (Togo)	87.75 (Rwanda)	50.98	94.46 (New Zealand)
Procedures (number)	12.1 (Nigeria)	3.0 (Rwanda)	6.2	1.0 (4 Economies[a])
Time (days)	288.0 (Togo)	9.0 (Sudan)	57.5	1.0 (3 Economies[a])
Cost (% of property value)	18.9 (Cameroon)	0.1 (Rwanda)	8.3	0.0 (Saudi Arabia)
Quality of the land administration index (0–30)	3.0 (Central African Republic)	25.0 (Rwanda)	8.4	28.5 (3 Economies[a])
Getting credit (rank)	185 (Eritrea[a])	2 (Rwanda)	118	1 (New Zealand)
Getting credit (DTF score)	0.00 (Eritrea[a])	95.00 (Rwanda)	35.85	100.00 (New Zealand)
Strength of legal rights index (0–12)	0.0 (Eritrea[a])	11.0 (Rwanda)	4.9	12.0 (3 Economies[a])
Depth of credit information index (0–8)	0.0 (26 Economies[a])	8.0 (Rwanda[a])	2.3	8.0 (26 Economies[a])
Credit registry coverage (% of adults)	0.0 (Guinea)	82.6 (Mauritius)	5.8	100.0 (Portugal)
Credit bureau coverage (% of adults)	1.0 (Lesotho)	62.8 (Namibia)	7.1	100.0 (22 Economies[a])

(continued)

Table 8 (continued)

Indicator	Lowest regional performance	Best regional performance	Regional average	Best global performance
Protecting minority investors (rank)	185 (São Tomé and Príncipe)	14 (South Africa)	125	1 (3 Economies[a])
Protecting minority investors (DTF score)	25.00 (São Tomé and Príncipe)	71.67 (South Africa)	44.68	83.33 (3 Economies[a])
Strength of minority investor protection	2.5 (São Tomé and	7.2 (South Africa)	4.5	8.3 (3 Economies[a])
Indicator	Lowest regional performance	Best regional performance	Regional average	Best global performance
Extent of conflict of interest regulation index (0–10)	2.3 (Ethiopia)	8.0 (South Africa)	4.9	9.3 (Singapore[a])
Extent of shareholder governance index (0–10)	1.7 (São Tomé and Príncipe)	6.7 (Nigeria)	4.1	8.0 (4 Economies[a])
Paying taxes (rank)	187 (Mauritania)	13 (Mauritius)	131	1 (United Arab Emirates[a])
Paying taxes (DTF score)	17.71 (Mauritania)	91.92 (Mauritius)	58.01	99.44 (United Arab Emirates[a])
Payments (number per year)	63.0 (Côte d'Ivoire)	7.0 (South Africa)	38.6	3.0 (Hong Kong SAR, China*)
Time (hours per year)	907.9 (Nigeria)	85.0 (Seychelles)	308.6	55.0 (Luxembourg)
Total tax rate (% of profit)	216.5 (Comoros)	13.6 (Lesotho)	46.5	25.9 (Ireland)
Trading across borders (rank)	189 (Eritrea)	30 (Swaziland)	136	1 (16 Economies[a])
Trading across borders (DTF score)	0.00 (Eritrea)	92.68 (Swaziland)	48.96	100.00 (16 Economies[a])
Time to export: Border compliance (hours)	515 (Congo, Dem. Rep.)	3 (Swaziland)	108	0 (15 Economies[a])

(continued)

Table 8 (continued)

Indicator	Lowest regional performance	Best regional performance	Regional average	Best global performance
Cost to export: Border compliance (USD)	1975 (Congo, Rep.)	17 (Mali)	542	0 (18 Economies[a])
Time to export: Documentary compliance (hours)	698 (Congo, Dem. Rep.)	3 (Lesotho)	97	0 (Jordan)
Cost to export: Documentary compliance (USD)	2500 (Congo, Dem. Rep.)	25 (Togo)	246	0 (20 Economies[a])
Time to import: Border compliance (hours)	588 (Congo, Dem. Rep.)	4 (Botswana[a])	160	0 (19 Economies[a])
Cost to import: Border compliance (USD)	2089 (Congo, Dem. Rep.)	98 (Botswana)	643	0 (28 Economies[a])
Time to import: Documentary compliance (hours)	360 (South Sudan)	3 (3 Economies[a])	123	1 (21 Economies[a])
Cost to import: Documentary	1025 (Burundi)	38 (Comoros)	351	0 (30 Economies[a])
Enforcing contracts (rank)	185 (Angola)	27 (Mauritius)	132	1 (Singapore)
Enforcing contracts (DTF score)	26.26 (Angola)	70.50 (Mauritius)	47.67	84.91 (Singapore)
Time (days)	1715.0 (Guinea-Bissau)	228.0 (South Sudan)	653.1	150.0 (Singapore)
Cost (% of claim)	119.0 (Mozambique)	14.3 (Tanzania)	44.9	9.0 (Iceland)
Quality of judicial processes index (0–18)	2.5 (Eritrea)	13.0 (Mauritius)	6.4	15.5 (3 Economies[a])
Resolving insolvency (rank)	189 (9 Economies[a])	39 (Mauritius)	128	1 (Finland)

(continued)

Table 8 (continued)

Indicator	Lowest regional performance	Best regional performance	Regional average	Best global performance
Resolving insolvency (DTF score)	0.00 (9 Economies[a])	65.94 (Mauritius)	30.32	93.81 (Finland)
Recovery rate (cents on the dollar)	8.4 (Liberia)	67.4 (Mauritius)	19.9	92.9 (Japan)
Time (years)	6.2 (São Tomé and Príncipe)	1.5 (Mozambique)	3.0	0.4 (Ireland)
Cost (% of estate)	76.0 (Central African Republic)	8.0 (Guinea)	23.1	1.0 (Norway)
Strength of insolvency framework index (0–16)	9.0 (Central African Republic[a])	14.5 (South Africa)	6.3	15.0 (4 Economies[a])

[a]Two or more economies share top ranking on this indicator. A number shown in place of an economy's name indicates the number of economies that share the top ranking on the indicator
Note The global best performer on time for paying taxes is defined as the lowest time recorded among all economies in the DB 2016 sample that levy the three major taxes: profit tax, labor taxes and mandatory contributions and VAT or sales tax."
Source Doing Business database

Table 9 Draft consolidated negotiating text

Article 1	Publication and Availability of Information
Article 2	Prior Publication and Consultation
Article 3	Advance Rulings
Article 4	Appeal Procedures
Article 5	Other Measures to Enhance Impartiality, Non-Discrimination and Transparency
Article 6	Disciplines on Fees and Charges Imposed on or in Connection with Importation and Exportation
Article 7	Release and Clearance of Goods
Article 8	Consularization
Article 9	Border Agency Cooperation
Article 10	Formalities Connected with Importation and Exportation
Article 11	Freedom of Transit
Article 12	Customs Cooperation

Source OECD Trade Policy Working Paper

References

Ackah C, Turkson FE, Opoku K (2012) Trade costs and intra-regional trade flows in ECOWAS. J W Afr Integr JWAI 1(1):1–35, EPAU, ECOWAS

Akinkugbe O (2009) Trade facilitation and Africa's manufactured goods' export: a panel data analysis. J Dev Areas 42(2): 77–88

Anderson JE, Van Wincoop E (2003). Gravity with gravitas: a solution to the border puzzle. Am Econ Rev 93(1): 170–192

Baldwin R, Taglioni D (2006) Gravity for dummies and dummies for gravity equations (No. w12516). National Bureau of Economic Research

Buys P, Deichmann U, Wheeler, D (2006) Road network upgrading and overland trade expansion in Sub-Saharan Africa, vol. 4097. World Bank

Djankov, S, Freund, C, Pham, CS (2010) Trading on time. *Rev Econ Stat* 92(1): 166–173

Draper P (2013) The shifting geography of Global Value Chains: Implications for developing countries, trade policy, and the G20. *Glob Summitry J* 1(1): 1–40

Hausman JA (1978) Specification tests in econometrics. Econ: J Econ Soc 46(6): 1251–1271

Head K (2003) Gravity for Beginners, Material presented at Rethinking the Line: The Canada-U.S. Border Conference. Vancouver, University of British-Columbia

Helpman E, Melitz M, Rubinstein Y (2008) Trading partners and trade volumes. Q J Econ 123: 441–487

Hummels D (2007) Transportation costs and international trade in the second era of globalization. J Econ Perspect 21(3): 131–154

Hummels D, Lugovskyy V (2006) Are matched partner trade statistics a usable measure of transportation costs? Rev Int Econ 14(1): 69–86

Hummels D, Skiba A (2004) Shipping the Good Apples Out. J Polit Econ 112(6): 1384–1402

Kien NT (2009) Gravity model by panel data approach: an empirical application with implications for the ASEAN free trade area. ASEAN Econ Bull 26(3): 266–277

Limao N, Venables AJ (2001) Infrastructure, geographical disadvantage, transport costs and trade. World Bank Econ Rev 15: 451–479

Lisinge RT, & United Nations. Economic Commission for Africa; United Nations. Economic Commission for Africa. African Trade Policy Centre. (2004). Trade Facilitation to Integrate Africa into the World Economy. *African Trade Policy Centre: Work in Progress* (4)

MacKellar L, Wörgötter A, Wörz J (2002) Economic growth of landlocked countries. In *Ökonomie* in *Theorie* und Praxis. Springer, New York, pp 213–226

Portugal-Perez A, Wilson JS (2012) Export performance and trade facilitation reform: Hard and soft infrastructure. World Dev 40(7): 1295–1307

Rose AK, Van Wincoop E (2001) National money as a barrier to international trade: The real case for currency union. Am Econ Rev 91(2): 386–390

Silva JS, Tenreyro S (2006) The log of gravity. Am Econ Rev 88(4): 641–658

Tinbergen J (1962) Shaping the world economy; suggestions for an international economic policy. *Books (Jan Tinbergen)*

Turkson FE (2011) Logistics and bilateral exports in developing countries: a multiplicative form estimation of the logistics augmented gravity equation. *CREDIT Research Paper* No. 11/06

Turkson FE (2012) Trade agreements and bilateral trade in Sub-Saharan Africa (SSA). CREDIT Research Paper (12/07)

Westerlund J, Wilhelmsson F (2006) Estimating the gravity model without gravity using panel data. Appl Econ 7(9): 1466–4283

Wilson JS, Mann CL, Olsuki T (2003) Trade facilitation and economic development: a new approach to quantifying the impact. World Bank Econ Rev 17(3): 367–389

Wilson JS, Mann CL, Otsuki T (2005) Assessing the benefits of trade facilitation: a global perspective. World Econ 28(6): 841–871

World Bank, World Development Indicators (2015)

Yang D (2008) Integrity for hire: an analysis of a widespread customs reform. J Law Econ 51(1): 25–57

Assessing the Role of Trade Liberalization in Facilitating Trade Flows and Economic Expansion: Evidence from ECOWAS Countries

Folasade Bosede Adegboye, Oluwatoyin A. Matthew, Jeremiah Ejemeyovwi, Olumide S. Adesina and Romanus Osabohien

Introduction

Economic development is known to be stimulated trade liberalization due to its effect resulting from the integration of the global economies and creating more enhanced markets. Globalization which is gradually enhancing more interconnectedness in regions and sub-regions globally improves free movement of trade, capital, financial activities, and information to boost economic advancement on the whole (Igudia 2004; Obadan 2004; Uwatt 2004). Globally, the merchandise trade increased in 2017 to 4.7%, from 1.8% in 2016. Africa also was not left out in growth trend, as Africa's trade rose to 10.6% in 2017, with the value of US$907.64 billion from US$820.76 billion in 2016 (ATP 2018). The African Continental Free Trade Area Agreement (AfCFTA) has the capability to improve the competence of African corporations. The required operational upgrade could as well accompany the operation of the policy as the proficiency and technological value of the export of the African countries are enhanced. For instance, 43% of merchandise traded in Africa are manufactured

F. B. Adegboye (✉)
Department of Banking and Finance, Covenant University, Ota, Nigeria
e-mail: folasade.adegboye@covenantuniversity.edu.ng

O. A. Matthew · J. Ejemeyovwi · R. Osabohien
Department of Economics and Development Studies, Covenant University, Ota, Nigeria
e-mail: oluwatoyin.matthew@covenantuniversity.edu.ng

J. Ejemeyovwi
e-mail: jeremiah.ejemeyovwi@covenantuniversity.edu.ng

R. Osabohien
e-mail: romanus.osabohien@covenantuniversity.edu.ng

O. S. Adesina
Department of Mathematical Sciences, Olabisi Onabanjo University, Ago Iwoye, Nigeria
e-mail: olumidestats@gmail.com

G. O. A. Odularu et al. (eds.), *Fostering Trade in Africa*,
Advances in African Economic, Social and Political Development,
https://doi.org/10.1007/978-3-030-36632-2_5

goods. Also, the technological value of trade within the African continent is greater than the trade of Africa with the remaining part of the globe (UNCTAD 2018).

Developing economies are quite unable to assimilate liberalization as ought in their economic and development programs, and this does not enable them to fully partake of the gains of liberalization and the global economy at large. Hence, several regions and sub-regions of the world came up with regional economic group such as the Organization of Economic Cooperation and Development (OECD), European Union (EU), and Organization of Petroleum Exporting Countries (OPEC), specifically aiming at coordinating trade strategies so as to earn economies of scale benefits. Therefore, the West African countries assembled together under the Economic Community of West African States (ECOWAS) body, to make the most of their endowment so as to realize the gains of trade openness (Osabuohien 2007).

The required need to promote formal trade within the ECOWAS region and the salient gains this will have cannot be overemphasized, essentially in the area of security of food as well as protection from international price volatility. The prominence of this factor was noted as a major challenge preceding the introduction of control on export by main global producers of rice at the inception of the global economic crisis from the year 2007 to 2008, which resulted into an over 300% rise in the price of rice globally. An assessment done by the OECD on the ensuing food crisis of 2008 in the ECOWAS region determines that, majority of countries in the region possess fertile land for the farming of rice, and however, the associated cost of production and sales results into small amount of production of rice. Due to this fact, the results showed that the ECOWAS region depends on inter-regional imports for about 40% of its source of rice. The region's trade core has thereby recognized worthy sequence of expectations, principally for primary food crop like cereals, as a basic element of its tactic to enhancing trade activities in the region. In 2017, the Trade Liberalization Scheme of ECOWAS (ETLS) focused on the Commission's paramount obligation to attain economic integration in the region by improving trade within the region amidits allies.

Though ECOWAS aspires to create regions without boundaries, where the residents could have the opportunity to its enormous natural deposits and the ability to utilize these resources to create prospects for a viable region, however, the only thing that ECOWAS has managed to produce is rather an integration of the region. This enhanced the ability of the people to have access to move freely, as well as to attain competent educational and health schemes and employ economic and viable activities, while there are harmony and serenity in the region. This explains the execution of salient and tactical schemes which could strengthen the interrelation and gradually eradicate the foreseen hurdles to the realization of total integration. Significant steps have been made over the years, in coordinating macroeconomic strategies as well as the advancement of the private sector in order to achieve economic integration.

In spite of the geographical and social influences, the countries in the ECOWAS region are objectively diverse in their economic characteristics. The core of the region's economic activities is Nigeria, having a Gross Domestic Product of $522.8 billion in 2013, which was 900% greater than the gross domestic product of the country that ranked next in size, Ghana. Cabo Verde had the highest per capita GDP at $3767 followed by Nigeria, with above $3000. The least gross domestic product for the region was from Gambia numerically, as well as the country with the population that was third least. The country with the least per capita GDP was Niger, a non-coastal country, with its total value at $415. Therefore, in contemplation of minimal range of development economically in West Africa, the aid of development stages in the region are much, for all countries in the ECOWAS region save Cabo Verde (ECOWAS External Trade Statistics 2009).

The export volume for the countries in the region increased by 260% subsequent from 2000, that is, in 2000, from a value of $34.5 billion to about $124 billion in the year 2014. Considering the said value, the portion of the exports that is ECOWAS channelled to other allies in the ECOWAS region has remained reasonably stable at around 7–11% of the overall export value. In 2016, ECOWAS inter-regional trade was 10.6% while trade with the rest of the world was 89.4%. Inter-regional export and import was 9.4%, whereas export and import with the rest of the world was 90.6% (UNCTAD 2018). Nevertheless, the trend and value of trade without the region has been substantially altered. For the region, both exports and imports for Asia, China (East Asia) in particular and for (South Asia) India, increased considerably whereas the portion of ECOWAS North American trade, to the USA precisely, was on the decline. The East Asian exports, for instance, included lower than 5% of the entire ECOWAS exports in 2000, whereas in 2014, it explained greater than 17% of the ECOWAS region. Conversely, for export in the region, about 35% was directed towards the USA in 2000, though there was a change in quite a lot of economic indicators, including a decline of the US demand for imported petroleum, which resulted into a further decline to 4% in 2014.

The degree of intra-regional trade for the ECOWAS region remains is still rather minimal, in spite of exertions to minimize the obstacles to trade amid West African allies. In 2014, not quite 10% of the total exports emanating from ECOWAS countries were directed to its ECOWAS allies. Nonetheless, there exists a great margin in the proportion for each economy's exports that was directed to ECOWAS allies. Nigeria, for instance, had the greatest worth of export to ECOWAS countries, which was greater than $5 billion. However, Nigeria's export to ECOWAS encompassed less than 6% of the nation's entire exports. That very year, exports from countries like Togo, Niger and Senegal accounted for barely 3% of the entire ECOWAS exports, even though every economy depended on ECOWAS allies for minimum 40% of their exports. Hence, though trade without the ECOWAS region does not instantly show as an essential necessity for the economic well-being of the region altogether, as certain economies depend on ECOWAS allies for a great proportion of their trade.

It is essential to take note that trade that is not accounted for in the form of informal cross-border trade (ICBT) is prevalent in West Africa, resulting into a high degree of unaccounted approved trade data, especially for trade without the region. Facts from the African Development Bank (AfDB) shows that ICBT for the ECOWAS region stands at the range between 20% for the Nigerian GDP and 75% for the Benin GDP. The annual percentage of real GDP for Benin was 2.1 in 2015 and 5.4 in 2017, while for Burkina Faso it was 4.03 in 2015 and 6.38 in 2017. For Cote d'ivoire, the real GDP was 1.24 for 2015 and 1.00 in 2017, Ghana had 9.01 in 2015 and a whopping 16.31

in 2017, whereas for Nigeria, 7.5 in 2015 and 11.80 in 2017. Concerns regarding control aggravate the subject of informal trade; whereas circumstances that pertain to unethical prosecution process for regulations and trade cliques portend impairment to formal trade. Hence, as the approved amounts of trade within the regional seem rather insignificant, a substantial volume of trade amid ECOWAS nations is persistently unaccountable in the records (The ECOWAS External Trade Statistics 2009).

This research work examined the extent to which trade liberalization exert on ECOWAS' members economies. The work will test the hypothesis: Trade liberalization has no significant effect on economic development of ECOWAS countries. The hypothesis will be tested with the use of pooled ordinary least square baseline regression, generalized least square, fixed and random effect model estimation techniques for 14 countries within the period 2000–2017.

Literature Review

Trade Liberalization is simply referred to removal or reduction of barriers to trade, liberalized external capital flows, and diffusion of technology and international migration of labour. It covers decontrol—the elimination of non-tariff measures—as well as policies that shift the trade regime towards neutrality—a reduction in the bias towards a particular activity, especially the production of import substitutes. Liberalization to trade is a vital element of economic liberalization, and this is hinged on the fact that trade liberalization involves the reduction of barriers to associated with trade, which includes barriers in form of tariffs and non-tariff, internal restrictions, such as directed credit and preferential purchasing (Matthew 2013). Again, trade liberalization is a mechanism used for measuring the rate of export promotion which involves the transfer of resources from import substitution to promote export. This is also comprises of the degree at which countries open to trade, the rate at which countries enhances th import and its export in the income of such countries as well as changing the structure of incentives and institutional framework (Mwaba 2000).

Liberalization to trade is a large scope which is made of the effect of exact policies to liberalization; these liberalization policies include inflow of foreign capital, reducing the rate of tariffs among other factors that constitute trade liberalization. Following the study of Chaudhuri et al. (2006) which was conducted to the impact of liberalization to trade and some major programmes that constitute expenditure on households welfare and the rate of labour force in developing countries in terms of a three-sector Harris–Todaro kind general equilibrium model. Also, the empirical work of Yabuuchi and Mukhopadhayay (2006) posited that there exists inflexibility in terms of wage rate in the urban sectors; this wage rigidity which result in instantaneous existence of open unemployment and an urban informal sector in the migration equilibrium.

The problem associated with liberalization to trade has brought about three various schools of thought which argued on the nature of trade liberalization. These three schools of thought are examined; thus, the first school of thought is the advocate of liberalization to (pro-trade liberalizationist), which are of the opinion that it is the best thing that could happen to this world. It has brought about a lot of benefits to the entire world. These benefits include access to modern technologies that are not available domestically, exchange of fruitful ideas, access to goods and services at relatively cheaper rates compared to the domestic economy, and it encourages specialization and competitiveness, enhances modernization, access to latest information and frontier of knowledge. The school argues that all these put together would enhance the economic activities in any country and thereby accelerate economic growth and development.

The second school of thought (anti-trade liberalizationist) believes that its advent has actually led to a more problem than good to various countries. This is because, the school of thought is of the opinion that liberalization to trade leads dumping of goods and services in countries which have no competitive power in the market, especially developing countries. It is also observed that it poses constraints to goods and services which are produced locally, bearing in mind that about 60% of goods produced by developing countries may not have the potential to compete favourably with goods produced by developed countries.

Given the fact that developing countries have limited potential to compete, this causes domestic organizations are in most cases crowding out in business, which in turn leads to massive layoff and thus, the rate of employment significantly declines in such countries. The third school of thought argued that trade liberalization may exert a positive or adverse impact on depending on the nature of strategy adopted by a given country to tacked of such issue. The school of thought is of the opinion that is based on the fact that while some countries have benefited from trade, others do not benefit from it. Similarly, the Asian Tigers gained due to their effective strategy to trade. But, in developing countries, the same thing is not experiences given the fact that most of the organizations which are locally based lack trade protection, which causes crowding-out of business as a result of international competition which in turn leads to diminish the rate of economic growth in such countries

According to Acha and Ukpong (2012), the development of an economy is made up of the procedure and programmes and where by a country enhances the economic, policies, and programmes which countries of the globe adopt to improve technological, scientific, cultural, and human capacity development of their citizenry. According to Blattnery et al. (2001), economic development has been noted since the Second World War (WWII) to involve economic growth, comprising of the improvement in income per capita, and improve the living standard of the people to match with the developed countries. Economic development can also be seen as astatic theory that documents the state of an economy at a certain time. Accordingly, the bottom line of economic development is hinged on prosperity building and living standard. The fact about economic development concept is that, the world lives and operates in a worldwide economy. Worldwide economy (commerce) means that in American (and indeed other parts of the globe) business must operate and corporate globally.

The underlying assumptions are that countries must think rationally, avoid isolationist practices, and build strong economic platforms for growth and emancipation. Thinking and acting regionally should be the key fundamental point of departure for economic development needs and goals; the same remains the focal point of this paper on trade liberalization in ECOWAS sub-region; its implication for economic development. Economic development is the long-term process of building a number of interdependent microeconomic capabilities and incentives to support more advanced forms of competition. These capabilities and incentives include the nature and extent of inputs required by the firms to produce goods or services; the rules, incentives and norms governing the type and intensity of local rivalry; the quality of demand for local services; and the extent and quality of local suppliers and related industries.

ECOWAS sub-region mission is made up of the following: regional trade promoting and economic integration via the creation of an economic and monetary union for promoting economic growth of member countries (Johnson 2003). The region mission also focuses on the promotion of the socio-economic and cultural activities among member states with the aim of improving the standard of living of the people, attainment of stability in the economy, enhancing cooperation among member states, and contributing to the overall development of the region in. However, ECOWAS has witnessed some draw back in the quest to achieve its goals. These range from political instability and violence, dearth of good governance in some member states, problem of national economies diversification; the inadequacy of reliable infrastructures, language differences between members, and difficulties in handling crises—especially those arising from religious and ethnic dispositions (Obadan 2003; CBN 2005).

A study carried out by Sachs and Warner (1997) posited that countries that engage trade openness witness significant economic development of 4.5% yearly in the late 1970s and the early 1980s. On the other hand, countries who are not open to trade experienced low growth rate of approximately 0.7% annually. Following the study of Sachs and Warner (1997) on binary measure of trade openness, the empirical study of Hoeffler (2002) affirmed that trade openness had significant and positive effect on economic growth of countries through improving the rate of investment stock. In a similar study, Ndiyo and Ebong (2004) conducted a study engaging the vector autoregressive (VAR) model in examining the dynamic effect openness to trade, foreign direct investment (FDI), and other macroeconomic factors on economic growth, and the study found and concluded that an adverse effect of openness to trade, volatility associated with exchange rate, fiscal deficit, average world prices and unfavourable balance of payments impact negatively on economic growth in Nigeria.

However, it is a widely known fact that the more a country is open to trade, the better inflow of FDI from developed countries to their developing fellows. Similarly, it has been observed that that the latter (especially ECOWAS members) have not been able to fully position their economies to align with the investment components in accelerating the desired economic growth of the region (Igudia 2004). This failure of alignment has been seen as to result from the inability of ECOWAS member countries to propound investment-driven programmes, political and social unrest, reliance on primary commodities to promote export, institutional and structural insufficiency, and inadequate infrastructural base (Fosu 1996; Obadan 2004; Aluko 2004; Osabuohien 2007). An empirical study conducted by Alege and Ogun

(2005) exploring the nexus between trade openness and industrialization by instigating the effect of difference indicators of globalization which include the rate of openness to trade, trade volume, FDI inflows and efficient innovation with respect to technology on aggregate manufacturing production in Nigeria. The study posited that trade openness, trade volume and increased information communication technologies (ICTs) have a positive impact on manufacturing output. The above is akin to the study of Akinlo's (2003) which concluded that using growth rate of export and FDI as proxy for degree of openness, that a 1%-point growth in exports increases stock market by 0.19% point in Sub-Saharan African economies.

Baliamoune-Lutz and Ndikumana (2007) in their study examined the growth effects of trade liberalization and the role of institutions in 39 African countries between 1975 and 2001 using pooled data. The result of their study showed that at high levels of trade, the quality of institutions plays a key role in the transmission of trade gains into growth. According to Mwaba (2000), he examined the impact of trade liberalization on economic growth in Africa using descriptive analysis. He found out that Africa has maintained the highest import barriers through tariffs and quantitative restrictions among the developing countries. Thus, measures should be embarked on to increase the competitiveness of their products.

Methodological Approach

The Empirical Model

This study formulates its empirical model by building on Matthew (2013) model on the examination of trade liberalization, institutions with emphasis on economic growth. The model proposed by Matthew (2013) was focused on the examination of the interaction effect of trade liberalization and institution on economic growth which verified if in effect, trade liberalization will affect economic growth more when we have economic, political or cultural institutions. This study differs from the model of Matthew (2013) by the examination of the effect of trade liberalization on economic development (beyond economic growth dimension) in ECOWAS. Hence, the empirical model expresses the components of economic development as trade to GDP ratio, government expenditure, tariff, infrastructure, domestic investment and foreign direct investment.

The implicit form of the empirical model is stated as follows:

$$Y = f(\mathrm{TAR}, \mathrm{FDI}, \mathrm{DOM}, \mathrm{GOVEX}, \mathrm{TRADE}, \mathrm{INFR}) \quad (1)$$

The explicit form of the model is given as:

$$\begin{aligned} Y_{it} &= \alpha_0 + \alpha_1 \mathrm{TAR}_{it} + \alpha_2 \mathrm{FDI}_{it} + \alpha_3 \mathrm{DOM}_{it} \\ &+ \alpha_4 \mathrm{GOVEX}_{it} + \alpha_5 \mathrm{TRADE}_{it} + \alpha_6 \mathrm{INFR}_{it} + \mu_{it}. \end{aligned} \quad (2)$$

The variables are transformed by taking the natural log and the result is seen in Eq. (3). The error term is hypothesized to be purely random while the parameters are hypothesized as follows: α_0, α_2, α_3, α_4 and α_6 as positive values while α_1 and α_5 are hypothesized as negative.

$$Y_{it} = \alpha_0 + \alpha_1 \mathrm{tar}_{it} + \alpha_2 \mathrm{fdi}_{it} + \alpha_3 \mathrm{dom}_{it} + \alpha_4 \mathrm{govex}_{it} + \alpha_5 \mathrm{trade}_{it} + \alpha_6 \mathrm{infr}_{it} + \mu_{it}. \tag{3}$$

where 'Y_{it}' represents human development index which is a proxy for economic development of country 'i' at time 't' as used in Ejemeyovwi and Osabuohien (2018) to proxy inclusive growth (economic development beyond growth), 'tar_{it}' stands for tariffs which is used as the trade liberalization variable whereby, the reduction or total removal implies the liberalization of trade; '$\mathrm{fdi}_{\mathrm{it}}$' represents foreign direct investment; '$\mathrm{trade}_{\mathrm{it}}$' stands for trade to GDP ratio; 'infr' represents infrastructure; '$\mathrm{dom}_{\mathrm{it}}$' represents domestic investment; and 'govex'''represents government expenditure.

Method of Analysis

The study utilizes four econometric techniques of estimation for the attainment of the study's objective. The selected techniques include the pooled ordinary least squares (POLS), generalized least squares (GLS), the random effect model (REM), fixed effect model (FEM) as well as the Sargan and Hansen Chi-square test. The pooled OLS method pools together the panel data set neglecting the cross-sectional and time series nature, hence getting a grand regression (Matthew 2013). The pooled OLS is utilized as a baseline estimation technique.

The generalized least squares technique caters to the possible heterogeneity issues in the data set given the panel nature of the data set. The fixed effect model (FEM) regression assumes that each individual unit has its own intercept, and the coefficient of the regressors vary across countries or overtime, hence implying that the explanatory variables and error term are correlated. The random effect model (REM), on the other hand, assumes that the intercept values are random drawing from a much bigger population of observations and have a common mean value for the intercept, hence assuming that the explanatory variables and error terms are uncorrelated. The Sargan and Hansen Chi-square test is a perfect substitute to the popular Hausman test and is utilized to determine the most appropriate model regression between the REM and the FEM given the data set (Gujarati and Porter 2009; Matthew 2013).

Data and Data Sources

The data utilized by this study encompasses data from fourteen countries that form the ECOWAS region, and the data covers the period 2000–2017. ECOWAS consists

Table 1 Variables' definition and source of data

Data	Identifier	Data source	Measurement
Economic development (human development index)	hdi	UNDP, 2018	a, b, c, d
Trade to gross domestic product (GDP)	trade	WDI, 2018	Per cent
Tariff	tar	WDI, 2018	Per cent
Foreign direct investment	fdi	WDI, 2018	Percentage (%) of GDP
Domestic investment	dom	WDI, 2018	Percentage (%) of GDP
Infrastructure	infr	WDI, 2016	Access to electricity; Percentage (%) of population
Government expenditure	govex	WDI, 2018	Percentage (%) of GDP

Note a = life expectancy at birth (to assess a long and healthy life); b = adult literacy (percentage of the population aged over 15 years who can read and write); c = educational enrolment rates (percentage of population in the relevant age cohort enrolled in primary, secondary, and tertiary education); and d = gross domestic product (GDP) per capita (to assess standard of living)
Source Compiled by the Authors', 2019

of fifteen countries of the West African region. The countries are Benin, Burkina Faso, Cape Verde, Cote d'Ivoire, Gambia, Ghana, Guinea, Guinea Bissau, Liberia, Mali, Nigeria, Sierra Leone, Senegal and Togo. The variables' identifiers, indicators, data sources and unit of measurement of the utilized data are presented in Table 1

Results and Discussions

The results for the baseline regression (pooled ordinary least squares), generalized least squares, fixed and random effect model (FEM and REM) estimation techniques utilized by the study are presented in this section. The section commences by the display of the results of the Sargan and Hansen which recommends the most appropriate model regression between the REM and the FEM. The rule of thumb for deciding the most appropriate model (between the REM and FEM) states that: given that the FEM was run first before the REM, if the Chi-Square probability value of the test is less than 0.05, the FEM is most appropriate and if the Chi-Square probability value is greater than 0.05, the REM is most appropriate for interpretation and policy recommendation. Table 2 shows the Hausman test result.

Worthy of note that FEM is necessary if a study is aimed to examine the effect of variables that are dynamic overtime for which there may be particular characteristics of the individual or entity (in this case country) that may impact or bias the predictor or outcome variables and hence a control will be needed for these fixed effects. This motivates the assumption of the correlation between the country's own error term and its independent (predictor) variables. FEM removes the time-invariant characteristics unique to the individual captured in the constant.

Table 2 Sargan and Hansen statistic test result

$\chi^2(4)$: 8.17	
Prob Value: 0.23	
Decision Rule	
Fixed Effect	**Random Effect**
Reject	Accept

Source Computed by the Authors', 2019

On the other hand, the random effect model (REM) was observed to be suitable if the variation across entities is assumed to be random and uncorrelated with the predictor (independent) but error term of an entity is correlated with the dependent variable In sum, the use of the FEM signifies the presence of individual-specific fixed effects which could affect the result if not taken care of during the estimation process while the choice of the REM indicates the absence of a correlation between the predictors and error term which allows for time-invariant variables to play a role as explanatory variables (Greene 2008; Osuma et al. 2018). The probability value of the Sargan and Hansen Chi-square test recommends the interpretation of the random effect result given that it is statistically insignificant (greater than 0.05).

Table 3 reports the empirical results of the study and the general interpretation show that the number of observations utilized for the study was 124 observations. The number of groups present within the data set was fourteen (14) while the R-squared for all the analyses were valued within the acceptable range (0.01–0.5] which indicates an acceptable goodness of fit (coefficient of determination). The F-statistics and its probability value that show the overall significance of the model and given that the probability value is close to '0.000' and more importantly less than 0.05, it implies a good overall fit of the model. The Wald test also indicates a similar overall model fit like the F-statistics and given that the values are not equal to zero, it is also acceptable. The correlation between the error term and independent variables show a negative correlation for the fixed effect model technique which indicates presence of time-invariant characteristics unique to the countries captured in the constant while the correlation between the error term and independent variables for the random effect model technique report the zero.

In terms of the variable-specific results, the major variable of interest for trade liberalization, tariff, firstly indicates statistically significant result for the pooled OLS while for the GLS, FEM and REM, statistically insignificant values were observed. This is shown by the probability values of the coefficient of Tariff for which the decision rule for the probability values (p-value) state that the p-value for should be less than 0.01 for statistical significance at 1% level, 0.05 for statistical significance at 5% level and less than 0.10 for statistical significance at 10% level of significance This economically implies that for Economic Community of West African States (ECOWAS) member countries, an increase in the tariff for importation may likely not affect economic development significantly. The result goes against 'apriori' expectation which states that a significant relationship is expected and furthermore, an increase in the trade liberalization (a decrease or complete removal of tariffs) will

Table 3 Econometric results (dependent variable: economic development)

Predictor variables	POLS	GLS	FEM	REM
Tariff	0.290 (0.002)	0.25 (0.24)	0.18 (0.18)	0.25 (0.24)
Foreign direct investment	−0.003 (0.015)	−0.004 (0.43)	−0.02 (0.36)	−0.004 (0.43)
Domestic investment	−0.047 (0.025)	0.04 (0.33)	0.03 (0.66)	0.04 (0.33)
Government expenditure	−0.207 (0.010)	0.22 (0.008)	0.27 (0.03)	0.22 (0.008)
Trade-GDP ratio	0.036 (0.66)	−0.12 (0.09)	−0.23 (0.04)	−0.12 (0.09)
Infrastructure	−0.077 (0.004)	0.06 (0.02)	0.04 (0.58)	0.06 (0.02)
Number of observations	124	124	124	124
Number of groups		14	14	14
F	7.99		2.20	
R^2	0.22	0.18	0.03	
Prob > F	(0.000)		(0.04)	
Root MSE	0.08			
Wald χ^2 (6)		17.83		17.83
Prob > χ^2		0.0067		0.0067
Corr (u_i, x_b)			−0.73	
Corr (u_i, x)				0

Note The values in the parenthesis '()' are the probability values; POLS: Pooled OLS; GLS: Generalized Least Squares; FEM: Fixed Effect Model; REM: Random Effect Model; *, ** and *** denotes that the coefficients are significant at 1, 5 and 10%, respectively. *Source* Authors' Computation, 2019

lead to economic development in ECOWAS countries. However, the insignificant result of this study is in line with Matthew (2013) who found that trade liberalization has no significant impact on an economy.

Interestingly, trade–GDP ratio and foreign direct investment (FDI) reported statistically insignificant result for most of the four analyses and surprisingly negative figures for the coefficients at 5% level of statistical significance. This economically implies that for ECOWAS member countries, an increase in the foreign direct investment and trade–GDP ratio may affect economic development insignificantly, and however negatively. The result also goes against 'apriori' expectation which states that a significant relationship is expected and furthermore, an increase in the foreign direct investment and trade—GDP ratio will lead to economic development in ECOWAS countries.

Theoretically, trade liberalization links up with economic development if there is over-sufficient presence of domestic high valued commodities and services produced by the ECOWAS countries. This will be a basis for economic liberalization hence sharing such proficient services and high valued goods will have a significant influence on the level of economic development across the various sectors of the ECOWAS communities. The various sectors that could be impacted positively and significantly include the education sector, health sector, agriculture sector, manufacturing sector through the production exchange of finances, goods and services among the ECOWAS member countries. The agriculture and manufacturing sector of ECOWAS countries may profit from trade liberalization if engaged in conversion from primary to secondary products because the two sectors should serve as the basis of majority of traded components.

Recommendations and Conclusion

The study investigated the effect of trade liberalization on economic development in Economic Community of West African States (ECOWAS) using pooled ordinary least squares (baseline regression), generalized least squares, fixed and random effect model (FEM and REM) estimation techniques. Evidence from the analysis covering 2000 to 2017—time period for fourteen countries reveal that the trade liberalization has an insignificant impact on economic development statistically at 5% level of significance.

The findings of this study supports the findings of Matthew (2013) that ECOWAS countries are not ready for trade liberalization as it has an insignificant impact on economic development. For obvious reasons, however, as it was noted that trade with other parts of the world is immensely greater than trade within the ECOWAS region, in spite of the liberalization efforts in the region. Also, more should be done regarding the accountability of intra-regional trade to ensure they are well documented and captured. These will correct earlier lapses and create sufficient possibilities of significant relationship to economic development.

Since development can also be noted to be much greater than growth in income, to other factors ranging from sustainable domestic market, education, better life expectancy alongside with sustainable socio-economic environment, it is essential that member countries' governments create enabling environments which will bring about the desired economic development and better living standards for the citizenry of member countries in the ECOWAS region (Adegboye 2014). Akin to the findings, ECOWAS member countries are tasked with identifying why trade liberalization's impact on economic development is insignificant and finding a lasting solution.

References

Acha I, Ukpong SM (2012) Micro institutions in Nigeria. Res J Finance Account. iiste.org/Journals/index.php/RJFA/article/view/328. Accessed on 21 Dec 2018

Adegboye FB (2014) Foreign direct investment and economic development: evidence from selected African countries. Phd thesis, Department of Banking and Finance Covenant University, Ota

Akinlo EA (2003) Globalization, international investment and stock market growth in sub-Saharan Africa. Visiting Research Fellow Monograph Series, No. 382. Institute of Developing Economies, Japan

Alege PO, Ogun TP (2005) Exploring the globalization-industrialization nexus for economic development: a case of Nigeria. Selected papers for the 2004 Annual Conference, Ibadan, Nigerian Economic Society, pp 245–274
Aluko S (2004) Background to globalization and Africa's economic development. Globalization and Africa's Economic Development, Ibadan, Nigerian Economic Society, pp 35–67
African Trade Report (2018) Boosting intra-African trade: implications of the African Continental Free Trade Area Agreement. *AFREXIMBANK Cairo*
Baliamoune-Lutz M, Ndikumana L (2007) The growth effects of openness to trade and the role of institutions: new evidence from African countries. Economics Department Working Paper Series, Paper 38, University of Massachusetts, Amherst, USA
Blattnery RC, Gerbz G, Thomas JS (2001) Customer equity, building and managing relationships as valuable assets. Harvard Business School Press, Boston, MA
Central Bank of Nigeria (2005) Economic Reports for the First Half of Year 2005. Central Bank of Nigeria, Abuja
Chaudhuri S, Yabuuchi S, Mukhopadhayay U (2006) Inflow of foreign capital and trade liberalization in a model with an informal sector and urban unemployment. Pac Econ Rev 11(1):87–103
ECOWAS External Trade Statistics (2009) http://www.ecostat.org/en/standard
Ejemeyovwi JO, Osabuohien ES (2018) Mobile technology adoption and inclusive growth in West Africa. Contemp Soc Sci. https://doi.org/10.1080/21582041.2018.1503320
Fosu AK (1996) Primary exports and economic growth in developing countries. World Econ 19(4):465–475
Greene WH (2008) Econometric analysis. Prentice Hall, Upper Saddle River, NJ
Gujarati DN, Porter DC (2009) Basic econometrics, 5th edn. McGraw Hill, New York
Hoeffler A (2002) Openness, investment and growth. J Afr Econo 10(4):470–497
Igudia P (2004) Globalization and economic development: Nigeria's experience and prospects. In: Globalization and Africa's economic development. Nigerian Economic Society, Ibadan, pp 347–375
Johnson E (2003) Economic community of West African states (ECOWAS), Country Analysis Briefs. http://www.eia.doe.gov/emeu/cabs/ghana.html
Matthew AO (2013) Trade liberalization, Institutions and Economic Growth in selected SSA countries. An unpublished Phd thesis submitted to the Department of Economics and Development Studies, Covenant University, Ota, Ogun State
Mwaba A (2000) Trade liberalization and growth: policy options for African countries in a global economy. Economic Research Papers, No. 60, African Development Bank
Ndiyo NA, Ebong ES (2004) The challenges of openness in developing economies: some empirical lessons from Nigeria. In: Globalization and Africa's economic development. Nigerian Economic Society, Ibadan, pp 571–598
Obadan MI (2004) Globalization and economic management in Africa. In: Globalization and Africa's economic development. Nigerian Economic Society, Ibadan, pp 3–34
Obadan MI (2003) National development planning and budgeting in Nigeria: some pertinent issues. Broadway Press, Lagos
Osabuohien ESC (2007) Trade openness and economic performance of ECOWAS members—reflections from Ghana and Nigeria. Afr J Bus Econ Res 2(2&3):57–73
Osuma G, Ikpefan A, Osabuohien R, Ndigwe C, Nkwodimmah P (2018) Working capital management and bank performance: empirical research of ten deposit money banks in Nigeria. Banks Bank Syst 13(2):49–61
Sachs DJ, Warner AM (1997) Fundamental sources of long-run growth. Am Econ Rev 87:184–188
United Nations Center for Trade and Development (2018) Trade and development report. United Nations Publications, Geneva
Uwatt BU (2004) Globalization and economic growth: The African experience. In: Globalization and Africa's economic development. Nigerian Economic Society, Ibadan, pp 129–158

Promoting Connectivity of Infrastructure in the Context of One Belt, One Road Initiatives: Implications for Africa in the Fourth Industrial Revolution

Musibau Adetunji Babatunde

Introduction

Africa is seen today as a continent of enormous opportunity, a destination for investors and development actors seeking high-growth markets. However, Africa's economic growth is being hampered by weak infrastructure especially on connectivity. Connectivity of a country, or of a port or airport, is usually defined as how central this location is on those networks. In part, connectivity reflects geography and the global structure of transport and logistics networks. Africa is the least connected continent as clearly evident from the 2012 NASA satellite image of the earth (Patel 2014). Thus, Africa's infrastructure networks are highly fragmentary, reflecting the continent's atomized nation-states.

Progress on the ground on improving connectivity (via better regional infrastructure and integration) has been and continues to be grossly inadequate. Roads, when present, are often unpaved and poorly maintained, rail networks are unreliable and limited and ports are inefficient and lack capacity. These problems increase production and transportation costs, harm product quality and lead to shipment delays. The World Bank estimates that Africa's infrastructure deficit holds back its economic growth by 2% each year (Foster and Briceño-Garmendia 2010). The connectivity bias is, however. more profound for landlocked economies. As a result, the level of intraregional connectivity is very low, when measured in the context of transcontinental highway links, power inter-connectors or intraregional fiber optic backbone. Thus, despite phases of economic growth in many African countries in recent years, these insufficient infrastructure networks have limited cross-border flows of trade, capital, information and people, drastically affecting Africa's growth and broader development performance and regional integration.

M. A. Babatunde (✉)
Department of Economics, University of Ibadan, Ibadan, Nigeria
e-mail: tunjiyusuf19@yahoo.com

G. O. A. Odularu et al. (eds.), *Fostering Trade in Africa*,
Advances in African Economic, Social and Political Development,
https://doi.org/10.1007/978-3-030-36632-2_6

Currently, there are four major transport corridors in Africa. These corridors are routes linking several economic centers, countries and ports. While some are only road transport corridors, most of them include more than one mode of transport. The formal designation of a specific set of routes as a corridor is generally part of an endeavor to focus effort on improving the quality of transport services to these routes. For example, the Northern Corridor comprises the transport facilities and infrastructure linking landlocked countries of East and Central Africa, namely: Burundi, Democratic Republic of Congo, Rwanda and Uganda to the seaport of Mombasa in Kenya. The corridor also serves Northern Tanzania, Southern Sudan and Ethiopia. Utilization of this corridor by the landlocked States was initially covered by bilateral agreements between countries. However, it was realized that some provisions of the agreements were contradictory and there were numerous transit charges payable by corridor users. Nevertheless, the central corridor comprises the Port of Dar es Salaam, the Dar es Salaam-Kigoma 1254 km long railway which interfaces with water transport on Lake Tanganyika to Bujumbura and DRC as well as a road route linking Dar es Salaam through Dodoma, Singida, Nzega and Lusahunga to Rwanda and Burundi.

The Dar es Salaam Corridor links the Port of Dar es Salaam in Tanzania to Lusaka in Zambia and Lilongwe in Malawi. Key infrastructure along the corridor includes the port, the TAZARA railway line and the TANZAM highway. The Walvis Bay Corridor consists of three trade routes linking the Port of Walvis Bay to neighboring countries. The three routes are known as: Trans-Kalahari Corridor (TKC); Trans-Caprivi Corridor (TCC); and Trans-Cunene Corridor (TCuC). The Trans-Kalahari Corridor is a highway connecting Walvis Bay to Johannesburg and Pretoria through Botswana. The Trans-Caprivi Corridor is a highway which branches off from the Trans-Kalahari Highway at Karibib and proceeds north-eastwards via Grootfontein to the Angolan border at Rundu, and then eastwards through the Caprivi strip to Katima Mulilo where a new bridge across the Zambezi River into Zambia onto DRC was opened in 2004 (ADB/UNECA 2003).

The Trans-Cunene Corridor consists of the northern part of the Namibian national highway from Otavi to Oshikango and shares the same route as the Trans-Caprivi Highway from Walvis Bay to Otavi. From Oshikango, the road continues to Lubango in Angola. This section is presently being repaired following damage during the civil war. As the Namibia rail network is separated from its eastern and northern neighbors, all three corridors are only partly supported by rail connections. The Walvis Bay Corridor concept is a complete regional development approach as the Port of Walvis Bay serves as an entry/exit point for landlocked countries—Botswana, Zambia and Zimbabwe—and markets in the hinterland of the DRC and South Africa (Gauteng Region) (Adzibgey et al. 2007).

The Maputo Corridor connects the Port of Maputo in Mozambique to Gauteng, the industrial heartland of South Africa. It comprises a concessioned road, a railway line and since recently a gas pipeline. It has emerged as one of the most successful implementations of the Spatial Development Initiatives (SDI), a concept developed in the mid-1990 s by the South African Trade Department and the Development Bank of South Africa (DBSA). The Lagos-Abidjan Corridor is the busiest passenger corridor in West Africa. It connects five countries—Côte d'Ivoire, Ghana, Togo, Benin and Nigeria—through the port cities of Abidjan, Accra, Lome, Cotonou and Lagos. Nevertheless, bilateral arrangements or agreements between neighboring states are still the most common forms of corridor management. These are found across Sub-Saharan Africa and were the first form of cooperation between the States of the Northern Corridor (Adzibgey et al. 2007).

The poor connectivity challenges can be seen in the unduly long transit times on African transport corridors due to factors such as unclear and sometimes conflicting rules and regulations, inefficient service providers, road blocks,[1] as well as cumbersome administrative and customs procedures. These have created a serious challenge to transport facilitation (connectivity) and trade on the continent. It leads to excessive traffic delays, resulting in substantial increase in transport costs. The current transport corridors in Africa therefore face the challenges of productivity. The existence of roadblocks and numerous checkpoints on African corridors has created a serious challenge to transport facilitation and trade in the continent. It leads to excessive traffic delays, thus resulting in substantial increase in transport costs.

Similar to the challenges faced by road transportation, the maritime transportation network in Africa is also inadequate. This is despite the fact that maritime transport is the most dominant mode of transport for moving freight from and to Africa. It accounts for over 92% of Africa's external trade. With a total coastline of 30,725 km, Africa has 90 major ports and a number of other ports providing services for fishing and tourism. African ports handle only 6% of global traffic, of which about six ports, three each in Egypt and South Africa, handle about 50% of Africa's container traffic (UNECA 2009). Africa is also endowed with a number of rivers and lakes that have great potential of being inexpensive, energy-efficient and environment-friendly inland waterways. Twenty-nine African countries have navigable bodies of water, but only a small number have been well developed for transport services. The ports and connecting sea corridors of the coastal nations are regional public goods that typically service multiple landlocked countries in the hinterland. While international norms for port performance (the number of days to get a container out) are 3–4 days from arrival, only Durban, Casablanca and Tunis are close to such performance with the average for Africa's other large ports being 16 days. State's role is predominant, the private sector, including global operators' role, being limited. Because of numerous constraints, port charges are high for shippers. Shipping lines face congestion costs and poor port productivity and pass these costs to the shippers. Consequently, African economies, as a whole, bear the costs of congestion and poor port productivity.

Landlocked countries are seriously disadvantaged as their shippers support very high transport costs owing to low traffic volumes along the Corridors but also to numerous abnormal practices and the limited use of modern technology. For example, West and Central Africa sub-region lags behind in terms of global trends affecting

[1]In 2008 the major corridors in West Africa had 1.7–2.40 roadblocks on every 100 km route. The Tema-Ouagadougou corridor had the most frequent check points, with 2.40 per 100 km (UNECA 2009).

port sector in the world. Contrary to most regions in the world, port concentration in West and Central Africa is limited. In terms of size and activity, the Port of Lagos is the most important. Its annual merchandise traffic is in excess of 30 million tons, which is approximately 55% of Nigeria's port activity (excluding hydrocarbon exporting terminals) and 25% of total ECOWAS member countries' port activity. The ports of Abidjan, Dakar, Douala, Tema, Lomé and Cotonou play a regional role. These ports can not only count on their national hinterland in order to thrive but also on traffic in transit. Should land transport be facilitated along the corridor Abidjan-Lagos, these ports would be in a situation of direct competition to serve landlocked countries.

The transport patterns in East Africa, as elsewhere in the world, are constantly changing and the coastal countries compete to serve as transit countries. A considerable number of landlocked countries border are to partly dependant on the two channels of Kenya and Tanzania on one hand as well as Sudan, Uganda, DR Congo, Rwanda, Burundi and Malawi on the other hand. Between these two coastal channels, and especially its ports, there is a constant competition to serve as transit ports for the hinterland.

Adequate air transport connectivity is important for tourism, business and high-value products. Although the number of airports and airfields in the region seem enormous, a significant number of them do not meet International Civil Aviation Organization (ICAO) standards and recommended practices. Only 117 of Africa's airports are classified as international airports (Jerome 2011). The share of global air transport remains modest at about 5.2% of the passenger traffic, approximately 3.6% of freight and roughly 8.5% of the number of departures for 2006 (Jerome 2011). Recent years have witnessed significant progress in air transport connectivity within Southern and Eastern Africa, with strong traffic growth and the emergence of three strong regional hubs and associated major African carriers—Ethiopian, Kenyan and South African. In addition, Togo and Cote d'Ivoire in West Africa are making progress after the vacuum created by the demise of several regional.

Rail links form an integral part of Africa's system of sea corridors. These sometimes provide the only connection to hinterland countries. More frequently, they compete with road connections. While rail has the competitive edge on certain bulk commodities, the volumes of traffic for these commodities in Africa are often below the minimum thresholds needed to make the rail corridors financially viable, particularly given that rail freight tariffs are effectively capped by intermodal competition from road freight. This is partly due to the fact that half of the railway lines are in poor condition with different network characteristics (gauge, clearance, axle load and signaling and communication systems) and use old technologies. Currently, there is the absence of a smooth interface between maritime and land transport systems in the continent which means that most of Africa's containers are stuffed and stripped in the vicinity of the port, rather than used as a mean of facilitating multi-modal transport. According to Ocean Shipping Consultants (2008), this practice, combined with inefficient port management, leads to truck cycle times of 4–10 h in Africa's ports, compared with one hour in other parts of the world. In addition, container dwell times range from 6 to 15 days compared with 7 in other parts of the world (Foster and Briceño-Garmendia 2010).

It is expected that the removal of these barriers would have a greater impact on economic growth and competitiveness of the continent. However, Africa's need is not just for an adequate, efficient and viable infrastructure stock, but for transformational infrastructure that will spur Africa to the next level of development and reposition the continent as a recognized player in the global economy. The essential benefits of a regionally integrated approach to infrastructure development are to make possible the formation of large competitive markets in place of small, fragmented and inefficient ones and to lower costs across production sectors so as to stimulate industrialization and growth. This is analyzed in the context of the One Belt, One Road (OBOR) initiatives to evaluate the implications for Africa in relation to the traditional sources of infrastructural support for the continent. Following this introductory section, section II discusses the responses (strategy, policies, etc.) to these challenges by African countries (regional level, selected national country level), while section III analyzes the responses to these challenges by Africa's development partners (bilateral, multilateral, public, private). The identification and analysis of responses to these challenges through the OBOR initiative is the focus of section IV, while a comparative analysis of the relative costs and benefits across the three response modalities is provided in section V. The identification and analysis of the specific arrangements, incentives and the capacity required to ensure that OBOR is beneficial to African countries is highlighted in section VI. The study is concluded with proposal and recommendation of options on how African countries can maximize the benefits from OBOR in section VII.

Identification and Analysis of the Responses (Strategy, Policies, etc.) to the Infrastructural Challenges by African Countries (Regional Level, Selected National Country Level)

In response to the infrastructure deficit and poor connectivity challenges, African countries have taken a number of concrete actions and made some progress toward the implementation of transport-related commitments and goals. Some of the initiatives that were developed in the early period include the United Nations Transport and Communications Decade in Africa (UNTACDA-I), which was launched in 1978. The second decade program, UNTACDA-II was launched in 1991 with the long-term objective of establishing an efficient and integrated transport and communications system as the basis for the physical integration of Africa. The UNTACDA-II incorporated four special initiatives: human resources and institutional development, the Yamoussoukro Declaration on a New African Air Transport Policy, the regional transport database and the Trans-African Highway Bureau. The level of resources mobilized for the projects was \$9.0 billion, compared to the financing requirement of \$16.6 billion, indicating 54% achievement for the program. The implementation of UNTACDA-II led to the expansion of the transport network in Africa, improvement of quality of infrastructure and services and strengthening of institutional capacity.

Also, to address this need for infrastructure, the African Union Commission (AUC), in partnership with the United Nations Economic Commission for Africa (UNECA), the African Development Bank (AfDB) and the New Partnership for Africa's Development (NEPAD) secretariat formulated the Program for Infrastructure Development in Africa (PIDA) in July 2010 and approved in January 2012. The purpose of PIDA is to provide strategic long-term planning for infrastructure development in a coherent way for all African stakeholders and address the many issues facing the transport sector along the African Regional Transport Infrastructures (ARTIN).

The overall objectives of PIDA are not only to recommend the building or modernization of regional transport infrastructures to increase capacity and satisfy the expected transport demand but also to establish regional transport systems, through policy reforms, that will not only encourage and facilitate regional trade and the movement of goods and passengers along the key corridors but also to speed up the economic development of both landlocked and transit countries and contribute to poverty reduction. The key output of PIDA is what is called the Priority Action Plan (PAP), a list of 51 immediately actionable projects across four key infrastructure sectors for implementation between 2012 and 2020. PIDA identifies the activities (both soft and hard) to be conducted by tranches of ten years (2010–2020; 2020–2030 and 2030–2040). Presently, the AUC, the NPCA, the RECs and the countries are implementing the PIDA-PAP, which cover the period 2010–2020. The transport section of the PIDA-PAP contains 24 programs. Majority of these programs are aimed at increasing (or building) transport infrastructure capacities to satisfy the expected traffic demand, in 2020 and to increase transport efficiency along the key corridors. Each program of the PIDA-PAP recommends to start with the conduct of studies and analysis to define the best technical and economical solutions to fill the identified gaps and to improve the overall efficiency of regional transport and then identifies and costs the required investments.

Unlike the UNTACDA initiatives, PIDA has true African ownership, as it was formulated with very close consultation from the outset with all key stakeholders—sector ministers, the Regional Economic Communities (RECs), the power pools, the water basin organizations, and others. Approval by the AU Heads of States in January 2012 represented a sign of strong political commitment. Besides identifying priority projects and associated basic technical and financial data (initial feasibility analyses), PIDA's other important outputs include several technical contributions such as approaches to raise financing, PPPs, institutional models (Table 1).

Table 1 PIDA: priority action program

	Energy	Transport	Water	ICT	Total
No of projects	15	24	9	3	51
Cost (US$b)	40	25	2	0.5	67.5
% of total cost	59.2	37	3	0.8	100

Source http://www.au-pida.org/pida-pap/

PIDA assumed that the average economic growth rate for African countries will be 6% a year between 2010 and 2040, driven by a surging population, increasing levels of education and technology absorption. This growth implies that, over the 24 years to 2040, the GDP of African countries will multiply sixfold, and the average per capita income will rise above $10,000 for all countries. This continuing growth and prosperity will swell the demand for infrastructure, already one of the continents greatest impediments to sustainable development. Under PIDA, roads and railways, which link a number of countries with ports, have been designated as *corridors* with the objective of providing a coherent transport service across and through states that can allow for more efficient import and export and growing inter-country trade. The focus is on enhancing inter-connectivity and facilitating trade by focusing on transport corridors as facilitators of integration and spatial development on the continent (Table 2).

Nevertheless, while the PAP was considered to be an entirely do-able program, both technically as well as financially, the total cost represented less than 1% of Africa's GDP in terms of annual outlays for the period up to 2020. The progress has been slow due to a number of problems:

- Weak connections between the economic analysis and the prioritization of projects;
- Inadequate discussion of PPPs and private investment options (despite it being a PIDA priority);
- Lack of clarity in institutional architecture for implementing the PAP—major confusion over how the projects would be prepared, who would do that, the role of the RECs, etc;
- Inadequate dissemination of information on PIDA including lack of user-friendly summaries of projects.
- Lack of resolution of these problems is the main constraint to moving faster on implementing the PAP.

In the railway sub-sector, the Brazzaville Declaration and Plan of Action on African Railways adopted by the first meeting of the African Ministers responsible for railway transport that was held in Brazzaville in 2006, reaffirmed the commitment of African governments to develop an effective railway system that would promote Africa's development and integration. A follow-up conference organized by AUC in collaboration with the Republic of South Africa for railway professionals looked into issues such as interconnection and interoperability of continental railway networks and made recommendations on harmonization of standards for infrastructure, equipment, practices and procedures. With regard to Africa's maritime transport, the first AU Conference of Ministers responsible for maritime transport adopted the *Abuja Declaration for effective revitalization of maritime transport in Africa*, as a key component of African socio-economic development policy and the associated Plan of Action on Maritime Transport for Africa. However, most of the contextual declaration did not solve the problem of infrastructural connectivity in Africa due to lack of financial support to execute the projects involved.

At the sub-regional level, ECOWAS countries adopted the West Africa Rail Master Plan with a focus on detailed engineering studies of the Kaya-Dory-Niamey link that

Table 2 Transport sector illustrative list of top five projects in advanced stages of preparation and/or readiness for funding and implementation

	Project	Description	Cost (US$ m)	Countries	Region
1	Yamoussoukro Decision Implementation	Accelerate Yamoussoukro Decision Implementation by identifying countries that are ready to fully implement It, and discussing and agreeing with both their government and airlines to launch the voluntary club on a full membership basis	5	Africa	Continental
2	Abidjan-Lagos Coastal Corridor	This program would modernize the most heavily traveled ARTIN corridor in West Africa (trade facilitation, OSBPs, capacity enhancement and implementation of PPP) for five countries: Côte d'Ivoire, Ghana, Togo, Benin and Nigeria	290	Nigeria, Benin, Toga, Ghana, Côte d'Ivoire	Western
3	North-South Multi-modal Corridor	This program is designed to modernize the highest priority multi-modal ARTIN corridor in, Southern Africa on modem standards and, facilitate travel of people and goods across the South borders between, Botswana, Africa, Zimbabwe, Zambia, Malawi and DRC	2325	DRC, Zambia, Zimbabwe, South Africa, Mozambique	Eastern

(continued)

Table 2 (continued)

	Project	Description	Cost (US$ m)	Countries	Region
4	Central Corridor	This program would modernize the third priority ARTIN corridor in East Africa and facilitate travel for people and goods across the borders between Tanzania, Uganda, Rwanda, Burundi and DRC	840	Tanzania, Uganda, Rwanda, Burundi, DRC	Eastern
5	Trans-Maghreb Highway	This program is designed to improve travel for people and goods across the Maghreb countries, which have had their trade and travel limited by artificial barriers between countries at the borders. This program would design and implement a smart corridor system along the highway and install one-stop border posts	75	Morocco to Egypt through Algeria Tunisia and Libya	Northern

Source http://www.au-pida.org/pida-pap/

connects the Abidjan-Ouagadougou railway line to the Republic of Niger. The project was funded by the European Union. In addition, there was also funding assistance of infrastructure projects including the construction of three bridges in Sierra Leone, the finalization and operation of Joint Border Posts as well as the facilitation of soft projects in conjunction with the UEMOA Commission. In the air sub-sector, the Community is effectively engaging its Air Transport Action Plan to bring into fruition, some recent air transport projects which include the implementation of the Yamoussoukro Decision for air transport liberalization, strengthening of aviation safety and security, promoting a viable airline industry in sub-region ECOWAS region as well as the implementation of ECOWAS air transport flagship projects.

Today, air service agreements with third parties, aeronautical cooperation and financial resource mobilization are being negotiated. Of great importance in this regard is the ECOWAS/UEMOA Yamoussoukro decision of July 2013. Heads of state and government have also since their July 2013 summit in Abuja decided to fast track the implementation of the decisions jointly taken. With respect to the ground transport system, the road sub-sector, which is the most utilized within the region, is now witnessing tremendous development. The principal activity in the roads sector is the continued implementation of regional road transport and transit facilitation program. Under this program, emphasis is placed on the ECOWAS Joint Border Posts (JBP) program which has seen the construction of Joint Border Posts in Seme/Krake (Nigeria/Benin) and Noepe (Ghana/Togo) and the drafting of the Legal Framework and Operational Manuals for the JBP which will guide the operation of the various JBP facilities.

On rail development, there is the Axle Load Harmonization Policy, the Road Transport Observatory and the Nigeria-Cameroon Multinational Highway, and Transport Facilitation Program developed as part of the Trans-Africa Highway program under which harmonization of norms, standard, vehicle size, axle load limit between Nigeria (in ECOWAS) and Cameroon in the Economic Community of Central African States (ECCAS) is being designed. Similarly, there is the existence of the Lagos-Abidjan Corridor Development Program and the Trans-Gambia Transport Corridor.

Transport infrastructure in terms of roads, railways and maritime transport facilities in the Eastern and Southern Africa region has evolved slowly over the years and can be described as barely adequate in most countries in terms of coverage compared with the developed and middle-income countries. Consequently, the COMESA sub-region has made effort to promote the development of road networks through construction of missing regional inks, upgrading and, rehabilitation of existing ones and increasing the capacity of current links where traffic volumes have surpassed the design volumes. In this regard, major road projects have been undertaken along the major transport corridors which include the Djibouti Corridor, Lamu Corridor, the Northern Corridor, Central Corridor, Dar es Salaam Corridor and the North/South Corridor of the sub-region. Also in the sub-region, there are plans for the construction of new railways along corridors such as Djibouti, Lamu, Nacala and the reconstruction of the legacy railway. With respect to the corridor development and management, discussions are being held under the auspices of the Tripartite on the North–South

Corridor, the Northern and Central corridors and the Djibouti Corridor on the development of physical infrastructure, including the establishment of one-stop border posts and the corridor management institutions. On the inland water transport, the Shire-Zambezi Waterways Project received funding from the African Development Bank to undertake more comprehensive studies to prepare for investment in requisite infrastructure in order to serve the growing traffic demands expected to arise from the exploitation of the coal deposits in Moatize (Tete) and the expected import cargoes to meet the needs of the mining industry.

The COMESA Infrastructure Fund is at an advanced stage of formation and is expected to provide funding for priority projects by raising capital for investment in trade-related infrastructure projects in the region. The Fund will provide seed capital and leverage resources from a mix of public and private investors' funds. On its inception, the Fund is planned to raise a minimum US$1 billion committed equity capital contributions, to be complemented with proportionate sub-ordinated debt offers depending on off-take for the equity offer. At the moment the, Fund is domiciled and hosted by the PTA Bank.

The Fund will target infrastructure assets in sectors which include transport, energy, water and sanitation, information and communication technology. The Fund is intended to provide seed money for the implementation of regional projects. This seed money is expected to play a great role in leveraging funds from other sources. Studies have been carried out to identify the technically feasible and financially viable physical infrastructure projects for the COMESA Infrastructure Fund where some priority projects have been identified. The projects estimated to cost US$ 6.554.0 million were identified by the Fund consultants.

Also, SADC has developed the Regional Infrastructure Development Master Plan (RIDMP) Vision 2027 to guide the development and implementation of priority infrastructure projects for the sub-region. The RIDMP identifies six priority sectors for development: energy, transport, tourism, information and communication technologies, meteorology and trans-boundary water. The RIDMP is being implemented in three phases: the short term from 2012–2017; the medium term 2017–2022; and the long term from 2022–2027. The strategy is to address trade facilitation issues simultaneously to ensure that the infrastructure developments are more effective. Such trade facilitation projects include the one-stop border post (OSBP) project that is supported by Trademark Southern Africa (TMSA), an example of which would be the Chirundu OSBP linking Zimbabwe and Zambia.

To implement the first five-year phase of the RIDMP (2012–2017), a short-term action plan was developed with the support from the UK Department for International Development (DFID) through the TMSA, as the principal funder of the RIDMP development process. Nevertheless, the support from DFID is being complemented by the EU and the Development Bank of Southern Africa (DBSA) within the framework of the SADC–International Cooperating Partner program. The North–South Corridor (NSC) has also been selected by the Tripartite Initiative as a pilot Aid for Trade Infrastructure Development program, as it covers a key set of corridors for the Tripartite Free Trade Agreement. The NSC comprises:

- Dar es Salaam with the copper belt in the Democratic Republic of Congo (DRC) and Zambia;
- Port of Durban with the DRC–Zambia copper belt via Zimbabwe and Botswana while connecting with Malawi via Harare; and
- Nacala, Beira, Maputo and Trans-Kalahari Corridors.

Once completed, it is anticipated that the NSC will reduce the cost of doing business in the sub-Saharan region. The NSC project is funded primarily by the Tripartite Trust Account, which has been managed by the DBSA. The projects themselves will be funded through development financial institutions (DFIs) and investors. The TMSA is also coordinating the OSBP projects to allow the simultaneous development of both infrastructure and trade facilitation. However, the TMSA is faced with a particular challenge with some SADC members regarding it as an external influence and therefore are not particularly receptive to its efforts. In summary, significant efforts were made by African countries at the regional, sub-regional and country level to address the issue of infrastructural connectivity of the African continent particularly with the design of various economic blueprints on infrastructural projects. However, lack of finances in some cases affects the effective implementation of some of the projects which explain the weak implementation of the projects under PIDA. The few projects that were implemented were based on loan support from development partners.

Identification and Analysis of Responses to These Challenges by Africa's Development Partners (Bilateral, Multilateral, Public, Private)

African development partners equally respond to the challenges of infrastructure connectivity in the continent. Stronger donor coordination became a huge necessity given the fact that financing requirements of infrastructure are greater than available resources, which clearly implies that no single financier is in a position to fund a large infrastructure project. Specifically, in 2005, the G8 summit in Gleneagles led to the creation of the Infrastructure Consortium for Africa (ICA). It was designed to help improve the lives and economic well-being of millions of Africa's people through encouraging, supporting and promoting increased investment in infrastructure in Africa, from both public and private sources. With a focus on regional programs and initiatives, the ICA has assisted to facilitate infrastructure development in the water, transport, energy and ICT sectors given that many African countries lack the essential building blocks of economic progress, such as well-maintained roads and railways, access to electricity and water and sanitation. Although not a funding agency, the ICA was designed to catalyze and facilitate the financing of infrastructure projects and programs. It also works to overcome technical and political challenges to building more infrastructures.

The ICA's bilateral members include the G8 countries (Canada, France, Germany, Italy, Japan, Russia, the UK and the USA). Membership is open to all countries in the G20, and the Republic of South Africa became the first non-G8 G20 member to join the ICA, in December 2013. Multilateral members include the World Bank Group, the African Development Bank Group, the European Commission, the European Investment Bank and the Development Bank of Southern Africa. Increasingly, the ICA is working to improve coordination among members, as well as between members and other significant sources of infrastructure development finance, such as China, India, Arab and Islamic financiers, African regional development banks and the private sector.

Total commitments to the African transport sector amounted to $24.5bn in 2016, a decline in the $32.4bn reported the previous year. This was largely accounted for by a decline in Chinese commitments, from $9.8bn in 2015 to $1bn in 2016. Nevertheless, funding from African national governments rose to $14.6bn in 2016, recovering from a notable fall in 2015. ICA member financing fell slightly from the record high reported in 2015, but still totaled some $5bn in 2016. India, South Korea and regional development banks all saw a significant increase in their financing of the African transport sector in 2016, with commitments of $513 m, $242 m and $403 m, respectively. The private sector also financed $1.3bn of transport infrastructure in Africa in 2016, having closed only $113.5 m worth of projects the previous year. West Africa received $6.6bn of commitments in 2016, representing 26.9% of the total. East Africa, which was the recipient of $11.3bn or more than one-third of commitments in 2015, received $5.3bn (21.7%) in 2016. Financing levels in 2016 in North, Central and Southern Africa (excluding the Republic of South Africa) were similar to 2015 levels, at $4.4bn, $2.9bn and $2.3bn, respectively. However, commitments in South Africa fell from $4.8bn in 2015 to $2.6bn in 2016.

Unsurprisingly given their political focus on the development of economic corridors, the AfDB is the biggest investor in transport infrastructure among the ICA members. The AfDB is the lead ICA member for the Eastern and Central Transport Corridors, which focuses on enhancing inter-connectivity in transport through infrastructure development and trade facilitation. The countries that are directly involved in the Eastern and Central Transport Corridors include Burundi, DRC, Kenya, Rwanda, South Sudan, Tanzania and Uganda. The total costs of priority projects were approximately US$1.8 billion under the ICA framework. These include five ports projects totaling US$990 m, four railway projects totaling US$465 m and eight roads projects totaling US$377. Also, funding totaling US$1.2 billion has been identified for a number of projects. However, the remaining projects require funding totaling of over US$560 million.

Also under the ICA framework, the implementation of the North–South Corridor program is coordinated and supervised by the Tripartite Task Force, with technical and financial support from TradeMark Southern Africa—a £100million, 5-year Program funded by DFID that is supporting deeper economic integration of the Southern and Eastern Africa region. The DFID is the lead donor and ICA Member supporting the Tripartite work program, which includes the North–South Corridor and is working in close partnership with other ICA Members including bilateral donors, the African Development Bank, World Bank, Development Bank of Southern Africa and EIB to deliver the North–South Corridor program. The countries that are involved are Botswana, Democratic Republic of Congo, Malawi, Mozambique, South Africa, Tanzania, Zambia and Zimbabwe.

The road network in the corridor covers 8599 km in seven countries while the costs of rehabilitating and maintaining the entire NSC road network to a good standard are estimated at US$9.1 billion (of which US$5.9 billion is for capital investment and US$3.1 billion is recurrent costs). In addition, the rail network is currently focusing on the upgrading of 600 km rail line at the value of US$800 m. The priority port upgrading and development for the corridor also includes the Dar es Salaam at US$800 m. Among other projects, the Horn of Africa Initiative focuses on delivering an agreed set of activities that will enhance the inter-connectivity in transport through infrastructure development and trade facilitation. The countries that are involved are Djibouti, Eritrea, Ethiopia, Kenya, Somalia, Sudan and Uganda. The priority projects have been identified, with costs totaling approximately €5.4 billion (this consists four ring roads which formed part of the ring corridor).

As part of the effort of donor partners to address the challenges of infrastructure in Africa, the Infrastructure Trust Fund (ITF) was created in 2007 in the framework of the EU-Africa Partnership for Infrastructure. The ITF comprises 13 donors—12 Member States and the European Commission. It aims to:

- Support regional investment projects in infrastructure in four sectors: energy, transport, ICT and water;
- Offer a blending mechanism through four financing instruments: interest rate subsidies, technical assistance, direct grants and insurance premia.
- Provide support based on a governance structure organized around three main bodies: the EU-Africa Partnership for Infrastructure Steering Committee providing strategic direction, the ExCom represented by the Donors and the European Commission providing an approval body for ITF grant operations, and the Project Financier Group (PFG) composed of development financing institutions, each of which is appointed by a Donor, who identify potential grant operations to be submitted to ExCom for approval.

The EU-Africa Partnership for Infrastructure was established as part of the overarching EU-Africa Strategy and targets the development of large regional infrastructure networks in Africa. The ITF is one of several funding instruments to enable the implementation of the Strategy. The objectives of the ITF are focused only on the delivery of the expected outputs of the ITF. The EU-AITF delivers on grant support to various stages of a project such as:

- Project identification—when a project aims to develop or prioritize other projects
- Project preparation—assessment of feasibility and design of a specific project
- Investment phase—project construction and implementation

Grants in the context of the EU-AITF are provided in the form of:

- Technical assistance for preparatory work like feasibility studies, Environmental and Social Impact Assessments, Resettlement Action Plans, etc., for project supervision, and also for targeted capacity building such as reinforcing the technical and administrative capacity of local staff in Africa.
- Interest rate subsidies to enable EU-AITF financiers to make long-term loan finance available in flexible ways in order to reduce the total amount of debt service. Such subsidies allow the final financing package to achieve the level of concessionality required by debt sustainability programs of, e.g., the World Bank or the IMF.
- Investment Grants are non-reimbursable contributions to finance tangible or intangible project components with the aim to decrease the total investment costs or to increase the concessionality level of the financing package of a project. Investment grants are also used to target the financing of specific project components which have substantial demonstrable social or environmental benefits or which can mitigate negative environmental or social impacts.
- Financial Instruments comprise, but are not limited to, guarantees, loan guarantee cost financing, insurance premia, equity or quasi-equity investments or participations and risk-sharing instruments.

The EU-AITF only supports projects which will improve regional integration and inter-linkages of infrastructure and so contribute to sustainable economic growth. The list of projects under the EU-AITF is shown in Table 3. The projects cut across the different sub-regions of Africa. An additional criterion is how this growth will contribute to social development and benefit the poorest citizens of the countries whether directly or indirectly. The use of blended grant-loan financing for projects, which clearly enables long-term financing for sustainable projects, is gaining importance and is strongly supported by African governments. African Ownership and project sustainability over the life of the project are therefore one of the guiding principles of EU-AITF support. In addition, blended financing requires one or ideally several of the EU-AITF eligible financiers to invest in the project through a loan or other financing. Among others, the EU-AITF Eligibility Criteria hence include:

- Project contribution to poverty reduction;
- Project contribution to economic development and trade;
- Economic viability of the project;
- Environmental viability of the project and mitigation of potential impacts;
- Provisions for the project/infrastructure's sustainable operation and maintenance;
- Projects may be implemented by public or private entities or entities with mixed public-private capital
- For operations in the context of the "Sustainable Energy for All-Initiative" priority will be given to projects providing increased access to modern, affordable and sustainable energy services.
- Projects must be trans-border infrastructure projects or national projects with a demonstrable regional impact on two or more countries or national projects in the context of the "Sustainable Energy for All" initiative, aligned to the partners' national policies, and, where applicable, to regional policies and/or plans

Table 3 Selected list of approved grant operations for projects under the EU-AITF context

Grant operation	Sector	Scope	Lead	Co-financiers	Grant amount	Approval date
Béroubouay-Malanville Road rehabilitation project	Transport	IG	AfdB		EUR 9,411,765	March 16, 2017
ASECNA EGNOS Phase B (re-approval of the grant under a new lead financier)	Transport	TA	AFD		EUR 5,000,000	September 20, 2016
IG for the Sirari Corridor accessibility and road safety improvement Isebania–Kisii–Ahero Road rehabilitation	Transport	IG	AfDB		EUR 10,000,000	December 9, 2015
IG for the Regional Road Corridor "South Sudan Link"	Transport	IG	KfW		EUR 22,200,000	December 9, 2015
TA for the Regional Road Corridor "South Sudan Link"	Transport	TA	KfW		EUR 2,800,000	December 9, 2015
TA for the Lake Victoria regional transport phase II	Transport	TA	PIDG		EUR 1,400,000	December 9, 2015
Kagitumba-Kayonza-Rusumo Road Rehabilitation Project	Transport	IG	AfDB		EUR 20,000,000	June 30, 2015
Technical assistance for the Lake Victoria Regional Transport project	Transport	TA	PIDG		EUR 600,000	December 12, 2013
GET FiT Premium payment mechanism	Energy	IG	KfW		EUR 20,000,000	October 24, 2013
Engaging Banks RTAP—Phase II	Energy	TA	AFD		EUR 2,100,000	June 27, 2013
ASECNA—EGNOS Phase B—CANCELED PRIOR TO DISBURSEMENT	Transport	TA	EIB		EUR 5,000,000	February 7, 2013
Technical assistance for the Kazungula Bridge Phase 2 project	Transport	TA	AFDB		EUR 2,000,000	December 13, 2012
Togo-Burkina Faso Road Corridor and transport facilitation project	Transport	TA	AfDB	KfW	EUR 2,340,000	April 19, 2012
Transmission Line Kafue-Livingstone—IRS	Energy	IRS	EIB		EUR 5,200,000	December 15, 2011
Eastern Africa Transport Corridor	Transport	IRS	EIB		EUR 16,600,000	December 15, 2011
Geothermal Risk Mitigation Facility (GRMF)	Energy	DG	KfW		EUR 30,000,000	October 20, 2011
Maputo Airport	Transport	TA	AFD		EUR 1,600,000	July 5, 2011

(continued)

Table 3 (continued)

Grant operation	Sector	Scope	Lead	Co-financiers	Grant amount	Approval date
Kazungula Bridge and border project	Transport	TA	AfDB		EUR 1,000,000	July 5, 2011
WAPP IC Ghana-Burkina Faso-Mali	Energy	TA	AFD		EUR 1,200,000	July 5, 2011
IRS for the rehabilitation of the Great East Road within Nacala Regional Corridor—Zambia Section	Transport	IRS	AFD		EUR 10,800,000 + EUR 2,900,000	July 5, 2011
Transboundary Water Supply Calueque (Angola)-Oshakati (Namibia)	Water	TA	KfW		EUR 2,400,000	May 25, 2011
Interconnection Côte d'Ivoire-Liberia-Sierra Leone-Guinée (CLSG) Project	Energy	TA	EIB		EUR 1,750,000	March 23, 2011
Integrated Transport Master Plan for Namibia	Transport	TA	EIB		EUR 560,000	November 9, 2010
Access to Douala	Transport	IRS	AFD		EUR 5,700,000	September 16, 2010
Lake Victoria WATSAN—Kampala Water (Uganda) TA	Water	TA	KfW		EUR 8,000,000	June 29, 2010
Lake Victoria WATSAN—Kampala Water	Water	IRS	KfW/ AFD	EIB	EUR 14,000,000	June 29, 2010
Rehabilitation of Great East Road, Zambia	Transport	TA	EIB		EUR 1,000,000 + EUR 500,000	June 29, 2010
Rehabilitation of the Great East Road, Zambia	Transport	IRS	EIB		EUR 25,000,000	June 29, 2010

Source http://www.eu-africa-infrastructure-tf.net/activities/index.htm

Nevertheless, Development Financial Institutions (DFIs) that are not ICA members made some interesting commitments to African infrastructure financing in 2013, despite being overshadowed in scale by the European ICA members. In 2013, more than a third of the commitments ($189 m of $512 m) made to Africa by non-ICA European DFIs were channeled to infrastructure-related deals. Leading the field, the highly active Dutch institution FMO committed $198 m in total, with $69.1 m allocated to infrastructure. Also noteworthy in 2013, Denmark's IFU committed $36.2 m to African infrastructure deals, which made up 85% of its total Africa commitments. Leveraging private sector investment remains a key focus among European actors, with DFI-backed credit lines gaining traction. In January 2013, FMO launched a landmark partnership with the multilateral Africa Finance Corporation (AFC) to establish a $15 m project development facility, which will fund equity investments in African infrastructure projects under development.

For 2013, total funding committed to infrastructure projects in Africa by members of the Arab Coordination Group reached almost $3.1bn. This roughly represents about $800 m drop on last year's $3.9bn total, but is consistent with the group's longer-term lending. During 2011, the group lent $2.9bn, and in 2010, it lent $3.3bn. North African projects accounted for just over 50% of total funding committed by the group for 2013, receiving $1.6bn in loans. North African projects have consistently received the majority of funding over the past three years, benefiting from $2.6bn in 2012 and $1.2bn in 2011. Of this, $878 m went to energy projects and $382 m to transport, while water projects received $359 m. The group made one commitment to ICT infrastructure, a $156 m loan to modernize railway signaling in Egypt.

Indian public financing to African infrastructure projects, administered through the country's Export–Import Bank largely in the form of lines of credit, amounted to almost $761 m in 2013. This represents roughly a $100 m increase on 2012's $667 m. However, while in 2012, some $450 m or 60% went to Africa's energy sector. Also, in 2013, energy projects on the continent received only $220 m. Instead, transport projects received the bulk of Indian financing, amounting to $450 m, or 60% of the total committed. India's Exim Bank lent no funds to North African projects during 2013. Instead, Southern African countries featured prominently, with funding going to water and transport projects in Mozambique, which received $20 m and $150 m, respectively. In total, it made eight commitments during 2013, with an average loan size of around $95 m. India looks set to continue making commitments of similar size in the medium term. It committed to providing $5.4bn in loans during an India-Africa summit in 2008, making an additional offer of $5bn over a three-year period in 2011. India is set to host the third summit in 2014.

In 2013, South Korea's Export–Import Bank, via its Economic Development Cooperation Fund, made a total of $175.44 m in two loan commitments to infrastructure projects in Africa. This contribution represents a significant reduction on 2012's contribution of around $677 m. Both loans were to transport projects, with Mozambique's Nampula-Nametil city road receiving $75.4 m and Ethiopia's Modjo-Hawassa highway project receiving $100 m. South Korea's funding of African infrastructure projects during 2013 is consistent with its public statements on the issue. As one of the global south's developmental success stories, the country has been providing expertise and advice, as well as funding.

In 2012, Brazil's state development agency Banco Nacional de Desenvolvimento Econômico e Social (BNDES) extended $530 m to African infrastructure projects, including a $300 m loan to the government of Mozambique to support infrastructure projects, including the construction of the Nacala International Airport. In addition, Russian companies are expanding their interests on the continent. During early June 2014, a Russian consortium, led by RT Global Resources and including VTB Capital and Tatneft alongside three other firms, submitted proposals for the construction of a Ugandan refinery, a project of vital importance for the region.

Also, funding for infrastructure projects featured prominently among the continent's regional development banks' lending during 2013. EADB directed some 42% of its total expenditure toward infrastructure projects, while 53.6% of Banque Ouest Africaine de Developpement (BOAD)'s commitments for the period went to infrastructure projects. ECOWAS Bank for Investment and Development (EBID) also continues to commit to infrastructure projects in the West African region. Between December 2012 and September 2013, EBID funded about $60 m of infrastructure projects in its region of operations. This is consistent with the Bank's activities during 2012, during which it lent $63 m, some $39 m of which was directed toward energy projects, with the remainder to transport projects. Meanwhile, BOAD was similarly active in infrastructure projects, with commitments totaling $876 m. The bulk ($672.1 m) of BOAD's 2013 commitments went toward transport projects. BOAD directed some $547.2 m, toward 17 separate road projects in West Africa.

At public-private partnership (PPP) level, DFI backed venture funds also made special infrastructure investments. Although typically reserved for financial services investments. The East Africa-focused Novastar Ventures, which closed at $44 m, received contributions from Norfund ($10 m) and FMO ($10 m), as well as from the UK Department for International Development's Impact Fund and several private investors. The fund has already made some infrastructure investments, including to Sanergy. The private sector also focused on Nigeria's transportation sector in 2013, with the Onne Port expansion and Lekki Deep Seaport projects attracting $2.9bn and $1.5bn, respectively.

Local company, Deep Offshore Services Nigeria Limited, is leading the Onne Port expansion and looking to attract some foreign investment in this project. The $1.5bn Lekki Deep Seaport features private capital provided by a Singaporean investor, the Tolaram Group with public sector stakes held by Nigeria's federal government via the Nigerian Ports Authority (NPA) and Lagos State Government. Lekki Ports LFTZ Enterprise, a PPP, would operate the seaport under a 45-year concession commencing after which it reverts to the federal government. Final negotiations to establish the value of land Lagos State Government is contributing in exchange for its equity may impact on the initial shareholding in which fund providers Tolaram Group and NPA would, respectively, take 61.5% and 20% stakes with Lagos State Government holding 18.5% of the equity. The port will compliment Lekki Free Trade Zone, which was created in 2002 with a vision of a deepwater seaport that was formalized in a 2009 Master Plan. A total of $800 m from the project cost would be funded through debt financing, while the balance would be contributed by equity.

Identification and Analysis of Responses to These Challenges Through the OBOR Initiative

Official Chinese engagement with Africa commenced with the establishment of the Forum on China-Africa Cooperation (FOCAC) in 2000 and marked an unprecedented level of multi-faceted engagement between China and African countries. FOCAC greatly facilitated equal consultation, enhanced understanding between high-level officials, expanded consensus and promoted cooperation between China and Africa. In the implementation of the latest FOCAC Action Plan (2016–2018) adopted in

Johannesburg in December 2015, China pledged USD 60 billion in financial support with a focus on infrastructure development and industrialization (FOCAC 2015).

However, since September 2013 China has been promoting the One Belt, One Road (OBOR) initiative. The initiative is a continuation and deepening of China's opening up and going out with a regional focus on Asia, Europe and Africa. The belt relates to the six economic corridors, namely Eurasian land bridge; China-Mongolia-Russia; China-Central Asia-West Asia; the China-Indochina peninsula; China-Pakistan; and Bangladesh-China-India-Myanmar. The route will emerge as a major logistics corridor and will create new opportunities for Central Asia and Eastern Europe as both a trans-shipment hub and commodities supplier. The maritime road is a densely populated consumer and industrial opportunity. Like the landlocked belt, it also connects China and Europe, but differs in that the road passes through Southeast Asia, South Asia, the Middle East and East Africa.

The OBOR strategy is centered on infrastructure development, especially regional transportation and connectivity projects. Improving the connectivity of the infrastructure in the countries along the Belt and Road is a priority area by improving the connectivity of infrastructure networks and technical standard systems by linking unconnected road sections, pushing forward port infrastructure construction, building smooth land–water transportation channels, advancing port cooperation, building platforms and mechanisms for comprehensive civil aviation cooperation, quicken pace in improving aviation infrastructure, building cross-border power supply networks and power-transmission routes, cooperating in regional power grid upgrading and transformation; and constructing cross-border and transcontinental sub-marine optical cables and creating an Information Silk Road. There are plans to build transport routes connecting major seaports along the Belt and Road.

It was only around early 2015 that Africa started becoming part of the initiative. Specifically, in January 2015, the African Union and China signed an agreement to help build railways, roads and airports to link all 54 African countries. While most African countries are FOCAC members, only a few African countries may become part of the Initiative initially. This implies that in the original design of the initiatives, none of the countries in sub-Saharan Africa were part of the OBOR initiatives out of the 65 countries identified along with the Belt and Road framework. The specific call for Africa's inclusion in the Belt and Road initiative was echoed by He Wenping, one of China's leading China-Africa researchers on the basis that the initiative and Africa's development strategy share the same spirit and that combining the two will not only create new momentum for Sino-African ties, but also present a new approach for South–South cooperation.

Given that the Belt and Road initiative has its own vision and action plan, dedicated political fora, financial institutions and resources, its design is not simply to account for FOCAC achievements, but to reinforce and expand the scope and depth of cooperation. For African Belt and Road initiative countries, this implies that resources in addition to those under FOCAC become available under the Initiative. Furthermore, in contrast to FOCAC, the initiative is not limited to bilateral relations between China and African countries, but aims to connect Asia, Europe and Africa. As such, the initiative continues to aim at bringing in technology, know-how and resources, but also strongly supports the going out of Chinese enterprises to facilitate industrial upgrading at home, pave the way for investments and trade abroad and advance the internationalization of the Chinese currency (NDRC 2015).

Since 2013 Chinese state media has published several different Belt and Road maps with varying indications of Africa's participation in the Maritime Silk Road. Most of the maps include a route through the Indian Ocean toward Kenya, passing Somalia, Djibouti, Eritrea, Sudan and Egypt before continuing in the Mediterranean Sea. Some of the maps show the Maritime Silk Road leading from the Indian Ocean directly to the Red Sea via the Suez Canal into the Mediterranean Sea. In most cases, the maps do not offer any indication on ports along the African part of the Maritime Silk Road. However, the latest version published by the Chinese news agency Xinhua (Fig. 1) shows Nairobi as part of the Maritime Silk Road. This is in line with the historic maritime route, which saw the first trade between China and Kenya during the early fifteenth century (Wekesa 2015). It is noteworthy that all other cities on the map are port cities, while Nairobi is almost 500 km away from the closest port located in Mombasa. This is not only an indication that China sees Kenya as part of the Belt and Road Initiative, but also that the new railway and economic corridor that China is currently building in partnership with Kenya from Mombasa to Nairobi is a part of the Maritime Silk Road.

Since its announcement, China has established dedicated financing mechanisms, such as the Silk Road Fund with an initial capitalization of US $40 billion, organized international fora and initiated the broad international promotion of the Initiative by Chinese state media. The Initiative comes with massive investments, which are likely to be mainly channeled through new financial institutions initiated or led by China,

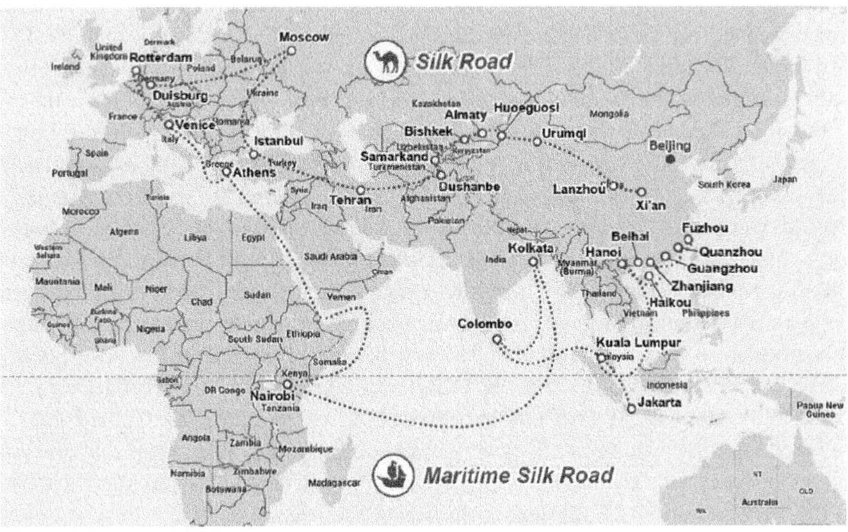

Fig. 1 Map of the silk road economic belt (silk road) and 21st century maritime silk road (maritime silk road)

such as the Asian Infrastructure Investment Bank. There are a number of examples how this agreement is already being implemented through large-scale infrastructure projects in cooperation with China on the continent. Egypt, Kenya, South Africa, Angola and Tanzania can be considered as immediate Belt and Road countries in Africa, while Republic of Congo, Ethiopia, Nigeria, Morocco and Mozambique are likely to become Belt and Road initiative countries in the near future.

Within Africa, benefits of the Belt and Road initiative can be seen in the transport and other infrastructure connectivity built by the Chinese, particularly in East Africa. For example, Kenya and Djibouti have had infrastructure projects carried out by Chinese companies, heavily financed by China's Export–Import (Exim) bank. Kenya's US$3.8bn standard gauge railway (SGR) project, the Mombasa-Nairobi SGR, has been completed and now carries 7000 passengers per week (Xinhua, June 7). At the Belt and Road Forum (BRF) in May 2017, Kenya and China agreed upon a US$3.6 billion credit in funds for the extension of the Kenyan railway line between Naivasha, near Nairobi and Kisumu which is a mere 100 km to the border of landlocked Uganda. The 609 km railway project is being developed by China Road and Bridge Corporation. China Exim Bank provided 90% of the funding, with the remaining 10% provided by the Kenyan government. Other phases of the SGR will seek to connect Mombasa to Uganda, Rwanda and South Sudan, fueling the potential for increased economic growth and development for all countries involved as well as broader international trade opportunities in the process. Thus, the Mombasa port will be extensively connected to Africa's inland, going far beyond Kenya China is also involved in the Lamu Port project in Kenya being built by China Communications Construction Company. The Chinese company has invested almost $480 m in the construction of three berths. Upon completion, the new port, part of the Lamu Port South Sudan-Ethiopia Transport Corridor, is expected to benefit the region. Another newly opened line links landlocked Ethiopia's capital Addis Ababa—with the Port of Djibouti (Xinhua, October 5). When finished, the network will connect Kenya with Ethiopia, South Sudan, Uganda, Democratic Republic of Congo, Rwanda and Burundi, as well as proving a link between Nairobi and the secondary Port of Lamu.

Thus, through the large-scale infrastructure projects of the Mombasa and Lamu deepwater ports, and the construction of the standard gauge railway from Mombasa Port to Nairobi and a new economic corridor along the railway line, Kenya is in a very good position to take the role of an international trading hub along the Maritime Silk Road. This is in line with China's selection of Kenya as a China-Africa industrial cooperation demonstration and pioneering country. Hence, the emerging oil and gas industries from East Africa shall be integrated with Asian market dynamics. In this sense, it is possible to observe that the OBOR initiative will knot together a set of great goals of the Chinese government. However, it has been argued that China carefully selected the route due to the discovery of oil on the route. The recent discovery of oil and gas deposits around the East African coast means that the extractive model is the main reason for the strategic selection of the route.

Egypt is also of great strategic importance for the Maritime Silk Road as it controls the Suez Canal, which links Asia and Europe through the Indian Ocean and the Mediterranean Sea. Therefore, Egypt is particularly crucial for the New Maritime

Silk Road. China is supporting numerous infrastructure projects in Egypt, including up to US$15 billion financing for the development of the country's US$ 45 billion new administrative capital. China also invests in the development of special economic zones (SEZs) and has a stake in Egypt's ports and shipping industry. Egypt has already signed a MoU with China on the Belt and Road initiative and as such can already be considered as a Belt and Road country. Egypt is also China's fourth largest trading partner on the continent (NBSC 2015) and receives a considerable amount of Chinese investment in infrastructure, industrial cooperation and power projects.

A Chinese company is already constructing the new multi-purpose terminal at Alexandria Port (Egypt) (AllAfrica 2015). The port is, however, being operated by the Hong Kong-based company Hutchison Ports. China Railway Construction Corporation is currently constructing a 70 km railway from the expanding capital Cairo to its surroundings. In Egypt's bordering state Djibouti, starting from 2015, Doraleh Port was built within less than two years jointly financed by China Merchant Holdings Intl. (CMHI) and the Djibouti Ports and Free Zones Authority (DPFZA). When constructing the Doraleh Port, it was ensured that it is well connected with Djibouti's resource-rich neighbor and newly developed production country.

Ethiopia is also a China-Africa industrial cooperation demonstration and pioneering country, in which China is investing heavily in industrialization through the construction of SEZs and major infrastructure projects. For example, the new 3.4 USD billion railway (750 km), linking Addis Ababa to Djibouti (Ethio-Djibouti), financed by China's Exim Bank and built by *China Railway Group* and *China Civil Engineering Construction* was inaugurated in November 2016. The Ethiopian section cost $3.4bn with 70% financed by China's Exim Bank and 30% financed by Ethiopian government. The railway is the first step in a 5000 km long network of rail, which Ethiopia hopes to build by 2020, connecting it to Kenya, Sudan and South Sudan. Ethiopia has received three loans worth more than $380bn from the Chinese government and the Export–Import Bank of China for the development of infrastructure in the country (two road construction projects and upgrading of the electric grid system). Both the Doraleh Port in Djibouti as well as the Ethio-Djibouti railway started operating in 2017. Addis Ababa with the African Union's headquarters is the political capital of Africa and it is of strategic importance to China.

The proximity of Djibouti to Ethiopia has made it to become a Belt and Road initiative country together with Ethiopia by default. Djibouti, a small lower-middle-income country with a 900,000 population, located in the Horn of Africa, is of strategic importance to China. It is strategically located between the Red Sea and the Gulf of Aden. In spite of its small size, the country is very important in the framework of the New Maritime Silk Road, sheltering the first Chinese ultramarine naval base—where the USA already have the Pentagon's African Command (AFRICOM), used for CIA (Central Intelligence Agency) drone operations.

The alleged goal of the Chinese government is to deploy facilities able to provide logistic support to efforts against piracy, humanitarian assistance and peace maintenance. In 2016, Djibouti signed an agreement with China to be used as a Chinese naval port. Djibouti has received increasing access to Chinese funds, which may prove beneficial in reducing its 41.9% extreme poverty (2012 estimate). Chinese infrastructure projects in the country include a new port, airports as well as the Ethiopia-Djibouti railway projects. Djibouti contributed $878 m for the railway project. Furthermore, the Chinese state-owned enterprise China Merchants Group is the second-largest shareholder of the Port of Djibouti and investing in expanding the port's infrastructure to make it its first Silk Road hub (*China Daily Asia* 2016).

Also, South Africa is the only other African country that has signed a MoU with China on the Belt and Road initiative and which therefore can also already be considered as a Belt and Road country. The inclusion of South Africa is significant as it expands the Maritime Silk Road beyond its ancient route to the South. South Africa is by far China's largest trading partner on the African continent (NBSC 2015) and has a broad portfolio of projects with China in the area of infrastructure and power projects as well as the financial sector and industrial cooperation. Besides Egypt, South Africa is the only other African founding member of the AIIB.

Angola received the largest share of China's loans between 2000 and 2014 and is China's second largest trading partner (NBSC 2015) and number one oil exporter on the continent. Angola has further been selected by China as a China-Africa industrial cooperation priority country, which makes it likely that industrial cooperation will significantly increase under the FOCAC Johannesburg Action Plan (2016–2018). With Angola, the Belt and Road initiative will further expand from its ancient route, venturing into the Atlantic Ocean.

Tanzania is another East African country with prospective benefits from the Belt and Road initiative. It is another country that is likely to be among the first African Belt and Road initiative countries. Similar to Kenya, Tanzania is cooperating with China on creating a strong industrial base as a China-Africa industrial cooperation demonstration and pioneering country as well as an international maritime hub through the construction of the massive Bagamoyo Port. The Tanzanian Port Authority recently announced its approval for a US$10 billion project to develop a port at Bagamoyo financed by China. Located about 60 km north of Dar es Salaam, Bagamoyo is expected to become the biggest port in Africa once completed, handling twenty times more cargo than Dar es Salaam Port. Bagamoyo Port will be connected to the central corridor railway and the TAZARA Railway through an extended link. Chinese state-owned companies also hold shares in the Ports of Dar es Salaam and Mtwara.

Another key infrastructure project that China is investing in is the revival of the Tanzania-Zambia Railway. Built by China between 1970 and 1975, it links the Port of Dar es Salaam in Tanzania with Kapiri Mposhi in Zambia's copper belt. Among other things, it served to transport Zambian copper to the Port of Dar es Salaam. At the time of its completion, the 1860 km railway was the single longest railway in Sub-Saharan Africa and with a construction cost of US$ 500 million, the largest single foreign-aid project undertaken by China at the time (Bräutigam 2009). However, over the decades the railway almost became almost completely dysfunctional due to mismanagement and a lack of maintenance. China has now proposed to restore the railway and link it with 1344 km Benguela railway, connecting Angola's Atlantic Port of Lobito to the eastern border town of Luau, which was completed by a Chinese state-owned enterprise in August 2014, 2015 at a cost of US$ 1.8 billion. This would be the first connection between the shores of Indian and Atlantic Ocean by rail.

In Mozambique, a consortium of Chinese companies has announced to invest USD 1 billion to construct a new port in Maputo (Macau Hub 2016). Mozambique was selected by China as a China-Africa industrial cooperation priority country. The building of two deepwater ports and adjacent SEZs in Maputo and Beira is making Mozambique another stop along the Maritime Silk Road on Africa's East coast. Nevertheless, China's engagement of the two lusophone countries Mozambique and Angola and its recent agreements with Portugal to strengthen triangular cooperation with African countries may also open the door for other African lusophone countries, such as Cape Verde, Comoros and Guinea Bissau to become Belt and Road initiative countries in the future. In addition, a railway link from landlocked Zambia via Malawi to Mozambique is under construction.

The Republic of Congo is the only China-Africa industrial cooperation demonstration and pioneering country that is located at the Atlantic coast. In the Republic of Congo, China Road and Bridge Corporation is building a new port at Pointe-Noire, Congo's economic capital. The port construction plans include an industrial park as well as an oil refinery and a power plant. China's plan of building a new railway line would most likely encompass the modernization of the existing Pointe-Noire-Brazzaville line and perhaps also the line branching off to Mbinda, which connects Congo to Gabon (CRBC 2016). With its inclusion in the Belt and Road initiative, the Maritime Silk Road would hence expand further up North from Angola into the geo-strategically important Gulf of Guinea. The large-scale Pointe-Noire deepwater port development project coupled with an SEZ and railway and road projects connecting Congo to its neighboring countries provides a solid basis for the country to develop into a Maritime Silk Road hub in the Gulf of Guinea.

The governments of Senegal and Mali have entered into USD 2.73 billion agreements with the China Railway Construction Corporation on the repair and reconstruction of the 1286 km railway between the port of Dakar and Bamako. The agreement includes staff training and the modernization of 22 railway stations (Railway Gazette 2016). On Africa's West coast, Chinese companies are also a shareholder or involved in the construction and expansion of ports in Walvis Bay, Namibia; Luanda, Angola; Libreville, Gabon; Sao Tomé and Principe; Kribi, Cameroon; Lomé, Togo; Takoradi, Ghana; Abidjan, Ivory Coast; Conakry, Guinea; Dakar, Senegal; and Nouakchott, Mauritania.

Arguably, other countries in West Africa, such as Nigeria seeking loans from China's Exim Bank for transport infrastructure, could also be considered interested in the Belt and Road initiative. Nigeria is Africa's most populous country and China's third largest trading partner on the continent (NBSC 2015). Although Nigeria was not given priority from China on industrial cooperation, China is financing and implementing a number of large-scale infrastructure and SEZ projects, including the Lekki Free Zone with the adjacent deepwater port. It is expected that with the completion of the Lekki Port, the Lekki Free Zone will become a major industrial zone in the country and the vast port facilities may function as trading hub, expanding the Maritime Silk Road further to the West on the African continent (UNDP 2015).

Other examples of such infrastructure projects in Nigeria include the coastal railway project from Calabar to Lagos and the Nigerian railway modernization project from Lagos to Kano. The China Railway Construction Corporation has recently completed the Abuja-Kaduna railway, which is the first phase of a larger railway modernization project connecting Lagos with Kano in Nigeria's north. In 2014, the Nigerian government and China Civil Engineering Construction signed an agreement for the $12bn coastal railway project to link all 10 coastal cities in Nigeria. Unfortunately, this did not materialize and a new deal was signed in 2016. In Nigeria, the China Railway Construction Corporation signed a US$ 12 billion contract to build a 1400 km railway along Nigeria's coastline, connecting Lagos with Benin and Cameroon. As expected, large shares of the Lagos-Ibadan railway, as well as the coastal Lagos-Calabar railway are financed by China Exim Bank and built by China Civil Engineering Construction Company (CCECC). However, growing security concerns and increasing administrative and business costs may be among the reasons why China has not given top priority to Africa's largest single future market.

With Morocco, the Maritime Silk Road may complete its full inclusion of the African continent continuing up North the Atlantic coast from Nigeria. In addition to Egypt, Morocco provides another direct link to Europe on the Maritime Silk Road. Morocco is also a member State of the Arab League with which the Chinese government is committed to jointly implement the Belt and Road Initiative. Morocco's deepwater Tanger Port is already the main gateway between Europe and Africa with 36 established shipping lines to 22 African countries (ChinaAfricaBlog 2015).

Similar to other countries, China has been active in Togo's transport infrastructure. Prior to the formulation of the OBOR initiatives, the Togolese Government in collaboration with China built a new $150 million passenger terminal at Gnassingbé Eyadéma International Airport (AIGE) in Lomé which include a terminal with three boarding bridges, a viaduct to the terminal and expanding the parking lot. It was financed by loans from China's Exim Bank and has made the country a transport hub in the West African sub-region. The China Airport Construction Group (CACG) and the fellow Chinese company, Wietec, carried out the design and construction. Work on the project began in 2012 and was completed in July 2015. It represented part of the global cooperation for China's aviation industry. Also, China Merchants Holdings International (CMHI) has invested in Lomé Port of Togo.

Cameroon in Central Africa is also reported to be pitching itself as the gateway to West and Central Africa. It has also had Chinese cooperation in its transport infrastructure, notably the new deepwater Kribi Port built by Chinese companies. In Cameroon, China Harbor Engineering Company constructed the US$ 1billion Kribi Industrial Port Complex with 85% of the costs financed by China Exim Bank. Cameroon's first deepwater port is being connected to urban areas, including Yaoundé via roads and railway links constructed by Chinese companies (*The Diplomat* 2015). Further, the infrastructural projects to be undertaken in Africa under the "Belt and Road" framework include the development of deepwater ports in coastal cities including Bizerte, Tunisia; Dakar, Senegal; Dar es Salaam, Tanzania; Djibouti, Djibouti; Libreville, Gabon; Maputo, Mozambique; and Tema, Ghana. These will be key sites of the transcontinental exchange of manufactured goods and commodities between

Asian and African economies along the Maritime Silk Road. These ports are also likely to be developed as industrial hubs, following the model of China's development of the new Cameroonian deepwater port of Kribi.

Algeria and China agreed to construct a US$ 3.3 billion trans-shipment port at Cherchell, 60 km west of the capital city of Algiers. The port will be constructed by China Harbor Engineering Company (CHEC) and China State Construction Engineering Corporation (CSCEC) (The BRICS Post 2016). In addition, the memorandums of understanding between the government of Chad and Chinese companies signed last year suggest that Chad might become an important east-west nexus as well. In summary, the OBOR initiatives of the Chinese government offered several opportunities for the African continent with respect to infrastructure connectivity. Obsolete transportation network of connection is being resuscitated with new ones also being opening up.

Assessment of the Costs and Benefits Associated with the OBOR

Obviously, African needs continued financial support in infrastructure development. While the One Belt, One Road initiative offers considerable with respect to infrastructural connectivity, it also presents many uncertainties and potential concerns. In terms of benefits, One Belt One Road has assisted many countries in developing infrastructural connectivity. This implies that any effort to support the development of Africa's infrastructure is welcome in the context of the OBOR initiative. Firstly, with China involved in all these infrastructural projects in Africa, coupled with OBOR's vision for improving connectivity among countries, the initiative will offer a centralized, clear vision, and concerted effort in streamlining infrastructural development in Africa. An illustration is the railway line in Angola which is complete on the country's side of the border, but under-utilized because neither Democratic Republic of Congo nor Zambia have linked up to connect to the port, hence hindering efforts to export their products.

Secondly, capital for infrastructural development in Africa comes from various Chinese bank loans under individual bilateral agreements entered into by these countries. Through OBOR, the capital inflow can be clearly centrally monitored through the Asian Infrastructure Investment Bank (AIIB), Chinese Export–Import Bank and the Silk Road Fund (SRF). This implies that the race to finance African infrastructure has many upsides. The push to lend increases the total financing available for infrastructure and encourages lenders to streamline their procedures and make funds more accessible for borrowers. Having numerous financiers increases the scope for joint financing, which can help to spread the risk inherent in large projects.

Thus, countries with dire need of infrastructure development will benefit from the OBOR investment in their construction of the much-need transport and amenities network. For several years, Gabon, a West-African nation, had wanted to improve the transport network of its crumbling French colonial buildings and dilapidated roads. Things changed in recent years when China Road and Bridge Corporation (CRBC) won the contract to build the first overland route from the capital city Libreville to Port-Gentil with the country's deepest harbor. The once dreadful road through seemingly impassable jungle and marshland is now a reality, and the economic and commercial value-added from this route adds up. Chinese firms are able to offer competitive pricing and their prices are usually lower than most United States or European Union companies. Chinese firms are also winning lucrative service contracts in Africa which once used to be the domain of US, European and Japanese firms, to run those completed infrastructures. In addition, products made in Africa are increasingly produced in Chinese owned companies: In the scope of restructuring its economy, China started to outsource labor-intensive branches such as shoe and clothing manufacturing as well as car assembling to African countries like, e. g., landlocked Ethiopia, which makes the Ethio-Djibouti railway essential.

In the context of OBOR, the benefits to Africa can be summarized as:

- Participating countries will get greater access to China as well as other interconnected markets along the proposed routes. Smaller and landlocked countries especially stand to gain from increased inclusiveness.
- Smaller countries will see inland infrastructure improvement through increased investment by China and other partner countries.
- Lowering of costs of transporting goods to countries given economies of scale and availability of better infrastructure.
- Infrastructure connectivity will result in lower transit costs.

Multinational brands will gain from enlarged catchment areas as a result of infrastructure upgrades. By connecting the ports with the inland provinces, China is making sure that products and resources can be transported to the coast and then exported to China. The intervention in the infrastructural connectivity has stimulated Special Economic Zones and Free Trade Zones in several African countries. More importantly, Africa is a crucial market for China's exports. This initiative seems to have made China supportive of Africa's homegrown development plan as set out in the African Union's Agenda 2063. This is strengthened with China signing a memorandum of understanding with the African Union (AU) in January 2015 to connect all 54 countries with high-speed rails, ports and roads. Thus, there are clear synergies with the Belt and Road initiative that support greater connectivity. In other words, the OBOR initiatives strengthen the bilateral relations of China with African countries. The initiatives currently represent the most comprehensive framework to interconnect African countries as against other interventions from Africa's development partners (bilateral, multilateral, public, and private).

However, the uncertainties and potential concerns are quite fundamental to the continent sustainable development goals. For example, the initiative is part of a massive restructuring of the Chinese economy as the country seeks to move from a *newly industrialized* economy to a *fully developed* one. The old drivers of development such as low wage and low-end export manufacturing have been widely successful. But the system has essentially run its course. Overproduction and cyclical crises have led to social and economic problems such as unemployment, increasing income disparity and an overheated housing market. In this regard, there is little doubt that some, perhaps many, Chinese see the One Belt, One Road initiative as a way of relieving overcapacity in certain Chinese capital goods and construction-oriented industrial sectors. Chinese private firms (POEs) are typically most active abroad when growth slows at home and as they look for alternative markets for either sales or margin growth.

As part of the costs of the OBOR project, China-sponsored infrastructural projects are often intended not to support the local economy, but to facilitate Chinese access to natural resources or to open the market for Chinese exports. Several countries that lie along the path of the OBOR project, having been a subject of historical neglect by institutional forms of investment coupled with urgent domestic infrastructural requirements, can fall prey to Beijing's advances. This implies that the need to have access to natural resources is very strategic in the selection of the maritime ports in the East Africa sub-region. From an Africa perspective, the One Belt seems to continue the colonial legacy of building infrastructure to get resources out of the continent, and not interlink the continent. Thus, most of the infrastructure connectivity projects are being done to enhance the ease of Chinese goods movement into Africa. The connectivity is are therefore being pushed along the transport corridors where it will aid the movement of natural resources such as crude oil, copper to China. It is just like a colonial-style arrangement in which transport links are simply created to shuttle resources out of the host country, without creating opportunities for growth.

Another concern is that of the long-term employment benefits to the host nation by awarding Chinese firms to manage infrastructure projects. The bulk of the infrastructure connectivity financing in the OBOR initiatives is contracted to Chinese national companies such as China Communications Construction Company, China Railway Construction Corporation and China Civil Engineering Construction among others. In many cases, China even sends its own construction workers as opposed to hiring locally, thereby minimizing the number of local jobs that are created. Hiring Chinese workers allowed the employers to impose exploitative labor conditions that locals would never tolerate. In most cases, the managers, foreman, and workers are usually brought in from China. There are evidences across other divides that even after the supply of work visas was exhausted, rather than offer a wage high enough to attract local residents, the companies arranged for more Chinese construction workers to enter the host countries as tourists. Senior managers are also usually expatriated from China to supervise the projects.

Public financing of infrastructure projects on the continent are mostly administered through the Export–Import Bank of China and the China-Africa Development Fund. China, through the OBOR, aims to support infrastructure projects in strategically located developing countries in the form of huge loans to their governments. Hence, loans to countries have therefore continued to form a prominent part of China's public investment portfolio in Africa. However, there are concerns with how the financing will be structured and deployed. While increasing infrastructural financing does not in itself address the shortage of bankable projects, on the contrary, it may actually increase the likelihood of unjustified projects being financed. Geopolitical and economic rivalries can see projects of questionable value get pushed through on political grounds, without proper assessment of their financial and economic viability, and cutting corners in technical, environmental and social due diligence. There is a growing risk that African countries will borrow for white elephant projects, saddling them with hard-to-service debt and lenders with nonperforming loans or default. For example, there are arguments that the China Development Bank (CDB) and China Exim lend on largely political grounds, do not have clear-cut debt sustainability limits and have recently incurred major losses in risky countries such as in Sudan and Zimbabwe.[2]

Chinese loans may have laxer requirements and carry a lower interest rate than those of commercial banks. But they are loans. China expects them to be repaid. For example, while Chinese loans used to have low-interest rates around 2.5%, they are now creeping up to near 5% or more. This will make them harder to repay. Historical precedent has shown that, as a result, countries become ensnared in a debt trap that leaves them vulnerable to Chinese influence. The heavier the debt burden on smaller countries, the greater China's own debt leverage becomes. Countries overwhelmed by their debt to China have in the past been forced to sell stakes in those projects to China. Additionally, China placed pressure on nations to award its additional contracts due to delays in payment on part of the dependent nation. Thus, while those who receive Chinese funds are happy to improve their roads, they may be mortgaging their futures. Many of the nations in the One Belt, One Road region are exceedingly poor, with limited experience in undertaking huge infrastructure projects, and considerable levels of corruption endemic in their countries. It has been argued that Beijing encourages dependency using opaque contracts, predatory loan practices, and corrupt deals that mire nations in debt and undercut their sovereignty, denying them their long-term, self-sustaining growth. This strategy has been referred to as debt-trap diplomacy which offers the honey of cheap infrastructure loans, with the sting of default coming if smaller economies cannot generate enough free cash to pay their interest.

For example, Sri Lanka's recent dealings with China offer a cautionary tale for many African countries. It is important to recall what happened in Sri Lanka. Post-civil war Sri Lanka went on a borrowing binge to reconstruct dilapidated infrastructure. To successive Sri Lankan governments, China was a benevolent friend, offering cheap, easy and addictive money—an attractive alternative to the strict conditionality of Western financing arrangements. But the country soon ran into economic woes, and when the debt burden became untenable, the Sri Lankan government was forced to relinquish majority control over the port in 2017 in lieu of repayment. This sparked outrage across Sri Lanka. To critics, it was confirmation of China's imperial agenda and demonstrated the pitfalls of Chinese financing: that despite a lack of explicit political conditionality, there is certainly no free lunch, and such arrangements pose a threat to the sovereignty of vulnerable countries. Thus, the way

---

[2]In Venezuela, for example, loans were secured against oil reserves, before prices—and the economy—collapsed. The losses have forced China's policy banks to reassess their approach to sovereign risk and their country lending priorities.

the island nation has ceded control of the strategic port of Hambantota[3] highlights the issue of debt-trap diplomacy—a predatory system designed to ensnare countries into a straightjacket of debt servitude. It poses the question of whether developing countries are naively mortgaging their resources and strategic assets to China. Given Africa's huge reliance on China as a source of funding, there is concern that African states might suffer a similar fate to Sri Lanka—and unwittingly become pawns in China's global strategic agenda.

Given that China's development financing is not free grant, people wonder whether Africa is capable of repaying Chinese loans, and, if so, how. The reason is that Chinese loans are collateralized by strategically important natural assets with high long-term value (even if they lack short-term commercial viability). In return for financing and building the infrastructure that poorer countries need, China demands favorable access to their natural assets, from mineral resources to ports. While, the recipient nations usually suffer from low credit ratings and have difficulty obtaining funding from the international financial market. China, however, makes financing relatively easily available—albeit with certain conditions and less *paperwork* than conventional sources. Through this method, China achieves the twin goals of economic penetration and strategic leverage. In addition, Chinese loans for infrastructure projects are often made with the understanding that the developing countries award construction contracts to Chinese companies. In short, China benefits from both the financing and construction of infrastructure projects, while developing countries must bear all of the financial risk.

It therefore appeared that Africa is merely borrowing money from China to pay itself back. Linked to the point above, is the fact that Africa is already deeply indebted to China. In Kenya, China owns half of the country's external debt. Kenya will pay about KES 60 billion to the China Exim Bank. Since 2013, for instance, Kenya's debt-to-GDP ratio has risen from 40 to 53%, far above the government-set preference of 45%. Kenya and Africa do not need more debt from China, and if this initiative is primarily debt-financed (in a non-concessionary manner), it will cause considerable concern in African capitals. Most of the OBOR funding is in the form of loans, not grants. This means, for example, that if Kenya or any of other counties in the initiatives cannot pay back its loans, China could own many of its ports and rail lines and therefore have enormous leverage over the Kenya government. In summary, extending loans for infrastructure projects is not inherently bad. However, the projects that China is supporting are often intended not to support the local economy, but to facilitate Chinese access to natural resources, or to open the market for its low-cost export goods.

While there are arguments that China had to forgive many of their debts which is about $3.9 billion in all, since borrowers could never repay them. But that is a small fraction of the total debts that developing countries owe it. For example, in 2015 China canceled $40 million in debt from Zimbabwe. But Zimbabwe still owes China over $1 billion. Moreover, at the time of China's modest debt cancelation, Zimbabwe

[3]The port of Hambantota straddles Indian Ocean trade routes linking Europe, Africa, and the Middle East to Asia and is quite strategic to the Chinese interest.

pledged that it would increase its use of the Chinese yuan in its foreign exchange reserves. It therefore seemed that China had used its debt cancelation to achieve its larger foreign policy goals.

Countries along the Belt and Road have highly diverse levels of development and sometimes rather dysfunctional governance conditions that impede infrastructure development as well as the development of trade and investment. Nevertheless, the risk of political instability in the countries it will pass through. Infrastructure projects such as railways, highways and power stations depend on continuing and constant government support. However, many countries in the OBOR region are subject to frequent political upheaval which can have an impact on policy and the implementation and success of projects. Other costs relate to the different regulatory and legal systems in the countries along OBOR. Many of these African countries are still developing so their legal and regulatory systems may not be so sophisticated, may be incomplete and may not have been tested for foreign investments.

For example, some OBOR projects have witnessed domestic opposition. There has been some opposition by civil society groups to various infrastructural projects which are deemed to have adverse effects on the community. In Kenya as a case in point, government has had to pay millions of dollars to communities affected by the standard gauge railway line as compensation for the project to take off. In some instances, the project had to be suspended by the courts until compensation has been carried out. In another case, environmentalists took the government to court in opposition to the railway line passing through the Nairobi National Park, arguing it will adversely affect the natural habitat of wildlife within the park. These issues will increase costs to the projects, while the duration of implementation might also be lengthened to counter for court appearances and consultations with the communities involved.

The complexity of developing sustainable infrastructure and combining infrastructure investments with improved policies for fostering trade and investment demands a comprehensive policy approach beyond a mere focus on individual projects. Countries will have to be supported in this endeavor through various channels of support—through policy advice and peer learning, through the engagement of development banks, and through the adoption of common standards to be developed in supranational fora, involving governments, private business and civil society. In terms of overview, some costs attached to the initiative include:

- China could use OBOR to export its surplus steel, cement and other materials, to smaller markets.
- Many countries along the corridor are credit-rated poor by top credit rating agencies and there is an associated lending risk therein.
- Many Countries in BELT and ROAD region are characterized by internal strife, poor governance and so on, and any domestic instability will increase associated costs of transportation and labor.
- Large financial investments relative to the small size of some economies could result in macroeconomic imbalances and high budget deficits.

- There are also attached social and environmental risks as infrastructure projects could displace communities and lead to environmental pollution.

It is therefore evident that China's African policy is driven by its self-interest and its own political and strategic considerations, not altruism. The bulk of the Chinese experience behind the New Silk Road, based upon infrastructure buildup as a way to boost new fluxes and partnerships, has been shaped through the existing Sino-African relations. In summary, there are more benefits and costs to be shared among countries involved in the One Belt One Road initiative. If the inherent risks, if properly managed, it should not hinder the progress of world infrastructure upgrading.

Identification and Analysis of the Specific Arrangements, Incentives and the Capacity Required to Ensure that This Issue Is Beneficial to African Countries

The realization of the BRI requires physical infrastructure—roads, rail, ports and aviation—underlined by a strong financing framework. With respect to funding arrangement in the OBOR initiatives. The first layer of the standard OBOR financing model involves China providing 80% of the funding for any given project in the form of long-expiry loans. The remaining 20% is provided locally through loans and stock shares. There are two main funding vehicles driving China's 80% contribution. The first is the $40 billion Silk Road Fund, backed by China's sovereign wealth fund, China Investment Corporation (CIC Capital), China Development Bank, the Export–Import Bank of China, and the State Administration of Foreign Exchange. The Bank of China and CITIC Bank have further committed $100 billion and $113 billion, respectively. Though not set up specifically for OBOR, the Asian Infrastructure Investment Bank, worth $100 billion, is planning to loan out between $10 and $15 billion per year to projects.

The second layer of the standard financing model involves the use of open tenders for construction contracts. This essentially favors Chinese contractors and workers, who charge cheaper rates than their international counterparts. This effectively produces the same results as a closed tender process. China has therefore been swift to adopt the interchangeable open tender system as an ostensible move toward transparency in order to alleviate international concerns about corruption. After terms are reached with a host country, funds are transferred directly into the Beijing-based bank accounts of China's state-owned enterprises, which build the project often with Chinese materials. This is a model Beijing has employed extensively in Africa. Once Beijing's political blessing for a project is communicated via funding from its policy banks, China's national- or provincial-level state-owned enterprises build it, often with little or no political or financial risk assessment or market research. This financing arrangement will not likely be beneficial to the African economies involved in the OBOR initiatives. Such loans should be domiciled in the banking system of the host economies rather than Chinese banks.

However, it is obvious that Chinese banks alone will not be able to fully fund the Belt and Road projects as the scale of the initiative expands. This is where private capital will come in and public-private partnerships (PPP) have an important role to play with respect to structural, economic and legal reasons. Many companies working on OBOR projects—especially high-speed rail—are contractors that work on a loan-and-build model; they often do not think like investors. With many OBOR projects being regularly launched, issues and questions will arise as to how best to structure them in other for them to be beneficial to Africa.

For African economies, they should key mainly into projects in which infrastructure gaps are looking for equity investments of the type that the PPP model strongly supports and which the OBOR strategy will encourage. This is of course a move away from the traditional procurement methods which used to see the engagement of Chinese enterprise solely for their construction capabilities. The Chinese government itself is now aggressively advocating and encouraging outbound investment in the form of equity stakes in projects and assets across the globe. The PPP arrangement is one of the more convenient and workable project models for contractors who are looking to get into joint ventures with foreign entities. Increasingly in recent times, Chinese enterprises are looking to commit to countries beyond just contracting work. They are now looking to invest with, and in, the nations which are looking to them for their expertise. By becoming a partner to governments, rather than mere employees, there is scope for significant mutual benefits to arise. In many of the African nations along the Silk Route, the mandatory position for one reason or another is for the host nation to have ownership (or at least strict control) over its own infrastructure. Without the resources to go it alone, the PPP model is an obvious choice for them to meet their infrastructure needs without ceding rights they wish to retain. By awarding a concession they can attract foreign know-how and investment while maintaining ownership (or the right to ownership at a later time). Currently, there does not seem to have been any major public-private partnership arrangements for the OBOR projects in Africa. If private funds were to be enticed to invest in these projects, then there would be greater demand by private investors for transparency and reasonably high rates of investment within a relatively short period of time. This would translate into a demand for setting up of some monitoring arrangements to scrutinize the viability of projects, based on rational economic calculations rather than political considerations.

Consequently, the collaboration between private and public partnerships involves numerous obstacles. To overcome these hurdles, effective communication is essential between all parties involved. Host African countries must provide policy support—ranging from educating companies about cultural norms to local law—and regularly engage with companies to ensure the project is successful. OBOR project collaborations between government and business also face working in remote or multiple locations throughout the process, creating challenges exchanging information with one another. In order to implement a successful OBOR project using a PPP model, communication and collaboration are essential. It is therefore important to introduce state-of-the-art technologies and expertise throughout the full duration of the project to ensure the quality and progress of the OBOR projects. Starting with the bidding process through project implementation, organizations must have transparent communication to ensure their projects are successful. This allows clients to put together larger, cross-border investment opportunities with fewer challenges.

On capacity building, a recent McKinsey report involving a study of 1000 Chinese firms in eight African countries found that a vast majority (89%) of firm employees were African and almost two-thirds of the firms provided some form of skills training to its employees. This drive to employ Africans is linked to rising labor costs in China. Nonetheless, the report also highlighted particular challenges, especially the failure of many Chinese firms to promote local workers IN African economies to management positions, the competitive threat of Chinese firms to longstanding African enterprises (and the jobs the latter provide), and instances of serious breaches of labor, health, and safety regulations. The projects planned under OBOR could help employ short-term construction crews, provide necessary infrastructure for the movement of trade (highways, ports, airports) and spur employment in trade-related industry and services. If this will be achieved, African countries as China's main commercial partners need to have strict laws against importing foreign labor. In addition, adequate arrangement must be provided in the contract with Chinese firms to transfer technology and technical capacity to African nationals in the course of entering into agreements in the OBOR projects.

In summary, for it to be beneficial to Africa, the OBOR projects must make adequate operating capital accessible. For instance, funds to maintain infrastructure projects must be made available as needed. The above represents serious challenges for the governance of projects in poorer countries in Africa. The OBOR projects can accelerate policy change, to better manage project risks, in favorable directions at all tiers of governance. This will require the review of the OBOR projects to understand the gaps in policies that need to be bridged to achieve best practices. These could be gaps of several types: in technical capacity, such as how to design a rail line network to achieve an effective connectivity; in managerial capacity, such as how to instill appropriate maintenance procedures after completion; and, in resourcing capacity, such as how to provide adequate access to operating capital. Each of these gaps will trigger recommendations for changes in regulations, systems and procedures and capacity building.

Concluding Summary

Infrastructural connectivity is a major challenge in Africa. However, different responses have been made by African countries (regional level, selected national country level), Africa's development partners (bilateral, multilateral, public, private) and through the OBOR Initiative to address the challenges. An emerging scenario is that most individual African countries are cash strapped and therefore cannot embark on huge infrastructural projects that involve massive financial resources. This is why investment in infrastructural resources for each country is muted. Nevertheless, the benefits of undertaking infrastructural projects that enhance connectivity using domestically mobilized resources lie in the ownership of such investments. However, this is not feasible for most African countries.

The regionally conceived arrangement to ensure infrastructural inter-connectivity in the context of PIDA is still a long way from meeting its potential. The reality gap is that PIDA has made some progress, but not fast enough to bridge the infrastructure gap by the deadline of 2040. The PIDA arrangement was created to address the failures of the previous regional infrastructure initiatives such as incomplete information, inadequate causal analysis, lack of politically accepted and technically justified priorities, poor implementation, and lack of regulatory frameworks and incentives. Consequently, PIDA employed a more comprehensive set of instruments such as the Service Delivery Mechanism for technical assistance, the Continental Business Network for public-private partnerships, the Policy and Regulatory Framework for the continental harmonization of the legislation, the M&E and Information Management Framework to evaluate progress and the Presidential Infrastructure Champion Initiative (PICI) to fast track project implementation by assigning project ownership to a government official or head of state.

Despite the development of these instruments and other mechanisms intended to create a new dynamic for timely and effective infrastructure development in Africa, only four of the 51 major programs reached advanced phases of implementation in 2015 (Signé 2017). Most projects are only in the early needs assessment or funding proposal phase. Given that, prior to PIDA, the continent had only secured 5% of its infrastructure investment needs between 2004 and 2013, the slow progression toward bridging the infrastructure gap by 2040 is unsurprising. The most fundamental bottleneck is still the challenge of financing the infrastructural projects. The challenge of finance is also the bane of infrastructural supply arrangement at the sub-regional levels. This explains why the interventions on infrastructural connectivity at the regional and sub-regional levels are muted.

The multilateral development banks' role has been and remains substantial in the framework of infrastructure in Africa, but this will require adapting to the changing context of infrastructural connectivity of the continent. They continue to represent an important financing source especially for the lower-income countries, and they are critical for establishing ways of leveraging other types of financing where the risks preclude other options. However, the specific impact interventionist impact of some of the arrangements is not clear. For example, the ICA is not a financing agency or a pooled financing facility. It does not purchase, finance or build projects but only produce data and analysis which could be useful for project promoters and those seeking financing. Also, it has created a tool called the Project Preparation FUND FINDER—which put countries in touch with funding facilities. This is not what Africa requires at this moment.

The EU-AITF has made substantial effort in Africa with the provision of loans and grants from the trust fund. The grants are distributed in a competitive manner that is compliant with the institution's procurement rules and procedures which in turn conform to internationally accepted standards open at least to all enterprises established in either an EU Member State or a member of the African, Caribbean and Pacific Group of States. However, the bulk of the intervention from the EU-AITF has located within the domestic economy which may not encourage multi-modal connectivity of infrastructure in Africa. The Africa Development Bank (AfDB) estimates that *Africa's infrastructure deficit* amounts to USD 93 billion annually between 2010 and 2020 to plug the continent's infrastructure deficit. Yet the bank distributes a paltry US$3 billion per annum in loans. This miserly amount will not make a dent in assisting countries to meet crucial infrastructure needs. It will also be impossible for the bank to finance other urgent economic development priorities. The bank has only financed 2858 projects to the value of US$47 billion over 40 years.

In order for Africa to maximize the benefits of infrastructural connectivity and reduce the inherent risks involved in the OBOR initiatives, there is a need to:

1. Financing Africa's infrastructure gap is essential for the continued prosperity of the region. But the current politically driven race to provide funding entails major risks. The specter of bad debt has reared its head. Borrowers and lenders should heed recent lessons and beware of the looming debt trap. With narrow revenue bases and undiversified economies, there are doubts about whether these countries will be able to service debt, especially against a backdrop of weak commodity prices. Hence, the loan from China should be appropriately structured to avoid the debt-trap diplomacy inherent in Chinese loans. Contractual arrangement in the loans should discourage the taking over of the projects by China in the event of loan default. Under this scenario, the interest rate and the payback period should be adequately arranged.
2. The commercial banks in the host economies of Africa should be integrated into the financing arrangements of the OBOR projects. The arrangements of domiciling the fund in China are not adequate. The bulk of the transactions should be internalized in the host economies to ensure the integration of projects into the host economies right from the outset. This has a way of strengthening the financial institutions of the host economies in Africa.
3. The Public-private partnership arrangement should be well explored. Most African countries are indebted and do not have the financial capacity required for such huge OBOR projects. Given the dynamics of the OBOR projects, only PPP arrangements that will be beneficial to Africa and will not lead to an eventual take over by China should be undertaken
4. The OBOR initiatives should be adequately institutionalized. While the FOCAC is currently institutionalized, there is no such institutionalization of the OBOR framework with respect to the Chinese-African relations. It has very much relied mainly on the pronouncement of the Chinese Authorities. If the potential of the Belt and Road initiative is to be realized, a variety of platforms, partnerships and governance mechanisms will have to be established. Improving infrastructure and connectivity is not a purely technical matter. It requires policy reforms in countries which want to benefit from stronger integration, and platforms among financing institutions to foster project development and common standards for financing as well as for environmental, social and governance standards.

5. The labor laws in African economies should be adequately reviewed to ensure that foreign labors are not imported from China. This is the only way in which African nationals can benefit from the OBOR initiatives.
6. Countries should identify the routes of their inter-connectivity such that the OBOR projects to be embarked on will deliver on sustainable growth framework. The current idea of china selecting the inter-connectivity routes to aid the movement of their products from Africa to China is counterproductive. This will be beneficial only to China and less benefits will come to Africa. This is because States and sub-regions throughout Africa already have infrastructure projects that can enhance intra- and inter-connectivity that they understandably wish to prioritize or are ongoing. It is quite fundamental that the OBOR initiative made arrangement to absorb such domestic projects to make it part of the BRI projects. However, the conditions of linking up such projects must be made flexible to incorporate the country's financial capacity into focus. Financing such projects should be done with respect to taking into consideration the ability of such a country to repay its debt.
7. The local content framework should be built into the OBOR projects. Nearly all the required construction materials are sourced from China. This is an indication that China is only interested in developing the local industries in his own country. China's domestic economy is slowing and that China is increasingly concerned about keeping its construction companies working. African based construction firms should also be made participatory in the initiatives. Perhaps, one of the conditions for Chinese construction firms to participating in the initiative is to negotiate partnership with domestic construction firms in the host economies.
8. There should be a program that incorporates the development of the technical capacity of the domestic workers into the OBOR initiatives. It is not enough for them to be part of the project when they are not able to maintain such projects after completion due to their technical deficiencies.
9. This is an opportunity for Africa to negotiate the specifics of the type of infrastructure that the continent requires and create a win-win situation where Africa leverages Chinese financing to not only address priority infrastructure gaps, but also better interlink the continent. The continent's infrastructural development has shown substantial progress behind the construction of highways, international seaports, railways and airports.
10. The OBOR initiative should be developed further from a bilateral Chinese initiative to a more multi-lateralized mechanism, which would include private business as well as national and regional government institutions. The institutionalization framework can be seen in the ICA and the EU-AITF context of assistance to Africa. An incremental multi-lateralization of the Belt and Road initiative would lend credibility to the whole process and would increase the scope for engagement of governments and private business, which is instrumental for scaling-up investments and put them in the context of the development aspirations of the populations. It is of utmost importance, for example, that local businesses participate in infrastructure investments as well as in the value chains to be developed across borders.

11. An alternative to the current standard debt model is direct investment. For struggling economies, China's debt-funded financing model is unsustainable compared to foreign direct investment whereby foreign investors—rather than the struggling economy itself—shoulder the financial burden. Direct investment into existing local companies by Chinese state-owned enterprises would involve a shrewder calculation of risk and return. If China continues its risk-blind debt-financing model, in the mid- to long-term it might itself become weighed down with enormous amounts of debt and resentment from debt-ridden host countries. Switching to a direct investment model, or adjusting to risk, Beijing will nonetheless need to address the challenge of offloading overcapacity in a way that ensures local economies are not locked out of OBOR.
12. Transport corridors were designed by sub-regional institutions to enhance inter-country connectivity in the pre-OBOR era. The OBOR initiative should not design new transport corridors in order to make its intervention on infrastructural connectivity but should rather absorb and work with the existing transport corridor arrangement in Africa. The OBOR framework will therefore be seen as beneficial if it can follow such existing arrangements. However, negotiations should be done with sub-regional institutions in that regards. This is to prevent the level of default from individual country with respect to repayment.

As against all other forms of intervention on infrastructural connectivity, China continues to be most important ally for the African continent to date as against the opportunities offered by the World Bank, the EU and other development partners. The One Belt One Road Initiative offers an opportunity to deepen Sino-Africa Relations and should be explored further by the leadership of both China and Africa. OBOR clearly has the potential to alter the trade and investment landscape of Africa and bring about greater economic gains, and positive collaboration among participating states, thereby improving the economic prosperity of the region. Successful implementation of the OBOR throughout the African continent will have the added effect of improving intra-Africa trade. The multiplier effect this has would most definitely propel Africa into the growth path. This has implications for achieving the Agenda 2063: The Africa we want. The need of the hour, however, is for participating countries to work together to draft strong policy-related objectives and feasible agreements, chart out clear rules and regulations in regards to areas such as the environment, human rights and so on, thereby ensuring OBOR's success in the long run.

Policy makers in Africa should adopt a more circumspect approach toward dealing with China. It is important to be aware of exploitative dangers associated with such arrangements, but it is also important to be strategic in how Chinese interest can be exploited to Africa's advantage. Here, a level of tactical nous and economic diplomacy is required. By exercising their agency and setting the terms of engagement, savvy countries could use China's involvement in Africa to grow their economies. They could also solicit renewed interest from previously disengaged foreign powers by using their relationships with China to bolster their political capital. If this is done properly, they could avoid the fate that befell Sri Lanka—and even ensure African nations emerge as winners rather than losers.

References

AllAfrica (2015) Egypt signs deal to set up multi-purpose terminal at Alexandria. https://allafrica.com/stories/201510191283.html

Adzibgey, YCK, Tesfamichael N Mitiku (2007) Institutional arrangements for transport corridor management in Sub-Saharan Africa. Sub-Sahara Africa Transport Policy Programme, World Bank, EU and UNECA. http://documents.worldbank.org/curated/en/743421468008450182/pdf/430390REPLACEM11Corridor1Management.pdf

African Development Bank/United Nations Economic Commission For Africa (2003, August 14) Review of the implementation status of the Trans African Highways and the missing links: vol 2: description of corridors. Retrieved 14 Jul 2007

Bräutigam D (2009) The dragon's gift: the real story of China in Africa. Oxford University Press

China Daily Asia (2016) CMG plans network of ports, terminals. 2 June 2016. Available at: http://www.chinadailyasia.com/business/2016-06/02/content_15443229.html

China Road and Bridge Corporation (2016) CRBC sings the business contract for Pointe Noire New Port Project in Congo-Brazzaville. 22 February 2016. Available at: http://www.crbc.com/site/crbcEN/companyNews/info/2016/3438.html

FOCAC (2015) The forum on China-Africa cooperation Johannesburg Action Plan (2016–2018). https://www.focac.org/eng/zywx_1/zywj/t1327961.htm

Foster V, Briceño-Garmendia C (2010) Africa's infrastructure: a time for transformation. The World Bank, Washington, DC, USA

Jerome A (2011) Infrastructure for economic development and poverty reduction in Africa. United Nations Human Settlements Programme, Nairobi

Macau Hub (2016) China's CHEC involved in investment of US$1 billion in the new port of Maputo, 25 April 2016. Available at: http://www.macauhub.com.mo/en/2016/04/25/chinas-chec-involved-in-investment-of-us1-billion-in-the-new-port-of-maputo

National Development and Reform Commission of the People's Republic of China (2015) Vision and actions on jointly building Silk Road Economic Belt and 21st-century Maritime Silk Road. Available at http://en.ndrc.gov.cn/newsrelease/201503/t20150330_669367.html. Accessed on 19 Jun 2018

National Bureau of Statistics of China (2015) China Statistical Yearbook 2015. Available at http://www.stats.gov.cn/tjsj/ndsj/2015/indexeh.htm. Accessed on 5 Jul 2016

Ocean Shipping Consultants, Ltd (2008) Beyond the bottlenecks: ports in Sub-Saharan Africa. AICD, Background Paper, World Bank, Washington, D.C.

Patel P (2014). Regional infrastructure in Sub-Saharan Africa: challenges and opportunities. African Regional Infrastructure. http://siteresources.worldbank.org/1818SOCIETY/Resources/1818AFRICApaperFINAL.pdf

Railway Gazette (2016) Senegal—Mali railway modernization agreements signed, 5 January 2016. Available at: http://www.railwaygazette.com/news/infrastructure/single-view/view/senegal-mali-railway-modernisation-agreements-signed.html

Signé L (2017) The road ahead for fixing Africa's infrastructure deficit. Africa in focus. Brookings. https://www.brookings.edu/blog/africa-in-focus/2017/11/16/the-road-ahead-for-fixing-africas-infrastructure-deficit/

The BRICS Post (2016) Algeria, China ink $3.3 bn mega port deal, 18 January 2016. Available at: http://thebricspost.com/algeria-china-ink-3-3-bn-mega-port-deal/#.V3VoO4TF70d. Accessed on 27 June 2016

The ChinaAfricaBlog (2015) Morocco positions itself as hub for China-Africa business relations. Available at: http://chinaafricablog.com/post/138224689353/morocco-positions-itself-as-hub-for-china-africa#.V2pbGoTF7zI

The Diplomat (2015) What's it like to have China build you a port? ask cameroon, 27 February 2015. Available at: http://thediplomat.com/2015/02/whats-it-like-to-have-china-build-you-a-port-ask-cameroon/. Accessed on 26 June 2016

United Nation Development Programme (2015) If Africa builds nest, will the birds come? Comparative study on special economic zones in Africa and China. United Nation Development Programme

UNECA (2009) Arica Review Report on transport: a summary. UNECA. https://sustainabledevelopment.un.org/content/documents/AfricanReviewReport-on-TransportSummary.pdf

Wekesa B (2015) China's silk road economic belt: African perspectives and implications. African East-Asian Affairs, Issue 1 & 2, June 2015, pp 144–161

Xinhua (2018) Kenya's SGR train a catalyst for regional transformation: CRBC executive. Xinhuanet http://www.xinhuanet.com/english/2018-06/01/c_137223618.htm

The US-China Trade War: What Is Africa's Gain?

Folasade Bosede Adegboye, Gbadebo Odularu and Oluwatoyin Augustina Matthew

Introduction

As trade wars arise due to the impression that a country's rival economy has an prejudiced trading system, domestic industries would rightfully strain the government to reduce the attractiveness of imported goods, hence, driving global policy in the direction of a trade war. This could even be as a result of a misconception of the extensive gains of free trade. The striking basics of trade wars is that as it is initiated in an industry, it could spread to affect other industries. In like manner, it could be initiated amid two economies and could affect other economies that were not primarily subsumed in the conflict, therefore resulting into a tradeoff of import conflicts from a protectionist bias. If appropriate controls are not set in place, trade wars result in salient sanctions for erring countries, thereby, posing adverse effects on the trading relations amid two countries and by ripple effect the global trade landscape.

F. B. Adegboye (✉)
Department of Banking and Finance, Covenant University, Ota, Nigeria
e-mail: folasade.adegboye@covenantuniversity.edu.ng

G. Odularu
Department of Economics and Finance, Bay Atlantic University, Washington, DC, USA
e-mail: odularu@comcast.net; godularu@live.com; godularu@bau.edu

Socio-Economic Research Applications and Projects (SERAP LLC), Washington, DC, USA

Center for Research on Political Economy (CREPOL), Dakar-Yoff, Senegal

Trade, Economics and Agribusiness Division, SSCG Consulting, Birmingham, UK

American Heritage University of Southern California (AHUSC), Ontario, CA, USA

O. A. Matthew
Department of Economics and Development Studies, Covenant University, Ota, Nigeria
e-mail: oluwatoyin.matthew@covenantuniversity.edu.ng

G. O. A. Odularu et al. (eds.), *Fostering Trade in Africa*,
Advances in African Economic, Social and Political Development,
https://doi.org/10.1007/978-3-030-36632-2_7

The Review of Earlier Trade War

Economic conflict is not a thing of today, it has been around for centuries specifically the nineteenth century. There also has been a number of trade wars till date, which would be outlined chronologically, beginning with the First Opium War which occurred within the years 1839 and 1842 between the British Empire and the Qing dynasty. The war was as a result of prohibition on export, and it resulted in the displacement of China's control on Hong Kong. The Second Opium War was within the years 1856 and 1860, and this war was as a result of Britain as well as France compelling free trade and elimination of all barriers in China.

Also in 1930, the USA endorsed the Smoot–Hawley Tariff Act, with the major aim of protecting the declining capital market and indigenous industry. This initially was to preserve the domestic farm sector, nonetheless, the coverage extended to other commodities from several industries. The USA was successful in reducing dependence on import, but the reprisal actions from other countries resulted in an enormous decline of US exports by 1933, further accentuating the Great Depression.

Three decades further by the early 1960s, there were the Chicken wars, and it was instigated by the imposition of huge tariff by both France and Germany on the importation of American chickens due to the demand decline of European chickens. The reaction of the USA was the imposition of tariffs that were higher on several other products. Nonetheless, both France and Germany persisted on their stance hence, resulting in loss for all the countries. Also, in 1985, the USA increased tariff on pasta imported from Europe because of the inaction regarding prejudicial action against its Citrus product which remained persistently unattended to. The Pasta War lingered on as Europe struck back with greater tariffs on American lemon and walnuts. However, the both sides endorsed an agreement in 1986, putting an end to the Citrus dispute and in 1987 putting an end to the pasta conflict. Furthermore, there was the Banana War in 1993, due to the restrictions on import by placement of huge tariffs on banana from Latin America to discourage US investors as they were the primary owners of the banana farms. The USA protested severally in the WTO and eventually, Europe conceded to lower the tariff steadily until it endorsed an agreement involving ten Latin America countries in 2012, thereby putting an end to twenty prolonged years of Banana War.

The Genesis of the US-China Trade Conflict

In 2018, the global trade war, which had the USA and China in the main front line, increased alarmingly to the point where it resulted into an ardent shift in the global structure both economically and politicalwise. This emanated from controversies of the bilateral trade agreements of the USA and China, as well as other contingent issues like the Anglo-German contention, which resulted in the collapse of the Concert of Europe in 1914. These and other petitions were highlighted summing up the effect that

China has had on the economy globally since it entered the World Trade Organization (WTO) in 2001.

All through 2018, the USA set forth tariffs; the reaction of other trading partners in reprisal has had effect of about $450 billion of trade globally, estimating to about 0.13 of import of goods for the USA and 0.025 of trade of goods globally. This has resulted in several reactions from trade partners as they were faced with issues of protectionism leading to their retaliation against the US' high tariffs. The consequence of these is a continuous waning of the trade-restraining policies employed by the G20 countries, to a level lower than the trends as far back as 2012 (WTO 2018).

The US-China trade has shown indices of increase from $125 billion to about $700 billion between 2001 and 2017 (US Bureau of Economic Analysis 2018). However, within this period, the economy of China had increased fourfold in foreign exchange magnitude, making it second largest economy globally, from the fourth largest previously in 2001. The support provided by the USA to China was with the aim of global integration with the anticipation that as China derived benefits from the global economic structure, as well as membership of the WTO, its essence would turn out to be an accountable participant, hence working with the USA in sustaining the global structure which has aided its success. This, however, has not been the picture, consequently, the birth of the US' tariff war.

According to Gulker (2019a), these tariffs are paid directly from American business to the Government's coffers. In other words, the Government charges tariffs to the U.S. owned firms that are directly importing these products, via middlemen who pass the tariffs down the supply chain in the form of higher prices, a portion of which is often borne by end consumers. Invariably, producers in exporting countries also suffer from lower demand due to the higher end price including the tariff or must lower their prices to offset lost demand (Gulker, 2019b). Nevertheless, the perception of the USA regarding China has gradually grown into viewing China more as a rival than a partner, thus informing the stance taken by the USA. This hence brought about theatrical changes in policies by the USA regarding the investment and trade fore with respect to China, since the expectations of international trade are increases in economic efficiency, job reallocation to more resourceful sectors (Krauss 1997). Regarding the US-China trade, jobs had been created in certain aspects of the US economy, for instance, in agriculture and services, however, loss of jobs in other industries, of essence in the low salary manufacturing. The US export between 1995 and 2001 were projected to have created jobs in the range of about 6.6 million (Feenstra and Akira 2018). Also, current statistics depict that exports of the USA to China sustains about 1.8 million jobs in the agriculture, capital goods, and service industries (Wang and Wei 2018). However, a greater volume of job losses was experienced within the manufacturing and non-manufacturing sector as well, thereby accounting for trade deficit for the USA (Feenstra and Akira 2018). The bilateral trade deficit has increased to $419 billion in 2018 from 81 billion in 2001 (US Bureau of Economic Analysis 2018). Stated in a different way, since China became part of the WTO in 2001, the US trade deficit with China has risen yearly by $18.3 billion, or 9.9%, on average (Scott and Mokhiber 2018).

The Cost and Benefits of Trade Conflict on Countries and Globally

Much has been said regarding the implications of the trade war between the USA and China, on other countries and regions in the world. However, would it be gains? or would it be losses for these other regions essentially the emerging regions? It could be deduced from the research of Carvalho et al. (2019), that the impact on both USA and China would be negative, with China having the greater shock and the entire world losing in terms of welfare. This being the consequence of a tangible decline in allocative efficiency for the USA as well as terms of trade loss for China, but what would it hold for the developing regions like Africa?

Quite a number of key countries have pursued trade liberalization endeavors, by seeking market entry access via regional trade agreements (RTAs). RTAs have been on the increase and have also been altering in nature over the years. In 1990, there were only fifty trade agreements in force, and this has increased to more than 290 by 2019. From 2017 till date, about ten (10) RTAs have been instituted the likes of those between Canada and the European Union, China and Georgia, and Canada and Ukraine. The Comprehensive and Progressive Agreement for Trans-Pacific Partnership (CPTPP) was endorsed in 2018 by eleven (11) member countries after the withdrawal of the USA from the Trans-Pacific Partnership (TPP) endorsed in 2016. This was subsequently succeeded by the endorsement of the African Continental Free Trade Area agreement (AFCFTA) by 54 African leaders (Devarajan et al. 2018).

How Africa Can Cash in

Trade Liberalization and Regional Trade Agreements of Africa

Africa has about thirty trade agreements both bilateral and multilateral alike, hence making Africa the most economically integrated continent. The appalling discovery, however, is that in spite of this degree of integration, intra-regional trade for Africa is sparse conceding barely 10% of Africa's total trade (Jung 2017). Accessing the number of African trade agreements within the regions, vis-à-vis the level if intra-regional trade, a lot can be said regarding the gains of these trade agreements, in stimulating trade in Africa.

Africa has seventeen trade blocs as well as quite a number of bilateral trade agreements. The major aims of the AfCFTA is to increase intra-African trade via improved coordination and systemization of trade liberalization and enabling administrations and mechanisms across the Regional Economic Communities (RECs) and Africa as a whole, as well as creating a sole universal market for goods and services, which would enhance the free flow of both investors and investments, thereby, initiating and advancing the institution of the Continental Customs Union, in addition to resolving the issues that bother on memberships that are both diverse and overlapping within the regions.

The presence of real and geographic borders within African countries has resulted in loss of cost advantage along with the absence of free movement structures across borders since the time of Independence. This hence has made regional integration a huge consideration for the continent in order to surmount this disservice. This was incessantly advanced to African countries by the European colonists between 1950 and 1960 in order to promote trade within Africa. At present, the African Union (AU) identifies eight main RECs as constituents of the African Economic Community (AEC); they are the Arab Maghreb Union (AMU), the Community of Sahel Saharan States (CEN-SAD), the Common Market for Eastern and Southern Africa (COMESA), the East African Community (EAC), the Economic Community of Central African States (ECCAS), the Economic Community of West African States (ECOWAS), the Intergovernmental Authority on Development (IGAD), and the Southern African Development Community (SADC).

The situation of Africa is a peculiar one, in spite of the laudable intention of the RECs, a vast majority of them have not been able to employ a full implementation of their policies due to issues bothering on political unrest, hostility, and conflicts. This thereby gives a good explanation of why in spite of the structures put in place, intra-regional trade has not advanced amid the countries in Africa. A very good instance is the Northern African case, in 1989, the Arab Maghreb Union (AMU) eliminated tariff and non-tariff barriers among participating countries, and however, issues like political tensions among participating countries, like Algeria, Libya, Morocco, and Tunisia, did not permit the efficiency of intra-regional trade. Also, over the years, it can be seen that in spite of barrier removal, inter-regional trade has remained very low for the subregion, a good instance was in 2015, only 3.4% of the regional trade in the AMU countries where traceable to the member countries, whereas the region's trade with non-African countries accounted for 93.9%.

The AMU region does not stand alone, the same goes for the other regional communities in Africa. The East African Community (EAC) also removed both tariffs and non-tariff barriers for participating countries without encountering a better fate than the AMU because just like the Arab Maghreb Union, the total intra-EAC trade was only 11.5% in 2017 leaving a whopping non-regional trade of 88.5% (EAC Trade & Investment Report 2017). The Common Market for Eastern and Southern Africa (COMESA) is no different especially if the European Union (EU) could singlehandedly account for about 42% of the COMESA's total imports and unitarily close to 30% of the trade export, in 2017, whereas amassing less than 12% from intra-regional trade. For the other regional communities, a similar progression could be observed; in the Economic Community of West African States (ECOWAS) in 2015, only 10% intra-regional trade was captured. The Southern African Development Community (SADC) had only 20.7% of intra-regional trade, whereas an atrocious 7.8 and 2.1% for the COMESA and Economic Community for Central African States (ECCAS), respectively. For ECCAS, in spite of the hideously low intra-regional trade range, over 90% of its total trade in the same 2015 went to non-African regions of the world.

With regard to intra-regional trade, there is still a long stretch for Africa to cover indeed. In 2008, the intra-regional trade was negative for Africa, of which within two years precisely by 2010, there was a sharp rise to almost 30%. Within then till date, there has been consistent rise and fall in the level of trade amid the region. At present, intra-regional trade explains 17% of Africa's export, in comparison to 59 and 69% intra-regional trade proportions for Asia and Europe, respectively. It is expected, however, that the implementation of the AfCFTA could be strong motivation to propel the region in the direction of enhanced degree of intra-regional trade which is much more required.

The Regional Economic Communities and Structure Benefits for Free Trade in Africa

The integration of trade could boost development for Africa, just like it has impelled remarkable successful outcomes for other regions of the world (IMF 2018). Majority if not all of the RECs in Africa have trailed distinctive, broadly awkward procedures, and targets of liberalizing trade among their participating countries, which consistently have not been realized over the years. These procedures have been patterned to fit into theoretical custom unions and the economic community, yet in spite of the laudable strategies much has not been achieved through the RECs, as several treaties advanced for trade integration have not seen their aims of free trade actualized (UNCTAD 2015). A huge free trade area in Africa would augment the potentiality for the region to be economically transformed. This will not only create avenue for intra-regional trade but also, pull foreign investors, enhance the upgrowth of regional value chains, by which other regions globally have utilized as vital components of economic transformation.

The RECs from previous reviews have been seen not efficient sufficiently to achieve set aims of facilitating trade adequately to provide the required trade integration in the region. Several things, however, have been accountable for these setbacks for the region; the advent of tariffs and colonist frameworks that made it easier for the region to engage more in non-African trade than trade within the region, as well as the challenge of overlapping membership of the RECs that have consistently hindered the regularity of trade activities as well as the ability to enforce set policies of trade integration in the region. The aims of the AfCFTA is to utilize the basic structure of the RECs in establishing a single continental market for the trade of goods and services within the region, hence increasing intra-regional trade in Africa by cutting tariff by 90%, as well as consolidating trade policies, thereby taking care of the risk of overlapping in addition to expanding intra-regional trade to more than triple in the next couple of years.

For more than two decades now, intra-regional activities of trade have increased swiftly vis-à-vis the brisk integration of Africa with the global trade system. There has been dynamic trade increase for Africa in recent years, between 1990 and 2017, and trade openness in the region rose to 67% of GDP from around 53% of GDP. This advancement reflects an expansion in the volume of trade in addition to a more promising growth of prices. Over this time span, the scene of trade for Africa trading had transformed alongside its trading allies. Africa over this period formed new alliances with emerging economies like China. As Africa's intra-regional trade increased considerably, the percentage of Africa's total intra-regional imports also increased to 12% by 2017 from about 5% in 1990. With the AfCFTA in force currently, trade in Africa would be enhanced by better coordination and improved degree of integration, hence maximally utilizing the inherent benefit of the RECs as a required structure for better facilitation of trade for the free trade agreements.

Critical Policies and Maximal Resource Allocation

Trade policy quotas are, basically, aimed at the sectors of goods and services where if traded they influence the incentive framework, thereby affecting the relative prices of imported and exported commodities. Through this medium, trade policies employ their effect by changing the structure and volumes of exports and imports (Heleiner 1992, 1995; Oyejide 1999). On the subject of trade policy in the developing economies, the study of trade liberalization is often restricted to import liberalization or the removal or decrease of tariff and non-tariff import barriers. Considering a true scenario, though, liberalization of trade should include both export boost and import liberalization.

The boost of export is essential because even in the advent of an extensive and profound import liberalization plan, the possibility of survival or viability is limited without effective export. The study of Michaely (1991) premised on trade liberalization activities of selected developing economies, found that "the stability of trade liberalization efforts patterns for these developing economies was sturdily associated to a positive attainment in the level of export, however, the failure of trade liberalization is intensely associated with an extremely poor performance of export." The African region needs to learn from this in the fact that as policies are being put in place, the commensurate actions that will facilitate their performance need to be put into place to enhance their effectiveness. More than any region of the world, the time has come for Africa to engage in intense export drive with corresponding policies of trade liberalization in order to attain maximal resource allocation and take absolute advantage of trade facilitation.

Protectionist Policies and Effects on Imports

Trade protectionism is a policy that protects domestic industries from unfair competition from foreign industries. The four primary tools are tariffs, subsidies, quotas, and currency manipulation. Protectionism is a politically motivated defensive measure. In the short run, it works, but it is very destructive in the long term. It makes the country and its industries less competitive in international trade. The most common protectionist strategy is to enact tariffs that tax imports. That immediately raises the price of imported goods. They become less competitive when compared to local goods. Governments also frequently subsidize local industries to help them compete in the global market. Subsidies come in the form of tax credits or direct payments. The most commonly used are farm subsidies. That allows producers to lower the price of local goods and services. This makes the products cheaper even when shipped overseas. Subsidies work even better than tariffs. This method works best for countries that rely mainly on exports. A third method is to impose quotas on imported goods. This method is more effective than the first two. No matter how low a foreign country sets the price through subsidies, it cannot ship more goods.

However, there is little emphasis on the fourth type of trade protectionism because it is subtle. It is a deliberate attempt by a country to lower its currency value. This would make its exports cheaper and more competitive. This method can result in retaliation and start a currency war. One way countries can lower their currency's value through a fixed exchange rate, like China's Yuan. If a country is trying to grow strong in a new industry, tariffs will protect it from foreign competitors. That gives the new industry's companies time to develop their own competitive advantages. Protectionism also temporarily creates jobs for domestic workers. The protection of tariffs, quotas, or subsidies allows domestic companies to hire locally. This benefit ends once other countries retaliate by erecting their own protectionism policy. In the long term, trade protectionism weakens the industry. Without competition, companies within the industry have no need to innovate. Eventually, the domestic product will decline in quality and be more expensive than what foreign competitors produce (Zhao and Parolin 2014).

Trade Expansion Policies

Trade policies are strategies that precisely impart on the volume of goods and services amid countries and regions of the world. They comprise of import tariffs and quotas, voluntary export restrictions, export taxes and subsidies, alongside others. Countries and regions around the world could make use of these policies in order to facilitate and enhance the volumes and velocities of their trade activities over time. There are also domestic policies, on the other hand, that could also affect trade activities in countries and regions alike. The way and manner domestic taxes are imposed or the conduct of subsidies could as well promote international trade, in spite the size or deprived condition of a country or region in the global markets (Suranovic 2015).

Production subsidy policies could be introduced to boost domestic production especially in the wake of the new continental free trade area, hence taking advantage of vast resource endowment instead of exporting our enormous natural deposits as a region to the developed regions as well as importing from the same regions of the world. The domestic production increase with likely large market and resources availability would allow the region to take advantage of economies of scale and possibly produce on a large scale sufficient enough to have substantial share of export of specific commodities. Also, the imposition of policies like consumption taxes could as well be utilized to reduce domestic demand and consumption of a commodity in order to purposely increase export capacity of a commodity, hence expansion of trade (Suranovic 2015).

Unit subsidy could also be borne by governing authorities for particular commodities that are produced by indigenous industries in order to encourage production capacity, efficiency and enabling the industries to produce at a competitive price. This prospect, as a result of comparative advantage, will further foster both domestic supply and increase export across the global market. The African region because of the duplication conflicts regarding the RECs has not been able to do much about harmonizing trade policies, and however, the advantage of single continental market should be such as would allow the unison of trade policies, as well as being assisted by domestic policies, which would also encourage the expansion of trade activities and intra-regional trade facilitation in the region.

Response to Market Signals and Exports

Economic Flexibility and Improved Market Access

The development efforts of the domestic industrial sectors impose great effects on the widening of market channels, by transforming the markets and enhancing economic strength, self-development abilities, and industrial reshaping. This is becoming increasingly important in several regions of the world, Africa alike. The flexibility of economies strengthens and makes it possible for operating improved access to trade activities. Especially, in the current setting of the decelerated growth of the world economy, there is the dire need for regional development, economic transformation, and industrial structure adjustment, for any region of the world desiring improved access to the global market.

Africa could go a long way by taking advantage of the great potential for high quality, green and ecological agricultural product market, and more attentions should as well be paid to support the breeding, industry base construction, post-harvest processing, market circulation, and brand cultivation of characteristic agricultural products. The flexibility quotient is quite essential and also goes a long way to determine the degree of ingenuity which is actually what is required currently in the world today to fit into gaps such as have been created even in the face of the current trade war. As much as the region desires to take advantage of the gap created by the trade war, it requires to put policies in place that would support enhanced domestic investment in the agriculture and other primary sectors. In addition to these, there is a need to source foreign capital, skill and technology transfer to better enhance efficient performance of production, trading activities and consequently domestic investment growth (Fang and Liu 2014).

Sequel to the advancement of globalization, urbanization, and industrialization, which is much required for improved access to the global market, as well as the ability to fully engage the abundance of natural resources, there is need for the African region to fully determine the areas of resource strength and advantage in order to determine the focus of indigenous industrial engagements. There is an urgent need to restructure the domestic market framework with the aim of flexibility in fitting into available resource gaps created by the trade war, which would give Africa the desired share of the global market in sectors where it has a comparative advantage (Li et al. 2015).

Redirection of Trade Opportunities

There are prospects of benefits for developing economies; the possibility of a decline in their trade balances as a result of advancement in several sectors and improved opportunities of trade is due to ongoing dispute between the huge trade partners. Also, the redirection of trade is furthermore a prospect for developing regions to tap into, just the same way it was for Asia; this gives them the opportunity to compete with regions that are affected by direct tariff (Abiad et al. 2018). Hence, making their prices cheaper, access to larger markets and opportunity to enjoy economies of scale production; which for Africa, could be timely with the take-off of the AFCFTA with the major aim of creating a single continental market for goods and services; which is further fortified with the strong intra-African trade expansion activities.

Institutions have an impact on international trade because they influence the costs for administration and contracting and the risk of opportunistic behavior. Efficient institutions facilitate trade by offering stable rules that reduce uncertainty, secure property rights, enhance law enforcement, and facilitate interpersonal exchanges that allow for A more complex and efficient ways of organizing production and trade (North 1991; Williamson 2000; Massini et al. 2010). Institutions can also affect the costs of monitoring and control. Since contract costs can determine whether a cross-border relationship will be established, effective institutions are central to facilitating trade.

Apart from reducing trade volumes, weak institutions may also affect the duration and the dynamics of trade (Aeberhaedt et al. 2011; Araujo et al. 2012; Söderlund and Tingvall 2014). As shown by Araujo et al. (2012), trade with countries with weak institutions is characterized by short-lived trade flows and small initial volumes. Subsequently, trade flows may increase as exporters become more familiar with their contractual partner and learn about the institutional environment in the target economy. These contributions constitute an important link between international trade and international business; in international business, it has long been hypothesized that internationalization is a gradual process, where firms enter distant markets cautiously and raise their level of commitment only after learning about their partners and the local market environment (Johanson and Wiedersheim-Paul 1975; Johanson and Vahlne 1977).

Investment in Primary Sectors of the Economy

There is the dire need for Africa to invest in the primary sectors of their economies, exporting our raw materials to developed countries and importing them back as finished goods in nothing but futility. There is an urgent requirement for the region to earnestly commit resources to the agricultural, mining, and the oil and gas sectors. Conceivably, the major ultimate argument regarding Africa's development past efforts could not be written overlooking the poor investment in her primary economic sectors.

Africa is endowed with over 25% of the global arable land, but it produces only one-tenth of the global agricultural output; also, eleven of its countries is positioned among the highest ten suppliers of minimum a key mineral resource. Africa by capacity produced about 13% of total worldwide oil in 2015, and from the 9%, it produced in 1998. Likewise, agriculture is the hugest economic sector for Africa, signifying about 15% of its entire gross domestic product. In spite of all these, the agro-ecological capability of Africa is far greater than the present productivity level it has, as well as its demand for food. There is the desperate necessity for Africa to invest in new industry templates, with access to finance, superior quality seedlings and other inputs like manure, transportation, preservation, storage and irrigation, which are also major requirements for the sector to begin to thrive on maximum level and develop the African green transformation (McKinsey 2010).

The African mining industry is a representation of an irony: though the region has immense endowment of natural deposits, mining is yet to be a steady mechanism for development economically. The need for development funding and investment is required in the African mining sector to enable it maximize its innate capability so as to take advantage of the increasing global demand for mineral resources. In the face of the continental market access, the possibility of industrialization would enable Africa to move from its present level of developing economy like many emerging economies have, thereby, gradually moving on. Investments in the sector requires infrastructural transformation, majorly in transportation of raw or partly processed minerals to their markets within the region, particularly since this sector have not harnessed sufficient foreign investment in comparison with the level of endowment it possesses.

The African oil and gas sector has been an essential feature for the global hydrocarbon demand and supply equilibrium. There are 19 African economies that are main suppliers in the sector, and this alone is enough justification that the region has sufficient resources to add value to these raw materials rather than export them and further import processed products. The region is required to look inward for investment avenues in extractive industries as well, instead of engaging only foreign investors, that rip off the benefits without much gains for the region in terms of development. As much as foreign investment is vital to close the seeming gaps of investment, skills and technology, there is need of guidance particularly in the African extractive industry to ensure that domestic firms are able to thrive in the face of foreign competition (McKinsey 2010).

Theoretical Underpinning of Trade Facilitation

The theories of international trade have evolved consistently over the years right from the Classical Country-Based Theories to the Modern Firm-Based Theories. The Porter's National Competitive Advantage Theory states that the level of competitiveness of a country for a sector of the economy is contingent on the innovative capability of the sector as well as the advancement capacity. It further dwelt on the justifications regarding the reasons why some countries are more competitive in particular sector of the economy. Certain explanatory factors were highlighted in the theory: the resource and capability of the domestic market; alongside the domestic market demand environment, as well as the domestic suppliers and interrelated sectors, together with the characteristics of domestic investment (Carpenter and Dunung 2012).

Africa is endowed with massive natural resources and arable land, and these are underlying provisions for the comparative advantage viewpoint. The linkage between the current disadvantaged position Africa is and the competitive position it desires is the innovative capability it must acquire and efficiently utilize. The huge space available to Africa in the new continental free trade area would only facilitate this advantage.

Trade Facilitation and Economic Progress in Africa

Trade Facilitation, Market Efficiency, and Growth

Increased trade activities are catalyst for enhanced economic activities, which in turn could create basic links that would drive intra-regional trade in the region. Intra-regional trade in Africa is sine-qua-non to efficiency of its markets and very essential for growth and development in the region.

Trade Diversification and Economic Progress

There are potential opportunities for developing economies of Africa to explore in order to advance the capacity of trade. A very good example is the China- Africa trade relationship, which presumably would assist in the stimulation of the African economies, as well as result in trade diversification and funding opportunities. This window if explored by Africa, could give access to large market, innovative prospects, which would enable the continent express the innate resources available in the domestic sector to maximize the opportunities of trade for development of the region (Adekunle and Korzun 2017).

However, are there inherent risks for developing countries of Africa? What threats could arise for infant domestic industries? Would they be able to compete with goods that are imported from China that have better competitive advantage? (Adekunle and Korzun 2017). The onus still rests on Africa, and its capability to look inwards at sector where it is endowed with huge resources and where it requires only innovation, critical policies and consistency to make a difference, though maybe slow but assuredly.

The Benefits of Economic Integration

Africa has great potential in terms of huge availability of natural resources and enormous arable land, rainfall and good weather for enhanced agricultural output. This implies for Africa, the competitive advantage, which must be maximized by consistent innovation in order to enhance capacity in the face of competition and inherent rivalry globally. The birth of the new free trade area the (AFCFTA), is an avenue for a large domestic market as well as an enormous demand environment, which also doubles as a supply source for export as the market has been described as the largest in the recent history of economic integration.

Addressing Limiting Factors that Affect Trade

Infrastructure, Poor Institutional Framework and Corruption

Advanced infrastructural facilities are a catalyst for trade, investment, and enhanced economic activities, which is extremely required in developing regions of the world, Africa alike. The dearth of these amenities have consistently been a limiting factor in the African region, with regard to trade and other economic activities, hence, reason for inefficiency in almost, if not all the sector performances in the region.

In spite of huge infrastructural spending in the region, the level that the infrastructures are, are yet deplorable and as good as just the beginning still.

In order for the aims of the continental free trade area to be accomplished, investment in infrastructure is a very germane issue of consideration. However, majority of African economies do not have the resources on their own to maintain the projects, hence there is need for foreign investment and aid to compliment governments efforts.

The needs for infrastructural development vary from country to country and from sector to sector of the region. The requirements range from electricity production, dissemination and transmission, transportation, water and waste, communications and technology. The presence of these amenities would attract foreign investment, encourage rapid development of industries in locations of high natural resources, enhance domestic investment, and thereby attaining the set goal of the free trade policy.

One of the major challenge asides from the deplored situation of the African region amenities is the concern of poor institutional framework that accounts for gaps in the performance of set policies for each country and for the region as a whole. There is a need for the region to work assiduously to enhance the framework of institutions as they are the structures that are required to be put in place for the vehicle of trade to work effectively. In addition, the control of corruption cannot be overemphasized as Africa tops the chart touching issues of corruption control. The essence of improved coordination and systemization of trade in the region can only be attained with these germane subjects' matters being thoroughly addressed.

The Dutch Disease Syndrome

Trade activities and exports in African countries that are rich in resources are basically concerted on natural deposit targeted commodities, yet the countries have nothing substantial to show with regard value addition performances asides the natural resource industry. These countries, in spite of their rich resource, lag behind the countries that are not rich in resource in several growth factors (Mulwa and Mariara 2016).

Quite a number of modern development theories come with the assumptions that the wealth of natural resources influences economic growth capabilities for developing countries (Broad 1995). This is further buttressed by standard economic theories; that rise in the asset stock of a country proffers better prospects for economic development (Bulte et al. 2003; Okidi 2007). The current condition of resource-rich countries in Africa has, however, violated earlier development theories which assume that deposit of natural resources could possibly sustain economic growth.

Further, the expectations of many early development economists (Nurkse 1953; Rostow 1960) that resource endowments could potentially support economic expansion by drawing capital from foreign investors into the primary industries in order to reduce poverty and hence, attain development, has been confirmed incorrect. The wake of this realization for Africa is the essence of not depending solely on these natural resource sectors, but rather invest more into other sector that will facilitate trade like agriculture, and possible put them in a better position economically to attain the vibrant economies that they have potentials to be.

Figure 1 highlights the trade benefits and opportunities available for Africa as a continental marketplace: a boost in economic progress, reduction of trade balances, and better involvement of local industry by improved domestic investment

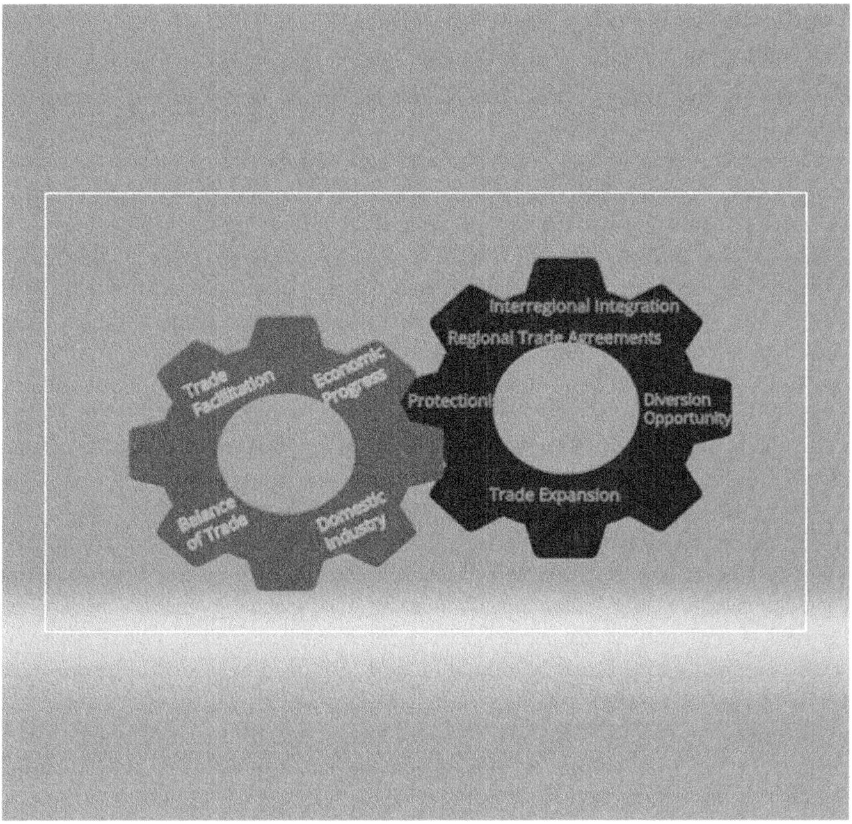

Fig. 1 Business opportunities and the continental market. *Source* Author

and enhanced facilitation of trade. This could be driven by engaging proactively in measures such as: taking available opportunities of regional integration as well as carefully maximizing the new free trade area (AFCFTA); fostering trade agreements with regions that are not related directly with the USA; making projections regarding trade diversions with the aim of filling up gaps created by tariff wars, by lowering prices; and cautious selection of protectionism stance in trade agreements in order to shield domestic industries and efforts to hugely expand trade with the available synergy of the continental free trade area (AFCFTA). These would then enable the region to establish a single central market for goods and services, which permits the free movement of trade, expansion of intra-African trade via the enhanced synchronization of trade across Africa. These activities would as well improve competitiveness of domestic industries by exploring all prospects highlighted for the advantage of economies of scale, better rationalization of resources, and economic progress.

Conclusion and Policy Prescriptions

The ongoing trade war between the USA and China has continued to intensify between the two largest economies in the world. On August 1, 2019, the USA announced new tariffs of 10% on $300 billion of imports from China to take effect on September 1, which is on top the previous $250 billion imports tariffs imposed on almost all Chinese imports. China's response was to offset the tariffs by reducing the dollar cost of Chinese exports by the Yuan slide below the previous boundary of 7 per dollar, thereby reducing the dollar cost of Chinese exports by encouraging local production and raising the Yuan prices of imports, while discouraging the purchase of foreign goods. Further, and in August, China announced imposing 5 and 10% tariffs on US imports in two rounds, on September 1 and December 15, amounting to $75 billion worth of goods. Consequently, the USA recommended to its China-based companies to immediately start looking for alternatives to doing business in China. This represents a fertile space for Africa to attract more US businesses, while unlocking the US-Africa trade relations opportunities.

Though it is said that in trade wars there are no winners; the US-China trade war alike, other regions of the world, including Africa will benefit or lose. Africa has a latent advantage via the new continental free trade agreement which is the hugest in size globally. With the AfCFTA in force, African commerce and economy could be enhanced by better coordination and improved degree of integration, as well as maximally utilizing the inherent benefit of the RECs structures for better facilitation of trade in the region. For Africa to enjoy the gains of ongoing US-China trade war, it must create an enduring business environment for domestic firms, increase investment opportunities in the primary sector for both public and private indigenous firms, as a medium for industrial development.

As the region engages critical policies which major aims are for increasing global market share as well as reducing trade deficits, the expectations of expansions of trade is gradually attained. Thus, the region can gainfully engage by bending back innovatively to fill the created gaps due to the trade war, in order to gain improved access to the markets, through the gains of trade facilitation, thereby attaining efficient market utilization and growth. What the RECs have not succeeded in doing for so many years, the AfCFTA would make it happen by creating a boost in economic progress, improved domestic investment and repositioning Africa in the global market.

References

Abiad A, Baris K, Bernabe JA, Bertulfo DJ, Camingue-Romance S, Feliciano PN, Mariasingham MJ, Mercer-Blackman V (2018) The impact of trade conflict on developing Asia. Asian Development Bank Working Paper Series No. 566

Adekunle B, Korzun M (2017) Trading with China: how can Africa benefit? In: Odularu G, Adekunle B (eds) Negotiating south-south regional trade agreements, advances in African economic, social and political development. Springer International Publishing

Aeberhaedt R, Buono I, Fadinger H (2011) Learning incomplete contracts and export dynamics: theory and evidence from French firms. Vienna Economics Papers 1006, University of Vienna, Department of Economics
Araujo L, Mion G, Orneals E (2012) Institutions and export dynamics. CEPR Discussion Paper 8809. Centre for Economic Policy Research, London
Broad R (1995) The political economy of natural resources: cases of the Indonesian and Philippine forest sector. J Dev Areas 29(3):317–339
Bulte EH, Damania R, Deacon RT (2003) Resource abundance, poverty and development. UCSB Working Paper. Department of Economics, University of California, Santa Barbara, CA
Carpenter MA, Dunung SP (2012) Challenges and opportunities in international business, vol 1. Retrieved from http://2012books.lardbucket.org/pdfs/challenges-and-opportunities-international-business.pdf
Carvalho M, Azevedo A, Massuquetti A (2019) Emerging countries and the effect of trade war between US and China. Economies 7(45):1–21
Devarajan S, Go DS, Lakatos C, Robinson S, Thierfelder K (2018) Traders' Dilemma: developing countries' response to trade dispute. World Bank Policy Research Working Paper. WPS8640
Fang YG, Liu JS (2014) The modification of North China quadrangles in response to rural social and economic changes in agricultural villages: 1970–2010s. Land Use Policy 39:266–280
Feenstra RC, Akira S (2018) The 'China shock,' exports and U.S. employment: a global input-output analysis. Special Issue Paper Rev Int Econ 6(5):1053–1083
Gulker M (2019a) Trump's tariffs did nothing to boost the steel industry. Retrieved 15 December, 2019 from https://www.aier.org/article/trumps-tariffs-did-nothing-to-boost-the-steel-industry/
Gulker M (2019b) This is how a nationalist raises your taxes. Retrieved 15 December, 2019 from https://www.aier.org/article/this-is-how-a-nationalist-raises-your-taxes/
Heleiner GK (1992) Introduction. In: Helleiner GK (ed) Trade policy industrialization and development: new perspectives. Clarendon Press, Oxford
Helleiner GK (1995) Trade, trade policy and industrialization reconsidered, World Development Studies No. 6, WIDER (UNU), Helsinki
International Monetary Fund (IMF) (2018) Growth challenges for the next decade and beyond. Regional Economic Outlook: Asia Pacific, Washington, DC, October
Johanson J, Vahlne JE (1977) The internationalisation process of the firm—a model of knowledge development and increasing market commitment. J Int Bus Stud 8(1):23–32
Johanson J, Wiedersheim-Paul F (1975) The internationalization of the firm: Four Swedishcases. J Manage Stud 12(3):305–322
Jung JW (2017) The impact of trade liberalization in Africa. Korean Institute for International Economic Policy (KIEP) Working Paper 17-05
Krauss M (1997) How nations grow rich: The case for free trade. Oxford University Press, New York
Li YR, Long HL, Liu YS (2015) Spatio-temporal pattern of China's rural development: a rurality index perspective. J Rural Stud 38:12–26
Massini S, Pern-Ajchariyawong N, Lewin AY (2010) Role of corporate-wide off shoring strategy on off shoring drivers, risks and performance. Ind Innov 17(4):337–371
McKinsey Quarterly (2010) Africa's path to growth: sector by sector. https://www.mckinsey.com/featured-insights/middle-east-and-africa/africas-path-to-growth-sector-by-sector
Michaely M (1991) The lessons of experience: an overview. In: Sheperd G, Langoni CG (eds) Trade reform: lessons from eight countries. ICEG, San Francisco
Mulwa R, Mariara J (2016) Natural resource curse in Africa: Dutch disease and institutional explanations. AGRODEP Working Paper 0029
North DC (1991) Institutions. J Econ Perspect 5(1):97–112
Nurkse R (1953) Problems of capital formation in underdeveloped countries. Cambridge University Press, New York

Okidi CO (2007) Application of environmental paradigm to tame conflict and poverty in natural resource-rich African countries. In: Daibert A (ed) Direito Ambiental Comparado. Belo Horizonte, Editora Forum 2008, Rio de Janeiro, Brazil

Oyejide TA (1999) Options for future trade liberalization in Sub-Saharan Africa. In: Oyejide ABN, Greenaway D (eds) Regional integration and trade liberalization in Sub-Saharan Africa, vol 4: synthesis and review. Macmillan, London

Rostow WW (1960) The stages of economic growth: a non-communist manifesto. Cambridge University Press, Cambridge

Scott RE, Mokhiber Z (2018) The China toll deepens: growth in the bilateral trade deficit between 2001 and 2017 cost 3.4 million U.S. jobs, with losses in every state and congressional district. Economic Policy Institute, Washington, DC. https://epi.org/156645

Söderlund B, Tingvall P (2014) Dynamic effects of institutions on firm-level exports. Rev World Econ 150:277–308. https://doi.org/10.1007/s10290-013-0181-2

Suranovic S (2015) International trade: theory and policy. FlatWorld, Boston, MA

UNCTAD (2015) Building the African free trade area: some suggestions on the way forward. United Nations, New York and Geneva UNCTAD/DITC/2015/1

U.S. Bureau of Economic Analysis (2018) International trade in goods and services. www.bea.gov/data/intl-trade-investment/international-trade-goodsand-services

Wang Z, Wei S-J (2018). Re-examining the effects of trading with China on local labor markets: a supply chain perspective. NBER Working Paper: 19

Williamson OE (2000) The new institutional economics: taking stock, looking ahead. J Econ Lit 38(3):595–613

World Trade Report (WTO) (2018) The future of world trade: how digital technologies are transforming global commerce. WTO, Geneva

Zhao D, Parolin B (2014) Merged or unmerged school? School preferences in the context of school mapping restructure in rural China. Asia-Pacific Educ Res 23(3):547–563

Strengthening the Future of US—Africa Trade and Business Relations

Gbadebo Odularu

Introduction

As science, technology and innovation (STI) become ever more complex and social media tools continue to play greater roles in transforming the global commercial landscape, the impact digital services on trade has been accelerated by many ICT innovations. Digitization implies that data will need to be exchanged between economic actors along the value chain. Digital and physical connectivity are interrelated in the sense that these latest technologies such as Blockchain, Artificial Intelligence (AI), internet of things (IoT) and machine learning, will enhance the facilitation of trade among nations. Globally, the adoption of digital technologies in global supply chains is resulting in a drastic shift towards intangibles and asset-like forms of international production. The global trade and investment policy climate have become generally less favourable due to many gaps, overlaps and inconsistencies in the more than 3000 investment agreements. In fact, most trade and investment policies are becoming more regulated and restricted at the expense of greater trade openness (UNCTAD 2019). By implications, for African countries which rely on investment in physical productive assets and on participation in global value chain, the U.S.-Africa trade relations will benefit maximally from the opportunities arising from digitization (UNCTAD 2019).

G. Odularu (✉)
Department of Economics and Finance, Bay Atlantic University, Washington, DC, USA
e-mail: odularu@comcast.net; godularu@live.com; godularu@bau.edu

Socio-Economic Research Applications and Projects (SERAP LLC), Washington, DC, USA

Center for Research on Political Economy (CREPOL), Dakar-Yoff, Senegal

Trade, Economics and Agribusiness Division, SSCG Consulting, Birmingham, UK

American Heritage University of Southern California (AHUSC), Ontario, CA, USA

G. O. A. Odularu et al. (eds.), *Fostering Trade in Africa*,
Advances in African Economic, Social and Political Development,
https://doi.org/10.1007/978-3-030-36632-2_8

The increasing number of African economic transformation agenda, by many accounts, is recording some progresses in building local business capacities. However, consolidating that success will require developing a critical mass of digital trade entrepreneurs and innovators who leverage digital technologies for business growth and expansion, thereby delivering well-paid jobs, wealth creation, productivity growth and improved social well-being. A pro-business policy approach is likely to yield superior results if a well-planned economy is structurally rooted in digital trade reforms and high-tech start-ups for fostering a dynamic local entrepreneurial sector. Digital trade will enhance a wide range of innovative activities across the spectrum of sustainable and inclusive development programs in Africa. Invariably, this holds immense benefits to American and African private sectors with focus on fostering trade by embarking on digital trade facilitation governance and reforms that would make it easier, simpler, faster and cheaper for businesses to comply with procedures which in turn reduces transactions costs.

Over the past couple of years (January 2018), most countries have increasingly re-prioritized their trade-related policies. One of the major challenges they face is how to take the emerging knowledge and experience garnered from digital trade to optimize market access opportunities today while ensuring we can adapt easily to what future challenges may confront our economies. This requires a whole new level of collaboration and creativity towards transforming the global trade architecture, therefore accelerating the adoption of new technologies as well as informing the vision of commerce in the future.

It is becoming more evident that better market access conditions alone do not translate directly into increased trade opportunities for African countries. A greater obstacle than tariffs is the high cost of moving goods across Africa and its borders. In addition to supply-side capacity constraints, behind the border barriers and non-tariff measures which are increasingly hampering African trade, its share in world merchandise trade remains a measly 2.7% in 2017. This chapter provides a brief understanding of US-African businesses with a special interest in sustainably enhancing US-Africa's business opportunities in this digital age. It identifies the innovative US-Africa trade facilitation policies, programmes, tools and initiatives towards fostering joint trade and business opportunities in the face of increasing non-tariff barriers, asymmetries and opacity that highly characterizes African business landscape. The author recommends appropriate and workable policy solutions towards fostering attractive and win-win U.S.-Africa trade relations.

Shifting U.S. Policy Towards China and the Political Economy of China-Africa Trade Relations

As the global trading system seemingly enters an uncertain era, one of its unending challenges which poses dire consequences of significant shocks to the world's trade systems are the origin of maldistribution of gains due to the U.S.-China trade war. The current United States Government under the leadership of President Donald Trump and its followers blame China for the ongoing American economic woes. Selected American politicians are allegedly referring to the Chinese as intellectual property spies such that the U.S.-China relations has assumed a national insecurity dimension. Thus, the U.S. administration argues that tariffs are necessary to level the playing field as well as protect American industry against unfair Chinese practices which have put American companies at a disadvantage. The Coalition for a Prosperous America (CPA) also opines that the tariffs are supporting targeted economic sectors, and well as addressing national security issues, and increasing the U.S.' independence from Chinese imports. It is however, pertinent to note that these U.S. macroeconomic challenges require deep, comprehensive, integrated and institutional paradigm shifts and policy reforms in health, trade, workforce, etc. More so that the USA has developed and also benefited considerably from the global trade architecture. However, these gains from trade appear to be poorly served by domestic policies and socio-economic institutions.

In a typically free, open, liberal and competitive economy, trade is a potent technological tool which allows households, firms and nations to achieve more with less. In other words, inappropriate protectionist policies may impede socio-economic growth, which is also capable of eroding the global division of labour that has so greatly enriched the world economy. More importantly, the interconnectedness of commerce in this digital age portends both extraordinary opportunities and challenges for both the developing and developed worlds.

Of significant implications is the rising alarm about the impact of the U.S.-China trade war on the global economy, as well as palpable signs of disappearing farms and weakening international demand for US manufacturing produce partly due to retaliatory tariffs. However, the US government is maintaining its stand on the use of tariff tool in order to enhance the productive capacities of American workers, farmers and manufacturers.

Tellingly, 'American First' policies focus on strategic tariffs and steep penalties for corporations that relocate jobs and factories overseas: Economic patriotism, free market principles in favour of protectionist trade policies to 'defend American jobs' as well as curbing wealth inequality. In fact, increased tariffs will raise taxes on Americans, reduce the number and variety of low-cost and innovative goods, like the iPhone, cheap avocados, lower-cost appliances like TV and washing machines, inexpensive, high-quality cars, etc., and reduce global trade.

Over the past two years, the global commerce landscape experienced trade wars between these two biggest countries in the world, resulting in the United States' $360 billion worth tariffs on Chinese goods, and huge levies on foreign steel and aluminum. Thus, both U.S. and China imposed tariffs on each other in 2018 covering more than half of their bilateral trade (approximately 70% of U.S. exports to China and almost half of U.S. imports from China) (World Bank 2019). According to Gulker (2019a) and Yandle (2020), the Trump administration placed 25% duties on imported steel in March 2018, in order to salvage the steel industry which was suffering from dumping by China during the pre-Trump era. It is relevant to note that the United States also imposed tariffs on other countries and on laundry list of goods such as solar panels, washing machines, wine, whiskey, cheese, English wool, steel and aluminum (Gulker 2019b). From the U.S.' perspectives, the tariff wars are aimed to deliver great free-trade deals, coerce other countries to change their protectionist policies and ultimately reduce U.S. trade deficits. Invariably, the trade wars seem to have increased global trade barriers at great cost to consumers in specific countries which implemented tariff practices, thereby reducing capital expenditures in the wake of the uncertainty. Since the current U.S. government began imposing multilateral tariffs, quite a number of nations have responded with retaliatory tariffs on US products. According to Gulker (2019c), higher tariffs (and the declining supply of foreign goods that as a result of such tariffs) compel Americans to allocate higher-cost resources to produce the goods previously purchased from foreigners, thereby increasing the prices of both tradable goods, and 'domestic' goods, based on the fact that many of the intermediate commodities that serve as inputs in our domestic production are produced abroad. For the American 'patriot' farmers, the trade wars have been quite devastating because selected U.S. farmers lost access to foreign markets due to retaliatory measures. In addition to the impact on disrupted supply chains, higher costs for businesses and consumers, new financial pressures which may result in job losses, vast costs in farmer-bailout funds, loss of U.S. negotiating credibility, a coalescing of new trading zones that are challenging U.S. dollar supremacy, and pressure on the Fed to ease money as a way of mitigating slower growth (Tucker 2019). Tariffs do not only harm American households and firms, they also fail to provide succor to ailing industries as promised by their proponents (Amiti et al. 2019). According to Gulker and Earle (2019), three striking findings on the recent U.S. tariff wars include inter alia: (i) 2018 tariffs directly snatched American households and firms of their savings from the 2017 cuts in individual and corporate tax rates; (ii) U.S. consumers incurred the greatest loss because U.S. importers passed a significant proportion of the tax burden to the households; and (iii) data from the steel and aluminum industries which were being protected with tariffs seemed to have realized negligible or no gain from the trade policy reform.

Science, Technology and Innovation (STI) competition and leadership remain one of the underlying reasons for the ongoing U.S.-China trade wars. For instance, the U.S.' insistence on Chinese 'forced technology transfer' intellectual property violation. Bearing in mind that technology transfer measures are core component of most foreign direct investment (FDI) policies towards fostering industrial development across all the 'catch-up' countries, including Japan, South Korea as well as China. For instance, with the U.S. bumping levies from 10% to 25% on $200 billion of Chinese goods in May 2019, Walmart increased its prices in response to the higher US tariffs.

The USA and China—the world's two largest economies and traders—have embarked on a spiralling tit-for-tat trade war that could imply huge and adverse spillovers to other countries, including Africa, and which could also pressure other countries to 'protect' their markets and also empower protectionists globally. For instance, the U.S. tariffs on steel and aluminum imports to protect American steel-makers and, putatively, to reduce trade deficits, as well as other protectionist measures aimed at China, may not have large, immediate economic effects but they also pose a bigger and long-term threat to the entire global rules-based system.

As the U.S. economy evolves, the Fed plans to respond to the higher tariffs either through a nominal GDP target, or alternatively through a contractionary monetary policy, reducing nominal spending and exacerbating the fall in real GDP. As against the case of the U.S. withdrawal from the Trans-Pacific Partnership (TPP) agreement, the U.S.-Africa economic relations will blossoms, thereby potentially enhancing the credibility of both American and African entrepreneurs. These business relations are being pursued in the renewed interest in 'America First' trade policy, which most African businesses will need to gain its understanding in order to paddle their canoe viably within the US-Africa trade corridors. Based on the current state of both American and African economies, their perception of increased economic interests and trade relations is encouraging in the sense that it provides more room for exploring triangular business opportunities and global value chain between USA, Africa and other countries in the North or South such as Brazil, South Korea, Russia, etc.

The ongoing US-China trade negotiations is at its crucial phase, which are intended to make China comply with the U.S. trade agreements but China's insistence that it is impossible to change its basic economic system leads to more divisions between these two biggest countries in the world. In other words, the central focus of U.S.-Sino trade talks is no longer the bilateral trade imbalance, but rather about protecting China's political security.[1]The idea of building a community with a commonly shared destiny and future for humanity is the centrepiece strategy of the Chinese 'New Era', that reflects the ultimate goal of the Belt and Road Initiative, and which is well-articulated in the Chinese Communist Party's constitution and the preamble of China's national constitution. Based on its Belt and Road Initiative, China has been making inroads into Europe, especially Greece, Italy and Portugal, gaining access via the continent's soft underbelly, the economically troubled southern states. Consequently, the European Union recently shifted its China policy, describing the country as a 'systemic rival'. It is relevant to note that China's tight control of information is well represented by its outright blockage of overseas social media platforms like Google, Facebook and Line. This ban on foreign social media is due to the fear that free flow of information could threaten the Communist Party's governance system, while WeChat and other Chinese social networks are freely used in Western nations, making the West believe that China uses its social networks to gather information from around the world into mainland China.

The U.S.' prevention of the world's information, including information about the USA, itself from flowing into China is the battle for supremacy over data, technologies, information and trade remains the foremost underlying factor behind the move to exclude Chinese tech giant—Huawei Technologies from providing infrastructure for next-generation 5G communication technology.

[1]While Washington insists that Beijing abolish subsidies for state-owned Chinese companies, strengthening state-owned enterprises is a pillar of Xi's new era, and spearheading calls for stronger, better and larger state-owned companies.

Having noted that at the centre of the US-China trade and economic tug of war is the fight over technology supremacy,[2] Washington has demanded that China withdraw from its big data mobilization as well as its 'Digital China' initiatives, which are important pillars of the 'Made in China 2025', a policy to develop Chinese high-tech industries.

Arguably, one of the most critical features of Africa's 'looking eastward' policies is the nature of the relations between the two partners. Deploying new tools and perspectives to measure and quantify the relations by collecting systematic evidence of the composition of China-Africa relations over a 50-year period for a large sample of sub-Saharan countries, this research will shed light on how governments' investment deals with China may affect economic outcomes, and how this will contribute to effective investment relations-policymaking and improve China-Africa international relations. Most Sub-Saharan African economies depend largely on China for the funding of its socio-economic infrastructure (health, sanitation, schools, police, housing, electricity or energy, highways, railways, etc.). African Governments increasingly depend on China for foreign direct investments and other forms of loan products. It is important to note the dominant role of the USA in leading and financing coordinated long-term health recovery and preparedness efforts in Africa (Ravi et al. 2019).

On the other hand, China is one of the world's fastest growing economies and hubs for innovation and global trade. Its implementation of e-commerce and associated technologies for facilitating global trade is among the fastest in the world. The understanding of illicit trade experience in trade relations is, however, empirically under researched and raises many challenges, especially, in U.S.-Africa-China trade relations whose commercial value has blossomed considerably over the last decade.

The China Government has continued to back Regional Comprehensive Economic Partnership (RCEP), the Japan-E.U. Free Trade Agreement (FTA), and TPP11(which is an effort by the remaining TPP signatories to sustain the agreement in some form. Meanwhile, China has stepped up its game in the field of development finance with the successful rollout of the Asian Infrastructure Investment Bank (AIIB) and the launch of its One Belt, One Road (OBOR) initiative. In the arena of economic diplomacy, Asians appear to be moving on without the U.S.

The current U.S. tariffs on China is averagely 21.0% (Bown 2019). Optimistically, both the USA and China agreed to sign an initial trade deal at the White House on January 15, 2020, while the talks for a second-phase deal would begin 'at a later date.' The U.S. will lower its tariffs to 7.5% from 15% on over $100 billion of Chinese exports when the agreement is implemented. This forthcoming trade agreement may provide some relief to manufacturers and other businesses that were affected by the prolonged trade war. Resume talks in October 2019, after which if no breakthrough

---

[2]The USA began sanctioning selected hi-tech Chinese companies with the enactment of the fiscal 2019 National Defense Authorization Act. In other words, beginning in August 2020, companies which use products made by five Chinese tech companies, including Hikvision and Hytera, in their offices will be banned from doing business with US Government organizations. China's grip on big data is to maintain a surveillance net it believes will prevent a colour revolution.

takes place, further escalation of spat and deepening of trade conflict is already scheduled.

Innovative Tools for Fostering Business Connections between USA and Africa

In the last few years, the U.S.-Africa trade and investment relations have received considerable attention because it offers an opportunity to optimize and foster win-win outcomes for both parties through new business innovation models based on continuous growth and limitless resources. For instance, Africa is currently experiencing an increasing demand for affordable, reliable high-speed connections, thereby enhancing business growth and spurring innovation and productivity. This will expand huge opportunities for US companies, and also developing high-quality information and communications technology infrastructure across Sub-Saharan Africa. Some of the novel initiatives which are aimed at fostering U.S.-Africa trade expansion are inter alia:

Africa's Growth and Opportunity Act (AGOA) is the U.S. Act which allows duty-free entry for a wide range of imports from qualifying African countries. AGOA is a globally matchless trade agreement initiative that has brought about reduction of duties and tariffs on approximately 6400 products originating from Africa into USA to zero. Prior to AGOA implementation, Africa's relationship with the USA had been characterized by donor–recipient relations, poverty alleviation through aids, emergency relief and cold war calculations. Thus, AGOA and related programmes have significantly and increasingly enhanced the rules of engagement between the U.S. and African Governments. This is evident in the evolution of trade relations between African countries and the USA, which culminated into investment by the USA as a driving force for economic transformation (Odularu 2008). The crux of AGOA towards its alignment with the Africa's Agenda 2063 is to stimulate economic ascent and democratic governance; accelerate manufacturing so as to serve as impetus for economic expansion, job creation through entrepreneurship, gender equality, youth (including girls) leadership and poverty reduction. AGOA continues to play a significant role in increasing Africa's exportability capacities of processed foods and related items with direct and targeted market access in the USA. In addition to AGOA and the President's Advisory Committee on Doing Business in Africa (PAC-DBIA), the U.S. government makes concerted efforts to expand and innovate its commercial tools for enhancing U.S.-Africa trade exchanges. Further, and over the past 4 decades, China has strategically strengthened its geo-economic relations with Africa, which has largely and increasingly prompted the USA to re-program its interests in Africa (Mlambo 2019; Adekunle and Korzun 2017).

Development Finance Corporation (DFC): The Overseas Private Investment Corporation (OPIC) and the Development Credit Authority (DCA) of the United States

Agency for Internatioanal Development (USAID) transitioned into the U.S. International Development Finance Corporation (DFC) on October 2019. DFC was created by the bipartisan Better Utilization of Investments Leading to Development (BUILD) Act of 2018, which was signed into law by President Donald Trump on October 5, 2018. This transformation empowers DFC to combine the OPIC and USAID's Development Credit Authority's joint capacities towards providing foreign aid though the financing of private development project. Further, the DFC will provide $60 billion in loans, loan guarantees, insurance and related financial tools to U.S. companies investing or operating in Africa and other developing countries.

Prosper Africa: was launched in December 2018, as the new vision for unlocking opportunities and expanding private sector activity between the U.S. and Africa. It is the US government initiative to substantially increase two-way trade and investment between the USA and Africa. For the very first time ever, Prosper Africa galvanizes 15 U.S. Government resource towards connecting U.S. and Africa businesses to new partners, buyers, suppliers and innovative business opportunities in this digital age.

EXIM: After two inactive years, the US Export–Import Bank (EXIM) has revived its Sub-Saharan African (SSA) Advisory Committee, therefore enhancing EXIM's capacity to serve as long term re-authorization tool for enhancing U.S. companies to up their business trajectory in Africa.

'**Access Africa'** is the USTDA's new initiative to support the development of quality ICT infrastructure and services across Sub-Saharan Africa. Access Africa represents a clear illustration of the joint public and private sectors' interests and presence of U.S. industries in Africa's ICT sector. Its mission supports 'Prosper Africa' towards developing high-quality ICT infrastructure across SSA. For instance, the US Trade and Development Agency (USTDA), in collaboration with selected US industry partners—Palo Alto Networks, Inc, the Corporate Council on Africa, Intel Corporation, Cisco Systems, Inc, General Electric Company, Symantec Corporation, and Adaptrum Inc, is enhancing America's role as Africa's most important ICT sector partner, and leveraging critical stakeholders and targeted programming to advance inclusive, secure and sustainable connectivity.

Conclusion

The most promising opportunity to strengthen Africa's rules-based economic order through AfCFTA is with the regional economic communities (RECs) (and other relevant initiatives). This is because RECs provide a natural opportunity to build a regional economy in defence of free and liberal trade, regional integration and economic cooperation. African leaders need a bold commitment to resist protectionism and to work with other countries within the established AfCFTA rules, thereby helping to minimize the damage of a protectionist agenda. If other AfCFTA countries would need to implement a strategic, coordinated and concerted strategy, Nigeria, being Africa's largest economy, has more to lose than most, but it also has the weight and interest to hold the line.

In the aftermath of U.S. approval of AGOA, the U.S. strategy for economic engagement with Africa in the face of increasingly fierce global competition, and related technological innovations, Africa needs to develop an effective strategy to up its trade game with the USA. While still maintaining an open trade policy, strategic responses from Africa and AGOA-CSOs reveal that there is increasing need for a comprehensive, innovative and effective programme or hub on best practices and quality management knowledge transfer. It is a great opportunity for selected CSOs to collaborate with strategically relevant partners towards deploying digital trade as a tool for fostering U.S.-Africa trade relations, as well as for promoting Africa's economic transformation.

African micro, small and medium scale enterprises (MSMEs) make up about 90% of its businesses and employs at least 60% of its national labour force. In addition, these SMEs are crucial levers to improving the livelihoods of vulnerable Africans, especially women and youth. However, based on the challenges that Africa faces in fostering U.S.-Africa business relations, and in order to enhance capacities of African enterprises to comply with the quality-related regulations, standards and other market-access requirements in the US market, there is a dire need for a comprehensive, innovative and effective program on best practices and quality management knowledge transfer. This should facilitate both American and Africa's enterprises capacity expansion, and integration in both regional and global value chains.

With increasing government emphasis on agro-processing and value addition, the capacities of African enterprises need to be strengthened towards unlocking opportunities in the US marketplace as well as the global arena. There is a need for a sectorally aligned comprehensive competitiveness- and productivity-targeted program which aims at creating jobs and wealth through regional and international (US) market access opportunities for American and African youth and women owned start-ups in both the U.S. and Africa. In response to the AGOA Strategy and the AfCFTA, there is increasing need for connecting producers (leather products, textile, handicrafts, etc.) with U.S. consumers, and also locating lucrative investments for American investors who are interested in investing in African business landscape.

According to UNECA, technological progress and ICTs contribute as much as 50% of economic growth rates. Thus, there is the need for a comprehensive programme towards solidifying selected countries as trade hubs within the AfCFTA, while making increased use of new technologies and e-commerce to strengthen Africa's digital trade capacities towards their competitiveness within the U.S.-Africa marketplace. The U.S. Government should leverage AfCFTA towards enhancing the digital trade innovations and opportunities within AGOA, Prosper Africa and other related initiatives. Further, the U.S. Government has continued to step up supportive efforts towards expanding its Africa strategy and ensuring that the different AGOA-related actors in the government are working together to achieve the vision and mission of the Strategy.

Another component to the argument is that multiparty trade agreements yield optimal economic and geopolitical benefits. By implication, several megatrade agreements that do not include the USA are being implemented on the African continent. Here, this article offers a series of recommendations on how to improve U.S.-Africa trade relations in the face of growing south–south RTAs (Odularu and Adekunle 2017; Odularu 2008):

1. Further re-articulate the AGOA strategy goals in order to take cognizance of the AfCFTA as well as South–South RTAs opportunities. This will help to understand the changing parameters of the relations under increasing competition and global megahurdles towards pursuing concrete initiatives that will create reciprocal benefits. This should generate and foster win-win economic relations for all partners and preventing marginalization from evolving regional economic architecture.
2. The establishment of a partnership on economic cooperation projects in Southeast Asia with the launching of AIIB, as its own quality infrastructure. In order to achieve this vision, the following action items are recommended: (1) Foreign Economic Policy: Complete ongoing trade renegotiations in a productive and timely way. Modernize an older trade agreement and ensure effective implementation of commitments. Successful completion of these renegotiations will inform what has changed, or not, under an AGOA trade policy, it will also inform their decisions on the merits about whether to negotiate bilaterally with the USA. In other words, the U.S' road to credible trade strategy for Africa should include Asia. (2) relaunch BIT negotiation with China as the negotiation continues. BIT is an important trade issue. BIT negotiation should be part of a larger strategy to encourage China to open up its economy. Putting the BIT on the back burner may play into the narrative that the USA is withdrawing from Asia and seemingly abandoning the U.S.-Asia-Africa business and commercial field to the Chinese.

References

Adekunle B, Korzun M (2017) Trading with China: how can Africa benefit? In: Odularu G, Adekunle B (eds) Negotiating South-South regional trade agreements. Advances in African economic, social and political development. Springer, Cham

Amiti A, Redding SJ, Weinstein D (2019) 'The Impact of the 2018 Trade War on U.S. Prices and Welfare.' The Center for Economic Policy Research (CEPR) International Trade and Regional Economics Discussion Paper (DP) 13564. Retrieved 16 December, 2019 from https://www.princeton.edu/reddings/papers/CEPR-DP13564.pdf

Bown CP (2019) 'U.S. – China trade war tariffs: an up-to-date chart' Peterson Institute of International Economics (PIIE). Retrieved 01 January 2020 from https://www.piie.com/research/piie-charts/us-china-trade-war-tariffs-date-chart

Mlambo V (2019) Exploitation dressed in a suit, shining shoes, and carrying a suitcase full of dollars: what does China want in Africa? J Pub Aff 19:e1892. Avaiable online at: https://doi.org/10.1002/pa.1892

Odularu G (2008) Nigeria–U.S. Trade relations in the non-oil sector. Retrieved 13 Oct 2019, from http://www.universal-publishers.com/m/book.php?method=ISBN&book=1599427036
Odularu G, Adekunle B (2017) Negotiating South-South Regional Trade Agreements | SpringerLink. Retrieved 13 Nov 2019, from https://link.springer.com/book/10.1007/978-3-319-45569-3
Ravi SJ, Snyder MR, Rivers C (2019, Feb) Review of international efforts to strengthen the global outbreak response system since the 2014–16 West Africa Ebola epidemic. Health Policy Plan 34(1):47–54. https://doi.org/10.1093/heapol/czy102
Gulker M (2019a) Trump's tariffs did nothing to boost the steel industry. Retrieved 15 December, 2019 from https://www.aier.org/article/trumps-tariffs-did-nothing-to-boost-the-steel-industry/
Gulker M (2019b) Protectionism sows the seeds of its own destruction. Retrieved 15 December, 2019 from https://www.aier.org/article/protectionism-sows-the-seeds-of-its-own-destruction/
Gulker M (2019c) This is how a nationalist raises your taxes. Retrieved 15 December, 2019 from https://www.aier.org/article/this-is-how-a-nationalist-raises-your-taxes/
Gulker M, Earle PC (2019) 'The trade war: a one-year assessment' American Institute for Economic Research (AIER) Publications. Retrieved 15 December, 2019 from https://www.aier.org/article/the-trade-war-a-one-year-assessment-executive-summary/
Tucker JA (2019) 'The trade war's new level of bizarre'. American Institute for Economic Research (AIER) Articles. Retrieved 02 January 2020, from https://www.aier.org/article/the-trade-wars-new-level-of-bizarre/
UNCTAD (2019) World investment report 2018 – investment and new industrial policies. Retrieved 02 January 2020, from https://unctad.org/en/PublicationsLibrary/wir2018_en.pdf
World Bank (2019) World development report 2020 – trading for development in the age of global value chains. Retrieved 02 January 2020, from http://pubdocs.worldbank.org/en/124681548175938170/World-Development-Report-2020-Draft-Report.pdf
Yandle B (2020) Tariff protection and big steel's struggle. Retrieved 03 January 2020, from https://www.aier.org/article/tariff-protection-and-big-steels-struggle/

Understanding the Role of Aid for Trade in Enhancing Corridor Development and Regional Integration in West Africa: Lessons and Policy Directions

Abiola Abidemi Akinsanya

Introduction, Rationale, and the Context

AfT is defined as 'a subset of the Official Development Assistance (ODA) provided by official agencies and multilateral institutions for programmes and projects identified in recipient countries' development strategies as trade-related priorities' (United Nations Economic Commission for Africa [UNECA] 2015, p. 7). It includes concessional loans and grants which must have grant element of 25% or more, calculated at a discount rate of 10% (Organization for Economic Development and Cooperation [OECD] and World Trade Organization [WTO] 2009). This means that the loans are granted at lower interest rates and must contain a grant share of 25% or more.

Furthermore, AfT to build economic infrastructure is one of the six categories through which AfT is allocated as shown in Table 3 in the appendix. These are aid for (1) trade development; (2) strengthening trade policy and regulations; (3) enhancing trade-related or economic infrastructure; (4) building productive capacity; (5) meeting trade-related adjustments costs; and (6) other trade-related needs (OECD 2011).

The single-issue ECOWAS faces the challenge of funding to finance its infrastructure needs. Hence, the need to examine the opportunities AfT offers ECOWAS to build road infrastructure networks and corridors that would strengthen integration of the sub-region and enhance its interconnectivity with the rest of the world. A corollary of examining the opportunities is to investigate the challenges that ECOWAS faces in using AfT to support its infrastructure and other developmental needs. These questions help to examine the linkages between AfT, infrastructure development, and regional integration. Transport and communication infrastructure has demonstrated considerable capacity to facilitate regional integration (Mbekeani 2010). Improving basic physical infrastructure, especially transport infrastructure, tends to also

A. A. Akinsanya (✉)
Federal Ministry of Industry, Trade and Investment, Abuja, Nigeria
e-mail: abiola.akinsanya@yahoo.com

G. O. A. Odularu et al. (eds.), *Fostering Trade in Africa*,
Advances in African Economic, Social and Political Development,
https://doi.org/10.1007/978-3-030-36632-2_9

have the biggest effect on export performance in comparison to other indicators like improving the business environment or investment reforms (Portugal-Perez and Wilson 2012). The effect of improving transport infrastructure is even greater for Africa's manufactured exports (Iwanow and Kirkpatrick 2009).

For instance, a study reveals that weak physical infrastructure contributes 25% on the average to trade costs arising from time delays in developing countries (Djankov 2010). Within Africa, transportation costs caused by transit delay add up to 15–20% on the average to the costs of goods from Africa, thus making the cost of intra-African trade to increase by 3–4 times higher than cost of goods from developed countries (Teravaninthorn and Raballand 2009). The quality and efficiency of ECOWAS transport infrastructure and services are the lowest in the African region (at LPI 2.19) based on World Bank's Logistic Performance Index (LPI) when compared with other African sub-regions (at LPI 2.27–2.73) or the globe (at LPI 3.01–3.99) (AfDB 2011). LPI deals with transshipment of goods through land such as haulage and logistic supply chain and facilitating the necessary documentation process. Poor transport infrastructure also inhibits the pace of using trade to alleviate poverty in Africa, especially as they are largely exporters of agricultural commodities, which often makes their produce to perish as a result of delay in linking the produce to the market (Mosley and Suleiman 2007; Cali and Razzaque 2013).

This study focuses on AfT to build economic infrastructure (road infrastructure) because poor infrastructure, particularly road infrastructure, remains a major obstacle to free and efficient movement of goods and services that is required to facilitate development and economic integration of ECOWAS. It identifies and explores the opportunities and challenges that Aid for Trade (AfT) to build road infrastructure brings to regional economic integration in Economic Community of West African States (ECOWAS). As this paper will establish, the lack of quality and efficient road infrastructure in ECOWAS limits the sub-region's capacity to integrate into the global market in order to benefit from the global value chain.

The Theoretical Underpinning and a Brief Review of Literature

Understanding the Theoretical Background

This article draws perspectives from development theory. Theory helps to support a case study approach by providing a body of knowledge that helps to evaluate and validate existing or new findings and propositions (Thomas 2011, 2017). Theory is a common or universal explanatory model articulated for clarifying, refining, and analyzing specific findings (Thomas 2017). For instance, theories have been used for analyzing international trade which includes trade theories like Adam Smith's absolute advantage theory which explains the capacity of a country to produce one particular product efficiently than the other country, or David Ricardo's comparative advantage theory which focuses on the need for a country to specialize in the production of one particular good in which it has relative comparative advantage. Theory helps to offer variety of concepts for explaining a phenomenon or for connecting analysis to pre-existing ideas in a systematic way (Silverman 2013; Thomas 2011).

Studies often trace the evolution of aid and AfT to the concept of development (Preston 1996; Pieterse 2001). Development theory provides an understanding of how the concept of development embodies the practice or idea of pursuing economic growth through planned intervention in the aftermath of the two World Wars (Preston 1996). Post-World War II, the USA initiated the Marshall Plan, which drew from the ideas of planned intervention from John Keynes, to reconstruct European economies (Peet and Hartwick 2009). For instance, aid or AfT constitutes a form of planned intervention between government and government aimed at facilitating global development.

Analyzing development theory often takes two trajectories, namely 'development sociology and development economic' (Pieterse 2001, p. 39). The former entails improving the social well-being and quality of life of the people, while the latter deals with gradual improvement in the wealth and transformation of States; however, both addresses reduction of global poverty and inequality. Analysis of AfT often takes the form of the latter because AfT is a development assistance created specifically for improving capacity to trade in order to facilitate economic growth and development. Consequently, reviewing AfT in the framework of development theory places it in the context of how AfT is used to promoting and complement free trade.

However, dependency theory makes us understand that aid has the potential to make developing countries dependent on developed countries or donors (Pieterse 2010; Preston 1996). In an effort to reform aid to prevent dependency, aid is now often being implemented in form of partnership to promote joint efforts toward capacity building rather than mere transfer of fund (Pieterse 2010). AfT takes this form as it entails technical assistance projects and programmes.

Definition and Background of Aid (ODA)

Official Development Assistance (ODA), generally known as aid, is defined as the flow of concessional financing granted through government agencies and multilateral institutions to facilitate economic development and improvement of welfare of developing countries (OECD 2003). From the definition, ODA (aid) as referred to in this paper are the funds allocated through formal channels including those allocated on a government-to-government (bilateral) basis or allocated by multilateral and regional donor institutions. In all cases, the funds are allocated specifically for economic benefits. Hence, humanitarian aid or military aid, which falls under other categories of aid, is not included.

As noted earlier, the concept and practice of AfT has a rich history and emanates from previous ideas of 'aid.' Indeed, prior to aid being formally introduced in 1947 after World War II through the Marshall Plan, colonial powers (Britain and France) used economic assistance schemes such as the Colonial Development and Welfare Fund to support their colonies (Ali and Zeb 2016; Van Bilzen 2015).

The Bretton Woods institutions, namely International Bank for Reconstruction and Development (IBRD) or the World Bank, the International Monetary Fund (IMF), and the defunct International Trade Organization, were created to facilitate the disbursement of that aid. The IMF was important in this regard as it provided aid to countries to address balance of payment problems (Karns et al. 2015). These institutions proffered financial assistance to developed countries to rehabilitate and rebuild their economies, especially their infrastructure, in the aftermath of the World Wars. Later, the functions of these institutions were expanded to cover other countries (World Bank, n.d.).

Economic prosperity of developed countries (donors) influenced the expansion in aid coverage to other regions in the world; however, the disbursement of aid fluctuated from time to time—decreasing and increasing over time (Addison and Tarp 2015; Jones 2015). The result of this inconsistency in allocation led the OECD's Development Assistance Committee (DAC) to adopt a target of 0.7% of donor's Gross National Income (GNI) for aid in 1970, and this target has continued to be accepted globally (OECD 2017; Kingsbury et al. 2016).

As the significance and supply of aid continue to rise, donors emphasize the need to ensure its effectiveness of meeting the objectives for which it is given. The OECD-DAC's Paris Declaration on aid effectiveness has been used as a guideline. According to this declaration, the objectives of aid are centered on facilitating economic development in the recipient nations. To determine whether aid achieves this benchmark, the aid provided should seek to address, among other things, three basic issues, namely reducing poverty, inequality, and unemployment (Seers 1970). Consequently, it is partly as a result of the measures of effectiveness that we begin to see scholars examining issues affecting aid in relation to socioeconomic factors such as development, public good, economic growth, and geo-politics. Some of these relationships relevant to this project are analyzed below.

Key Issues on Aid and the Case for AfT

Aid and Development

Africa remains the largest recipient of aid by region at US$54,193 billion in 2014 (OECD 2016), yet Africa still accounts for the largest number of the world's poorest nations. Thirty-four out of the world's 48 poorest nations are in Africa, and 11 of them are located within ECOWAS (UNCTAD 2016). This tends to create doubts in the minds of some scholars on the potential of aid to fulfill its objectives of assisting developing countries, especially LDCs to use aid to come out of poverty.

Those who hold concerns over aid have argued that aid, particularly tied aid or any politically motivated aid, is 'dead aid' because it compels African countries to absorb the exports of donors, thereby making them overly dependent on donors as opposed to attracting domestic and foreign investments (Moyo 2010, p. 78). This cannot facilitate development since they are not specifically created for such purposes in the first place, hence the need for Africa to progressively detach itself off aid dependence in order achieve an aid-free world (Moyo 2010). Early critics of aid are also of the view that developing countries and LDCs can achieve rapid economic development on their own without foreign aid just as developed countries have done (Bauer 1969). These critics point to how aid has not been effective at increasing economic welfare of poor countries. Boone (1996) notes that rather than using aid for development, the political elites of the recipient countries use aid to enrich themselves. Therefore, short-term aid (the AfT) targeted at specific sectors is necessary as opposed to the omnibus aid (Boone 1996, 2005). The AfT is sector-specific aid that focuses on using trade to address developmental challenges of developing countries and LDCs in order to assist them to achieve economic development through increased exports, as expressed in the Hong Kong Ministerial Declaration establishing AfT (Jakupec and Kelly 2016).

Contrary to the anecdotal view that aid has not done much to address development challenges, Tarp (2006) points to how a developing country like South Korea has used aid to facilitate its development and industrialization over a period of time. Botswana (Kaya et al. 2012) has also been held out as more positive example of an African country that has used aid to transform its economy. In a recent study, Asongu and Nwachukwu (2017) using Generalized Method of Moments (GMMs) to examine whether increased aid enhances inclusive development among 53 African recipients find a synergy effect between aid for economic infrastructure and inclusive development in Africa, suggesting that aid to African countries does not only help to improve infrastructure of those countries, but it also helps them to meet their development agenda. Development moves in tandem with poverty reduction because a country cannot develop while its people are wallowing in abject poverty.

Alvi and Senbeta (2012) using dynamic panel estimation techniques on 79 recipient countries provide evidence that there is a positive impact of aid on poverty reduction. The authors argue via their conclusion that aid in the form of grants disbursed through multilateral agencies tends to have much significance on poverty reduction than bilateral aid and loans. Another study of 46 recipient countries based on panel data analysis supports the assertion that aid directed toward agriculture, a sector in which rural poverty is highly prevalent, can be effective at alleviating poverty and facilitating development (Kaya et al. 2013). This is important in the African context since agriculture is the major productive sector and source of livelihood to many African countries, especially the LDCs. Agriculture contributes about 64% of the source of revenue to rural population in Africa (Moyo et al. 2015).

The studies mentioned above examined the impact of aid on economic infrastructure and poverty in Africa as a whole, while this research focuses on the specific challenges that might limit the positive impact of AfT, with particular attention on road infrastructure and ECOWAS. Various studies above did not capture the peculiarity of infrastructure needs of each sub-region that make up the African continent.

Aid and Economic Growth

Similar to the analysis above on aid and development, which explains the extent to which aid can be used as a means of addressing global poverty through provision of basic, affordable amenities and economic infrastructure for improving the welfare of the people, aid and economic growth is another contentious issue. The relationship between aid and economic growth helps to explain how aid targeted toward productive sectors like manufacturing or agriculture can increase export performance and economic activities in developing countries.

The literature examining the economic growth effects of aid is contradictory. While there is some literature (Nowak-Lehman et al. 2012; Rajan and Subramanian 2008) that have argued that aid is inconsequential on stimulating overall economic growth, especially per-capita income in recipient countries like ECOWAS (Adom 2012), there is another body of work that offers the contrary view (Lof et al. 2015; Minolu and Roddy 2010). The latter notes how aid is effective because it increases investment inflow (Clemens et al. 2012). This divide in perspectives constitutes another challenge to aid, which has prompted scholars to suggest an emphasis on reduction of inequality as the best measure for evaluating aid performance (Asongu 2016; Asongu and Nwachukwu 2017). The varying criteria and indices for measuring the usefulness of aid constitute a challenge in its implementation. The unpredictability and fluctuation in aid allocation have been identified as another challenge to implementation of aid, as these characteristics tend to limit its impact on growth in developing countries (Kodama 2012).

Studies (e.g., Doucouliagos and Paldam 2011, 2015) also affirm the role that aid can play in facilitating growth despite its shortcomings. These studies, however, assert that the reason for this is partly due to donors and scholars using statistical techniques and methods that provide the best suitable assessment outcomes. The inconsistency in aid allocation and the bias of some literature can create further challenges to the accuracy of aid data available to developing countries for their national development planning. More so, the role of aid in driving economic growth in various African countries often vary from sector to sector, which is why countries are encouraged to prioritize each sector in their own national development strategies in order to help identify sectors that can drive growth. This is why African countries like Botswana and Mauritius remain popular examples of countries, which have used aid to drive their economic growth because they have been able to support the aid received with effective domestic policies.

Another challenge is that it sometimes takes a longer time for the impact of aid in stimulating economic growth to be fully reflected in developing countries (Clemens et al. 2012). This may make some donors more committed to helping recipients address their social problems like health and education, where the impacts are easily measured, as opposed to assisting them to resolve more complex economic challenges and to alleviate poverty (Younas 2008). Ilorah (2008) notes that aid to African countries can also cause 'Dutch disease' which provides them with large financial inflow and imports from donors, which they cannot effectively absorb, thereby making Africa exports less competitive.

Skarbek and Leeson (2009) posit that any aid that cannot bring about 'economic successes' or provide solutions to economic challenges has failed in its objectives and needs no justification for continuity. Economic growth is often driven by multiple factors like good economic policies, good governance reforms and regulations such as anti-corruption, improvement of investment climate to encourage private sector development, especially SME development. Hence, to evaluate economic growth principally on capacity to utilize aid effectively may not give the accurate outcome. Perhaps, it is because of this complexity around measuring the effectiveness of aid that scholars proposed the need for aid to be allocated mainly to countries implementing sound domestic economic policies (Dollar and Levin 2006). Others conclude that 'if a country cannot develop without aid, it is unlikely to develop with it' (Bauer 1969, p. 89).

However, the result of an empirical review of aid studies from 2004 to 2016 shows that on average, scholars largely uphold the conclusion that aid stimulates growth despite varying levels of impact across countries (Glennie and Sumner 2016). An example is a finding from a study of 36 sub-Saharan African (SSA) countries, using country-based time series analysis, which revealed that aid facilitates growth and investment inflow in the long term in recipient countries (Juselius et al. 2014). These authors found that aid has significant positive impact on the GDP of 12 countries as well as on the investment inflow in 15 others. Arndt et al. (2015) used reduced-form regression model to investigate the opportunity that aid provides in addressing growth, inequality, structural performance and poverty over a duration of 40 years, finding that aid helps facilitate overall economic growth and improves socioeconomic welfare in developing countries in the long run, as opposed to harming their developmental pursuit.

Studies have also shown that aid toward agricultural development in Africa (Kaya et al. 2012), particularly agriculture infrastructure and assisting small farmers (Mosley and Suleiman 2007), provides opportunity to facilitate growth faster in the short term. Other studies, however, reveal that, on the average, aid provides a significant positive effect on economic growth in recipient countries with good domestic macroeconomic policies, effective institutions, and political stability (Burnside and Dollar 2000; Tarp 2006; Wagner 2014; Wickstead 2015; Sumner and Glennie 2015) including if the aid constitutes between 6.6 and 14.4% of the recipient countries' GNI (Gyimah-Brempong et al. 2012). In essence, there is growing consensus that some aspects of aid such as those targeted at building physical infrastructure and human capital provide opportunities to effectively facilitate growth and development faster than others (Asongu and Nwachukwu 2017; Doucouliagos and Paldam 2011).

Aid and Corruption and Poor Accountability

Corruption is another major challenge affecting aid allocation. It is perceived that opportunities in aid are often undermined by systemic corruption largely in recipient countries, and especially in Africa (Asongu 2015). Lopez (2015) argues that aid encourages corrupt practices in developing countries, especially through irregularities in aid disbursement. However, Stockemer et al. (2011) note that aid can reduce corruption because many donors often use aid to promote and enforce anti-corruption values, transparency and good governance in recipient countries in order to enhance economic growth (Stockemer et al. 2011).

Despite this contradiction, the perception is that aid encourages corruption. Isopi (2015), however, states that aid allocation may not be influenced by donors' perceptions of corruption in recipient countries because donors are more committed to maintaining their economic, political, and strategic interests in recipient countries rather than address corruption. Sometimes the prevalence of corruption does not stop the aid from being effective. However, it can undermine the level or depth of effectiveness, which could have been higher if corruption is tackled.

A study of 27 European Union (EU) donors shows that the concern about corruption perception in recipient countries is minimal in 15 EU donors because of their strong conviction in using aid to facilitate good governance and poverty reduction in developing countries (Bauhr et al. 2013). On the other hand, the other 12 donors put their national interest above corruption perception in recipient countries. Asongu and Jellal (2013) argue that while aid to support government expenditure in recipient countries raises corruption, aid disbursed as private investments reduces it. In essence, the divide is between donors who are not deterred by the prevalence of corruption and those who are concerned about it, and thus tie their aid to 'good governance.'

Using quantile regression analysis to examine 120 recipient countries, Okada and Samreth (2012) discover that aid helps to minimize corruption in recipient countries, especially multilateral aid, which tends to strengthen institutions and governance process in recipients countries. In contrast to this, Asongu (2015) using GMM techniques examines the impact of aid on corruption and institutions in 53 African countries and finds a positive causal link especially in landlocked countries, non-oil producers, and countries with poor institutional capacity to effectively absorb the aid. Also, Okada and Samreth (2012) look more broadly at all OECD donors, while Bauhr et al. (2013) limit their study to only EU donors; the two studies, however, give similar outcomes.

In addition, poor accountability by donors and the fact that increased foreign aid has not been based on effectiveness, but rather on global public sympathy campaigns, Shleifer (2009) further adds to the farce of aid. Many of the aid donor agencies tend to be more interested in their loans and reports as opposed to increasing the effectiveness of the aid itself (Easterly 2008). Lopez (2015), however, posits that corrupt practices in aid disbursement process are more prevalent in humanitarian aid and much lesser in aid for infrastructure development. In order to diminish the impact of aid on corruption, Osternhaus (2015) calls for enhanced channel of reporting corrupt practices and strengthening ethical regulations in public institutions dealing with aid funds in both recipient and donor countries as mismanagement of fund is peculiar to both. Easterly (2006) suggests the need for developing countries to devise their own development initiatives as opposed to relying on handouts of financial aid from developed countries.

Aid and Geopolitical Influence or Interests

The use of aid as a tool of influence and geo-politics constitutes another challenge to the effective use of aid. Hunt (2016) and Alesina and Dollar (2000) assert that donors use aid as an instrument for exerting influence, gaining political and economic advantages such as increased exports to recipient countries. Historically, major colonial powers, for example, France and Great Britain, granted development assistance to their former colonies, while the USA and the former USSR also used aid to exert geopolitical influence and promote liberal market and socialist values, respectively, during the Cold War (Tarp 2006; Wickstead 2015). Consequently, aid is sometimes termed 'latter-day imperialism' (Browne 2006, p. 11). However, Hoeffler and Outram (2011) reveals in their study of 22 OECD donors and 168 recipients that, with the exception of few countries like the USA and UK, which use aid to secure votes at the UN Security Council, many donors tend to use aid mainly to assist in addressing developmental needs of recipients more than they use it for geopolitical gains.

Notwithstanding the challenges of aid, this paper maintains that it still possesses great opportunities for developing countries, especially LDCs to utilize it to facilitate their developmental objectives as industrialized nations have done. However, to better maximize these opportunities, effective coordination of aid programmes and projects in developing countries would be of great importance. It is in response to this that the AfT was specifically created to ensure better and effective coordination of trade-related aid programmes and projects among donors and recipients globally. These aspects of AfT are espoused in the following section.

AfT: What Does It Have to Offer?

This section of the review will analyze existing theoretical and empirical literature on AfT, the challenges and the opportunities that it provides for developing countries especially ECOWAS member. As set out in the introduction to this paper, AfT has been identified as having the potential to facilitate economic growth and development in developing countries, especially low-income countries. However, these countries are often limited by supply-side constraints, which hamper their capacity to fully benefit from the opportunities in global trade. Hence, AfT was created as the mechanism for assisting them build the capacities they need to maximize these opportunities by overcoming barriers to trade. The literature on the various ways, which AfT has been assisting developing countries, especially those in Africa and ECOWAS in particular as well as its challenges, is analyzed in the second part of this review.

Analysis of Some Challenges of Aid in the Context of AfT

Introduction

This section reviews existing literature on how some of the challenges of aid can affect AfT too even though the challenges seem more prevalent in aid allocations. The findings from this review would provide us with analytical framework that would be used to analyze whether AfT is assisting ECOWAS to enhance its road infrastructure and identifying areas where it is helping to do so.

Donors' Economic Interests

A large share of AfT funding comes from OECD's DAC members through their development agencies, and this does tend to mean that AfT allocation is influenced by donors' economic interests. Although recipients devise their own development needs, donors sometimes still influence which of the needs they channel their funds to. This is evident in the fact that only one LDC, Tanzania, made it to the top 10 recipients of AfT from 2006 to 2015 (as indicated in the OECD and WTO 2017 report), while large economies like India, Vietnam, Turkey, and Indonesia, which offer donors greater economic opportunities, continue to be among the largest recipients. No ECOWAS country was among the top ten recipients, despite, as previously mentioned, 11 out of its 15 members are counted among the world's poorest nations. Similarly, despite the EU's increased AfT to Africa, the allocation to LDCs was only 22% which falls far below its AfT commitment (Holden 2014).

Also, AfT allocation sometimes experience some inconsistency in disbursement especially as projects or programmes often have timelines. For instance, donors keep enlarging the agenda of what constitutes AfT programmes or projects in line with their own interests like the addition of gender and climate issues into the AfT work plan of 2012–2013 (de Melo and Wagner 2016). Their commercial and political interests continue to limit the actualization of the main objective of AfT, which is to achieve a pro-poor economic development through fair trade (Langan and Scott 2011). Clearly, more consistent and increased allocation of more AfT to LDCs would be a better idea, as this would help to rapidly reduce their level of poverty.

Difficulty in Measuring AfT and Inadequate Statistical Data

There are also difficulties around measuring the full impact of AfT projects and programmes, partly due to the broad scope of what constitutes AfT. These difficulties are compounded by the problem of insufficient statistical data on AfT. Pettersson and Johansson (2013) note that the difficulty in separating AfT from ODA poses a challenge because some projects may not directly impact on export enhancement, but have positive effect on overall economic development. Jakupec (2016), Razzaque and te Velde (2013), and Hoekman and Wilson (2010), on the other hand, argue that paucity of data and varying methods of evaluation makes it difficult for scholars to conduct adequate qualitative empirical studies on impact assessment of AfT except those conducted by donor institutions. Sometimes data on AfT are marred by discrepancies and overly reportage by donors of AfT disbursement (Cali and Razzaque 2013). For instance, Cadot and de Melo (2014) point out that in 2011, a joint OECD and WTO report stated that the World Bank contributed about US$5 billion via AfT in 2008, while the World Bank in its own 2008 financial year report indicated the amount to be US$1.42 billion. This discrepancy, according to Cadot and de Melo (2014), is a result of the two reports using different evaluation criteria to identify, which project falls under AfT. The vagueness of some categories of AfT, especially AfT to build productive capacity, which consists of vast areas of activities and virtually all sectors of the economy, also makes statistical calculation very complicated (Holden 2014). For instance, it is difficult to determine how AfT to build productive capacity impacts on export diversification, and in addition to the lack of precise activities that constitute each category of AfT, all these add to the complexity of measuring its impact on economic performance (de Melo and Wagner 2015).

Lack of Effective Coordination and Ownership of AfT

Poor coordination of some AfT projects and programmes by both donor institutions and recipients makes implementation of AfT challenging. Some recipients do not have comprehensive AfT needs' strategies nor do they mainstream trade and AfT into their national development plans. Poor financial resources sometimes also deter recipients from owning or continuing some AfT projects and programmes. AfT priorities are sometimes not harmonized by recipient countries and donor institutions, thereby making effective coordination difficult (Turner and Fink 2013). Inconsistency of AfT allocation also limits recipients' ability to make proper planning and effective coordination of the AfT projects and programmes (Hoekman and Wilson 2010). Hence, Bigsten and Tengtam (2015) suggest more disbursements of aid through multilateral agencies since they have greater capacity to monitor effectively.

Bureaucratic and Institutional Delays in AfT Disbursement

Bureaucratic procedures in accessing AfT fund are often rigorous, thereby resulting in delays or totally making it difficult for some countries to benefit. For instance, Basnet and Engel (2013) find that only 10–15% of recipients note that delay in AfT allocation has no negative effect on their budgetary plans while the remaining recipients acknowledged the negative effect of delays in AfT allocations on their budget policy. The delay, according to the authors, is more common in implementation of AfT projects like infrastructure and agriculture development.

Overview of Opportunities of AfT

Despite the challenges associated with AfT outlined above, it still offers numerous opportunities, especially in providing financial and technical benefits to help recipient countries improve their productivity and facilitate their trade. AfT provides developing countries with additional funding from donors, which is why both donors and recipients often support the need for funding to trade initiative to help reduce global poverty and facilitate development (Cadot and de Melo 2014). Studies reveal that AfT provides opportunities for improving export competitiveness (Vigil and Wagner 2012; Hühne et al. 2014a; Bearce et al. 2013) and fostering regional integration (Deen-Swarray et al. 2014; Udvari 2014; Oyejide and Bankole 2010). It also plays a key role in helping to develop the capacities of the private sector to stimulate economic activities. For instance, AfT helps to support harmonization of regional policies, institution building and reforms and enhance private sector development (Ash 2011; Tembo 2011) which consequently facilitates integration process. It is for this reason that we often see donors like the EU providing assistance to developing countries, especially those in Africa to enhance their regional integration process. The EU gives special consideration to AfT to support regional integration by disbursing large share of its AfT to transport infrastructure mostly through regional level (Holden 2014). This is not surprising because the EU itself is a regional grouping and is seen as a model to other regions, especially those in Africa.

AfT is a veritable tool for enhancing and easing movement of goods and services between trading partners(Akpan 2014; Cadot and de Melo 2014) and reducing trade cost (Cali and te Velde 2008). It is as a result of this that categories like AfT to improve economic infrastructure, trade-related adjustments, or productive sector are designated to address specific challenges (see Table 3 in the appendix). It provides forms of assistance and capacity building for developing countries, particularly poor countries, hence perceived as public good (Wang 2011). Studies also uphold AfT as a tool for enhancing economic growth (Morrissey 2006; Lopez 2015), reducing poverty and meeting development needs (Mosley and Suleiman 2007). These are analyzed further in subsequent paragraphs. However, there are divergent views or perspectives on the concept of AfT. Based on this, this review will first analyze the perspective that makes critique of AfT, followed by the perspective of literature that is in support of AfT. This review sort of makes a comparative analysis of the divergent views on AfT.

Although there are numerous studies on aid, not much has been researched on AfT despite the fact that AfT is a large component of aid (Lee et al. 2015). AfT accounts for 30% of total ODA (de Melo and Wagner 2016), with half of it disbursed as grants and the remaining half as concessional loans (OECD and WTO 2013). Critics of AfT, just as in the case with aid (ODA), assert that the objective of AfT is faulty, thereby making it potentially impossible to achieve meaningful results. Evenett (2005) points out that AfT is created as a form of compensatory measure to developing countries, which may lose from trade liberalization in the Doha Development Round in order to deter them from blocking future progress in the Round. This, according to Evenett

(2005), constitutes a challenge to the objective of the initiative in providing the desired opportunities for developing countries.

Langan and Scott (2014) assert that AfT is used as a means to shift the blame away from the imbalance in the multilateral trading system and WTO rules, which puts developing countries at a disadvantage in gaining market access, and then placing those blames on the systemic domestic challenges in developing countries. Stiglitz and Charlton (2006), however, reject these ideas and argue that AfT is rather an essential measure initiated to complement market access opportunities in the Doha Development Round for developing countries, especially LDCs, as opposed to it being a compensatory measure. The WTO Hong Kong Ministerial Declaration emphasizes this by stating that AfT should not be construed as a substitute for development opportunities and market access in the Doha Round but rather as a necessary complement to the Round (WTO 2005). For instance, AfT helps recipients to remove non-tariff barriers to trade and build private sector capacity in order to enable them fully utilize market access opportunities in international market. Donors like the USA established trade hubs in various regions like the West African Trade Hub for ECOWAS members to help their exports meet US technical standards and regulations to gain access into the US market.

Analysis of Major Opportunities of AfT

Opportunities of AfT on Export Competitiveness

The opportunities that AfT provides on export performance are substantially covered in the literature. However, the outcome of these studies shows varying results. Some literature note that AfT provides the opportunity mainly to facilitate donor exports more than it does to recipients' exports, thereby making some scholars to conclude that AfT confers less opportunity for improving exports performance of recipient countries, especially LDCs. They argue that this is partly because AfT, especially bilateral aid, is often donor-driven and largely dependent on donors' sectors or products of interests and priority, which is why donors tend to grant more aid to recipients that trade more with them (Martinez-Zarzoso 2015).

For instance, a study by Younas (2008) concludes that donor countries allocate more AfT to recipient countries, which imports products such as capital goods in which donors have comparative advantage or commercial interest. The author finds that ample share of AfT is allocated to recipients that have higher capacity to import capital goods from donors, which is why countries like Egypt, Indonesia and Israel are receiving the largest AfT of US$1524 million, US$1390 million, and US$994 million, respectively, compared to LDCs like Togo receiving US$25 million. Also, using gravity model to examine the advantages that AfT provides to expand exports of OECD donors and their recipient countries, Wagner (2003) finds that aid causes a significant increase in donor exports to recipient countries by 35%, especially if the aid is tied or directly meant to support aid-financed projects in recipient countries.

This increase can sometimes reach as high as 133% in some countries. In essence, the study reveals that a US$1 aid would generate increased exports of about US$2.30 for donors.

Recent study also reveals that every US$0.50 aid spent on recipient countries in the short run brings about a US$1.80 increase in exports for donors in the long run, and much higher for donors which tie their aid (Martinez-Zarzoso et al. 2014). Their research investigates the linkages of aid on donor exports using gravity model, Martinez-Zarzoso et al. (2014) find that aid enhances exports of donors like Germany, Australia, USA, and Japan, which tie their aid, while having less impact on exports of other donors like New Zealand, Belgium, Ireland, and Netherland, which rarely tie theirs despite being some of the largest providers of AfT. However, it is worth mentioning that the use of tied aid has decreased since 2005 when OECD encouraged donors to prohibit its use (Martinez-Zarzoso 2015). Consequently, the opportunities of donors' tied aid may not be as high as this anymore.

The result of a country-specific study of how AfT provides opportunity for increased exports, based on dynamic and static gravity model, discloses that a US$1 aid provided by Germany to the 138 recipient countries examined increases Germany's exports in the short run by an average of US$0.05% (Martinez-Zarzoso et al. 2009). The authors, however, find that in the long run, it increases to an average of US$1.4 for every US$1 dollar aid, approximately 140% increase. Adding that, this increase can, however, diminish when other EU members tie their aid in the recipient countries, thereby displacing German exports. It is also revealed that AfT, when disaggregated from the broad ODA, increases mainly donor exports since certain part of AfT, especially those to build trade-related infrastructure and productive sector are often tied to donor exports (Pettersson and Johansson 2013). Similarly, using gravity model to investigate the impact of AfT on the exports of 123 recipient countries, Nowak-Lehmann et al. (2013) uncover that AfT tends to have less overall positive contribution to increase recipient exports to donor countries, hence concluding that AfT has not been beneficial to recipient countries.

However, contrary to these views, AfT does not only offer opportunities to increase donors' exports. It also increases recipients' exports. For instance, a study finds that aid for trade facilitation increases recipients' two-way trade, that is, export and import (Helble et al. 2012). Their research shows that a US$1 increase in aid for trade facilitation results in a US$1.33 increased exports for recipient countries. Another finding from a study of 180 countries using asymmetric gravity model reveals that AfT directly increases the trade of recipient countries with donor by 13% when compared with donors' trade between non-AfT receiving countries (Silva and Nelson 2012). Using asymmetric and aggregated gravity model to study opportunities of AfT on 170 countries' exports, findings also reveal that doubling AfT will cause exports of recipient countries to increase by about 5% and donor exports by 3% (Hühne et al. 2014b). In essence, the 5% increase in recipients' exports supports the fact that recipients' exports tend to benefit significantly from AfT.

Further, using gravity model analysis, a US$1 increase in AfT will lead to a US$5 increase in global trade, estimated at an increase of US545 million annually (Helble et al. 2009). Another study to examine whether AfT offers opportunities to increase bilateral exports of 184 countries based on gravity model finds that AfT does not only enhance donor exports, it also significantly increases recipients' exports and reduces the associated trade cost (Pettersson and Johansson 2013).

The result of another study, which used simple partial equilibrium model to investigate how AfT helps to increase exports of specific products from recipients' countries, discloses that AfT targeted at development of definite exportable products is more highly effective to increase recipients' exports to donor countries and to the rest of the world (Brenton and Vonuexhull 2009). Findings from study of AfT provided by specific donors also show positive results for recipients' exports. For instance, AfT provided by Sweden increases the exports of AfT recipients more than it does to exports of non-AfT receiving trading partners (Skärvall 2012). Finding also shows that a US$1 increase in AfT provided by USA to recipients will result in US$69 increase in exports of recipients over a period of two years (Bearce et al. 2013). Lee et al. (2015) assessed 105 recipient countries using regression model and revealed that AfT enables recipients to receive more financial commitments of up to 24.1% and additional 43.3% increase in AfT projects from donors when compared to what is granted to non-aid receiving trading partners. Perhaps it is as a result of the numerous positive impact of AfT on developing countries' exports that Cali and te Velde (2008) in their study conclude that a 1% increase in global AfT would result in a 0.15% reduction in trade costs on developing countries exports. In essence, AfT provides a win-win opportunity for exports of both donor and recipient countries.

AfT, Economic Growth, and Development

Some literature also infers that aid has little impact on economic growth, stressing that it has only been successful in addressing social challenges like health and education with so little on improving export-led economic growth in developing countries (Skarbek and Leeson 2009). Economides et al. (2008) investigate the impact of aid on growth in 75 aid recipient countries, finding that the overall effectiveness of aid on economic growth is mostly limited by rent-seeking vices inherent in aid allocation procedures adopted by public sector of recipient countries. Meschi and Vivarelli (2009) also discover that AfT has also not fully addressed the pro-poor economic development challenges like inequality and market failure arising from trade liberalization. Jakupec (2016) focuses on the importance of developed countries to remove trade barriers like subsidies in agriculture and high tariffs that hinder market access for developing countries' exports as opposed to providing AfT. This, he asserts, tends to be a more effective way of using trade to enhance economic growth and development in developing countries and LDCs. On the other hand, a study shows that AfT can facilitate economic growth, and hence, AfT should continue to be a supplementary measure to trade to stimulate economic growth (Morrissey 2006). Cadot et al. (2014) in their investigation on the impact of AfT on trade and growth in developing countries find that AfT directly targeted at export promotion or to support exporters in adapting new technology or improving standard and quality does have positive impact to increase trade and thus contribute to economic growth.

AfT and LDCs or Pro-poor Development

Some scholars argue that AfT has not achieved its objective of facilitating pro-poor development in developing countries, particularly in LDCs. For instance, Langan and Scott (2011) point out how more AfT has not been allocated to LDCs that need it the most while big developing countries like India, Egypt, and Iraq are some of the largest recipients of aid. Similar view is shared in the study by Gamberoni and Newfarmer (2014), which reveals that poor countries in SSA like Zambia, Niger, Mali, and Burkina-Faso, which are some of the poorest nations, are not receiving as much AfT as they should. Also, only three LDCs, namely Afghanistan, Ethiopia and Tanzania, are part of the top ten recipients of AfT disbursement between 2006 and 2013 (OECD and WTO 2015). Hühne et al. (2014a) assert that, just like aid conditionality, the stringent requirements for accessing AfT also make it difficult for poor countries to adequately benefit from AfT. For instance, many of US AfT requirements are subject to the capability of recipient countries to show flexibility or progress in the Doha Round (Langan and Scott 2011). On the contrary, a study conducted by Hoekman and Wilson (2010) shows that 93% of every AfT disbursed by multilateral aid agencies goes to low-income countries, valued at US$6.6 billion of every US$7.1 billion disbursed, while it accounts for 46% through bilateral disbursement, the remainder of this is allocated to middle-income countries. de Melo and Wagner (2015) by investigating AfT in relation to per-capita GDP as opposed to real GDP also find evidence that AfT tends to reduce poverty in 109 developing countries examined, which includes LDCs. More so, fund provided as AfT has the capacity to raise the welfare of both donors and recipients, especially recipient with low income tax (Naito 2012). It is as a result of the needs of LDCs that a dedicated framework on AfT (i.e., Enlarged Integrated Framework) was created to assist in their developmental objectives. Recent figure shows that AfT allocations to LDCs have improved when compared to other groups. Out of the total of US$252.4 billion disbursed to income groups between years 2006 and 2015, LDCs received the sum of US$80.43 billion (31.9% share) relative to low-middle-income countries at US$102.74 billion (40.7%), upper-middle-income and other low-income countries at US$61.98 billion (24.6%) and US$7.27 billion (2.9%), respectively (OECD and WTO 2017).

Conclusion and Recommendations: Overcoming Challenges Faced in Deploying AfT Toward Meeting Infrastructure Needs

AfT has assisted ECOWAS to improve its road infrastructure. It has helped in understanding how AfT contribution to economic infrastructure in general and road infrastructure in particular is helping to facilitate the integration of the West African sub-region through improving the efficiency of road linkages within ECOWAS and between ECOWAS and other African sub-regions and the global market. It finds that despite an increase in AfT to ECOWAS, government budgetary finance remains the largest source of road infrastructure finance in ECOWAS. More so, road infrastructure is capital intensive; hence, the need for multiple sources of financing is required, which include a mix approach of AfT, government finance, and private sector investment. This would minimize the indebtedness that may arise from external borrowings. The two road examples show the commitment of ECOWAS countries and donors' support to cooperate with ECOWAS in its efforts to deepen integration through trade and infrastructure development, with a view to accelerating full integration of the African continent into a single continental free trade area.

Despite divergent results in views and study outcomes in the existing literature examined, one of the predominant opportunities that AfT provides to developing countries is additional source of funding to assist them in meeting their developmental needs. These financial and technical supports help them to put in place mechanisms that help facilitate their export performance regionally and globally. These mechanisms include those related to building trade-related infrastructure like road networks, port development, strengthening private sector capacity, and removal of other barriers that increase trade costs in developing countries, especially ECOWAS. However, the capacity to effectively utilize this AfT varies across countries. Literature also reveals that AfT for economic infrastructure tends to be more effective in facilitating exports of both donors and recipients. AfT provides opportunities to ECOWAS to strengthen its regional road interconnectivity as a way of boosting regional trade and integration in the region. Extant studies conclude that without effective and sound domestic macroeconomic policies and institutions, AfT may not successfully deliver the desired outcome of facilitating growth and sustainable development in developing countries. It therefore becomes imperative for developing countries like ECOWAS to intensify efforts toward strengthening regional economic regulations and institutions so as to better harness the opportunities that AfT provides and mitigate the challenges therein.

Appendix

See Tables 1, 2, 3, and 4.

Table 1 Total AfT commitment and disbursement to transport and storage infrastructure in 2015

AfT sector and code	Commitment 2015 current prices (US$ million)	Disbursement 2015 current prices (US$ million)	AfT sector and code	Commitment 2015 current prices (US$ million)	Disbursement 2015 current prices (US$ million)	AfT sector and code	Commitment 2015 current prices (US$ million)	Disbursement 2015 current prices (US$ million)
Transport and storage infrastructure			Communications			Energy generation and supply		
Transport policy and administrative management (21010)	315.45335	307.511888	Communication policy and administrative management (22010)	25.118289	58.703757	Energy policy and administrative management (23110)	952.509185	842.74214
Road transport (21020)	2990.185657	2647.203994	Tele-communications (22020)	117.521475	83.247507	Energy education and training (23181)	9.240747	5.139039
Rail transport (21030)	242.899429	380.744119	Radio/TV/Print media (22030)	4.328194	6.343326	Energy research (23182)	3.746887	10.134184
Water transport (21040)	1015.599744	200.670612	Information and communication technology (ICT) (22040)	85.222033	53.8123	Energy generation, renewable sources—multiple technologies (23210)	341.589625	389.668186
Air transport (21050)	123.931634	184.165308				Hydro-electric power plants (23220)	327.449993	199.989685
Storage (21061)	3.6	0.250874				Solar energy (23230)	411.717181	486.497975

(continued)

Table 1 (continued)

AfT sector and code	Commitment 2015 current prices (US$ million)	Disbursement 2015 current prices (US$ million)	AfT sector and code	Commitment 2015 current prices (US$ million)	Disbursement 2015 current prices (US$ million)	AfT sector and code	Commitment 2015 current prices (US$ million)	Disbursement 2015 current prices (US$ million)
Transport and storage infrastructure			Communications			Energy generation and supply		
Education and training in transport and storage (21081)	0.103184	0.201853				Wind energy (23240)	79.953412	132.020383
						Marine energy (23250)	0.086522	0.1797
						Geothermal energy (23260)	13.128159	101.782989
						Biofuel-fired power plants (23270)	38.663785	14.804959

(continued)

Table 1 (continued)

AfT sector and code	Commitment 2015 current prices (US$ million)	Disbursement 2015 current prices (US$ million)	AfT sector and code	Commitment 2015 current prices (US$ million)	Disbursement 2015 current prices (US$ million)	AfT sector and code	Commitment 2015 current prices (US$ million)	Disbursement 2015 current prices (US$ million)
Transport and storage infrastructure			Communications			Energy generation and supply		
						Energy generation, non-renewable sources, unspecified (23310)	201.800408	160.489955
						Coal-fired electric power plants (23320)	——	——-
						Oil-fired electric power plants (23330)	30.493682	16.892453
						Natural gas-fired electric power plants (23340)	277.45708	46.363394

(continued)

Table 1 (continued)

AfT sector and code	Commitment 2015 current prices (US$ million)	Disbursement 2015 current prices (US$ million)	AfT sector and code	Commitment 2015 current prices (US$ million)	Disbursement 2015 current prices (US$ million)	AfT sector and code	Commitment 2015 current prices (US$ million)	Disbursement 2015 current prices (US$ million)
Transport and storage infrastructure			Communications			Energy generation and supply		
						Nuclear energy electric power plants (23510)	16.783835	5.453608
						Electric power transmission and distribution (23630)	2474.181892	1394.909143
						Gas distribution (23640)	77.648364	8.430394
Total	4691.772998	3720.748648		232.189991	202.106908		5226.450757	3807.067793

Source OECD CRS database (n.d.), viewed from http://stats.oecd.org/qwids/ and http://www.oecd.org/dac/aft/Aid-for-trade-sector-codes.pdf, accessed on 19 August 2017

Table 2 Total AfT to disbursement to transport infrastructure in Africa in 2002 and 2015

Transport infrastructure sub-set	Year 2002 (US$ millions)	Year 2015 (US$ millions)
Transport policy and administrative management (21010)	246.32905	315.45335
Road transport (21020)	917.864026	2990.185657
Rail transport(21030)	106.214584	242.899427
Water transport (21040)	143.026614	1015.599744
Air transport (21050)	42.674528	123.931634
Storage (21061)	–	3.6
Education and training in transport and storage (21081)	0.926396	0.10384
Total	US$1457.034198	US$4691.772996

Source OECD CRS database (n.d.), viewed http://stats.oecd.org/qwids/and.http: / /www.oecd.org/dac/aft/Aid-for-trade-sector-codes.pdf, accessed on 19 August 2017

Table 3 Categories of AfT

Aid for Trade (AfT)

⇩

Trade-related or economic infrastructure	Productive capacity	Trade development	Trade policy and regulation	Trade-related adjustment	Other trade-related needs
Electricity transport and storage telecommunications, etc.	Mining agriculture financial services Industries, etc.	Private sector development and engagement export diversification	Improving trade regulations and policies building capacity to negotiate, formulate and implement trade agreements	Support to reduce impact of tariff cut and preference erosion	Any other trade need

Table 4 Total AfT to Africa's transport infrastructure, 2005–2015

Commitments, US$ millions (current price)											
Transport sub-category	2005	2006	2007	2008	2009	2010	2011	2012	2013	2014	2015
Transport policy and administrative management 21010)	377.1	398.0	373.8	860.3	543.5	599.9	293.4	356.2	388.3	333.7	315.5
Road transport (21020)	1757.7	1837.6	2517.9	3345.4	4269.2	3835.6	2551.6	4555.1	3477.6	2954.6	2990.2
Rail transport (21030)	176.5	332.4	462.5	1090.9	426.2	405.3	166.3	1264.08	1122.7	705.2	242.8
Air transport (21050)	86.3	45.6	189.7	158.1	64.2	265.7	296.6	10.4	128.6	186.6	123.9
Total	2397.6	2613.6	3543.8	5454.7	5303.1	5106.5	3307.9	6185.6	3994.5	4180.1	3672.5
Disbursements, US$ millions (current price)											
Transport sub-category	2005	2006	2007	2008	2009	2010	2011	2012	2013	2014	2015
Transport policy and administrative management (21010)	157.9	160.9	270.0	329.5	356.1	337.8	359.7	480.8	466.0	433.9	307.5
Road transport (21020)	1375.7	1482.4	1814.0	2217.4	2061.6	2600.4	3035.1	2976.1	3360.6	3337.5	2647.2
Rail transport (21030)	117.1	215.0	223.0	253.7	269.3	362.0	458.5	367.6	494.1	439.2	380.7
Air transport (21050	24.7	27.9	47.0	66.0	70.6	129.2	191.3	162.6	166.0	156.9	184.2
Total	1675.4	1886.3	2353.9	2866.4	2757.4	3429.4	4044.6	3619.5	4486.7	4367.6	3519.6

Source OECD CRS database (n.d.), viewed from http://stats.oecd.org/qwids/; and http://www.oecd.org/dac/aft/Aid-for-trade-sector-codes.pdf, accessed on 5 September 2017

References

Addison T, Tarp F (2015) Aid policy and the macroeconomic management of aid. World Dev 69:1–5. https://doi.org/10.1016/j.worlddev.2014.02.009

Adom AD (2012) Investigating the impacts of intraregional trade and aid on per capita income in Africa: case study of the ECOWAS. Econ Res Int. https://doi.org/10.1155/2012/297658

African Development Bank (2011) Regional integration strategy paper for West Africa 2011–2015. Retrieved from https://www.afdb.org/fileadmin/uploads/afdb/Documents/Policy-Documents/RISP%20for%20West%20Africa%20-%20REV%202.pdf

Akpan U (2014) Impact of regional road infrastructure improvement on intra-regional trade in ECOWAS. Afr Dev Rev 26(2):64–76. https://doi.org/10.1111/1467-8268.12093

Alesina A, Dollar D (2000) Who gives foreign aid to whom and why? J Econ Growth 5(1):33–63. https://doi.org/10.1023/A:1009874203400

Ali M, Zeb A (2016) Foreign aid: origin, evolution and its effectiveness in poverty alleviation. Dialogue: Q J 11(1):107–125. Retrieved from http://www.qurtuba.edu.pk/thedialogue/The%20Dialogue/11_1/Dialogue_January_March2016_107-125.pdf

Alvi E, Senbeta A (2012) Does foreign aid reduce poverty? J Int Dev 24(8):955–976. https://doi.org/10.1002/jid.1790

Arndt C, Jones S, Tarp F (2015) Assessing foreign aid's long-run contribution to growth and development. World Dev 69:6–18. https://doi.org/10.1016/j.worlddev.2013.12.016

Ash K (2011) Aid for trade and the private sector: a partnership that works. Int Trade Forum (4):8–9. Retrieved from http://web.a.ebscohost.com.ezproxy.lib.monash.edu.au/ehost/pdfviewer/pdfviewer?vid=1&sid=0dbc220d-35a6-4251-a6c0-fe7a04a6c080%40sessionmgr4007

Asongu S (2015) The evolving debate on the effect of foreign aid on corruption and institutions in Africa. In: Arvin BM, Lew B (eds) Handbook on the economics of foreign aid, pp 313–322. http://dx.doi.org.ezproxy.lib.monash.edu.au/10.4337/9781783474592.00028

Asongu S (2016) Reinventing foreign aid for inclusive and sustainable development: Kuznets, Piketty and the great policy rehearsal. J Econ Surv 30(4):736–755. https://doi.org/10.1111/joes.12109

Asongu SA, Jellal M (2013) On the channels of foreign aid to corruption. Econ Bull 33(3):2191–2201. Retrieved from http://dx.doi.org.ezproxy.lib.monash.edu.au/ https://doi.org/10.2139/ssrn.2493353

Asongu SA, Nwachukwu JC (2017) Foreign aid and inclusive development: updated evidence from Africa, 2005–2012. Soc Sci Q 98(1):282–298. https://doi.org/10.1111/ssqu.12275

Basnett Y, Engel J (2013) Aid for trade in practice: addressing political economy of barriers to improve development outcomes. In: Rassaque M, te Velde D (eds) Assessing aid for trade: effectiveness, current issues and future directions, pp 128–150. http://dx.doi.org/10.14217/9781848591646-en

Bauer PT (1969) Dissent on development. Scott J Polit Econ 16(3):75–94. https://doi.org/10.1111/j.1467-9485.1969.tb00038.x

Bauhr M, Charron N, Nasiritousi N (2013) Does corruption cause aid fatigue? Public opinion and the aid-corruption paradox. Int Stud Q 57(3):568–579. https://doi.org/10.1111/isqu.12025

Bearce DH, Finkel SE, Pérez-Liñán AS, Rodríguez-Zepeda J, Surzhko-Harned L (2013) Has the new aid for trade agenda been export effective? Evidence on the impact of US AfT allocations 1999–2008. Int Stud Q 57(1):163–170. https://doi.org/10.1111/isqu.12027

Bigsten A, Tengstam S (2015) International coordination and the effectiveness of aid. World Dev 69(5):75–85. https://doi.org/10.1016/j.worlddev.2013.12.021

Boone P (1996) Politics and the effectiveness of foreign aid. Eur Econ Rev 40(2):289–329. https://doi.org/10.1016/0014-2921(95)00127-1

Boone P (2005) Effective intervention: making aid work. IDEAS Working Paper Series from RePEc, 1–7. Retrieved from https://ideas.repec.org/p/cep/cepcnp/187.html

Brenton P, Von Uexkull E (2009) Product specific technical assistance for exports—has it been effective? J Int Trade Econ Dev 18(2):235–254. https://doi.org/10.1080/09638190902916444

Browne S (2006) Aid and influence: do donors help or hinder?. Earthscan Publications Ltd, London, UK

Burnside C, Dollar D (2000) Aid, policies, and growth. Am Econ Rev 90(4):847–868. https://doi.org/10.1257/aer.90.4.847

Cadot O, de Melo J (2014) Evaluation in aid for trade: introduction to the symposium. World Econ 37(4):511–515. https://doi.org/10.1111/twec.12137

Cadot O, Fernandes A, Gourdon J, Mattoo A, Melo J (2014) Evaluating aid for trade: a survey of recent studies. World Econ 37(4):516–529. https://doi.org/10.1111/twec.12138

Calì M, Razzaque M (2013) Aid for trade: impact on Sub-Saharan Africa. In: Rassaque M, te Velde DW (eds) Assessing aid for trade: effectiveness, current issues and future directions, pp 102–127. http://dx.doi.org/10.14217/9781848591646-en

Calì M, te Velde DW (2008) Towards a quantitative assessment of Aid for Trade. Retrieved from https://www.odi.org/sites/odi.org.uk/files/odi-assets/publications-opinion-files/4432.pdf

Clemens MA, Radelet S, Bhavnani RR, Bazzi S (2012) Counting chickens when they hatch: timing and the effects of aid on growth. Econ J 122(561):590–617. https://doi.org/10.1111/j.1468-0297.2011.02482.x

de Melo J, Wagner L (2015) Aid for Trade as finance for the Poor. IDEAS Working Paper Series from RePEc. Retrieved from http://www.ferdi.fr/sites/www.ferdi.fr/files/publication/fichiers/wp125_demelo_wagner.pdf

de Melo J, Wagner L (2016) Aid for trade and the trade facilitation agreement: what they can do for LDCs. J World Trade 50(6):935–969. Retrieved from http://www.kluwerlawonline.com.ezproxy.lib.monash.edu.au/abstract.php?area=Journals&id=TRAD2016038

Deen-Swarray M, Adekunle B, Odularu G (2014) Policy recipe for fostering regional integration through infrastructure development and coordination in West Africa. In: Seck D (ed) Regional Economic Integration in West Africa, pp 29–56. https://doi.org/10.1007/978-3-319-01282-7

Djankov S, Freund C, Pham CS (2010) Trading on time. Rev Econ Stat 92(1):166–173. https://doi.org/10.1162/rest.2009.11498

Dollar D, Levin V (2006) The increasing selectivity of foreign aid, 1984–2003. World Dev 34(12):2034–2046. https://doi.org/10.1016/j.worlddev.2006.06.002

Doucouliagos H, Paldam M (2011) The ineffectiveness of development aid on growth: an update. Eur J Polit Econ 27(2):399–404. https://doi.org/10.1016/j.ejpoleco.2010.11.004

Doucouliagos H, Paldam M (2015) Finally a breakthrough? The recent rise in the size of the estimates of aid effectiveness. In: Arvin BM, Lew B (eds) Handbook on the economics of foreign aid, pp 325–349. http://dx.doi.org.ezproxy.lib.monash.edu.au / https://doi.org/10.4337/9781783474592.00030

Easterly WR (2006) The white man's burden: why the West's efforts to aid the rest have done so much ill and so little good. Penguin Press, New York, NY

Easterly WR (2008) Reinventing foreign aid. MIT Press, Cambridge, MA

Economides G, Kalyvitis S, Philippopoulos A (2008) Does foreign aid distort incentives and hurt growth? Theory and evidence from 75 aid-recipient countries. Public Choice 134(3):463–488. https://doi.org/10.1007/s11127-007-9239-9

Evenett SJ (2005) Some tough love on 'aid for trade'. Intereconomics 40(6):326–329. https://doi.org/10.1007/s10272-005-0163-2

Gamberoni E, Newfarmer R (2014) Aid for trade: do those countries that need it, get it? World Econ 37(4):542–554. https://doi.org/10.1111/twec.12139

Glennie J, Sumner A (2016) Aid, growth and poverty. https://doi.org/10.1057/978-1-137-57272-1

Gyimah-Brempong K, Racine JS, Gyapong A (2012) Aid and economic growth: sensitivity analysis. J Int Dev 24(1):17–33. https://doi.org/10.1002/jid.1708

Helble MC, Mann CL, Wilson JS (2009) Aid for trade facilitation. Retrieved from https://elibrary-worldbank-org.ezproxy.lib.monash.edu.au/doi/pdf/10.1596/1813-9450-5064?download=true

Helble M, Mann C, Wilson L (2012) Aid-for-trade facilitation. Rev World Econ 148(2):357–376. https://doi.org/10.1007/s10290-011-0115-9

Hoeffler A, Outram V (2011) Need, merit, or self-interest—what determines the allocation of aid? Rev World Econ 15(2):237–250. https://doi.org/10.1111/j.1467-9361.2011.00605.x

Hoekman B, Wilson JS (2010) Aid for trade: building on progress today for tomorrow's future. Retrieved from https://elibrary-worldbank-org.ezproxy.lib.monash.edu.au/doi/pdf / https://doi.org/10.1596/1813-9450-5361

Holden P (2014) Tensions in the discourse and practice of the European Union's aid for trade. Contemp Polit 20(1):90–102. https://doi.org/10.1080/13569775.2014.881607

Hühne P, Meyer B, Nunnenkamp P (2014a) Does aid for trade from the north promote south–south trade? Appl Econ Lett 21(17):1230–1233. https://doi.org/10.1080/13504851.2014.922665

Hühne P, Meyer B, Nunnenkamp P (2014b) Who benefits from aid for trade? Comparing the effects on recipient versus donor exports. J Dev Stud 50(9):1275–1288. https://doi.org/10.1080/00220388.2014.903246

Hunt J (ed) (2016) Aid and development, 3rd edn. Palgrave Macmillan, London, UK

Ilorah R (2008) Trade, aid and national development in Africa. Dev South Afr 25(1):83–98. https://doi.org/10.1080/03768350701837796

Isopi A (2015) Aid and corruption: an incentive problem. In: Arvin BM, Lew B (eds) Handbook on the economics of foreign aid, pp 305–312. https://doi.org/10.4337/9781783474592

Iwanow T, Kirkpatrick C (2009) Trade facilitation and manufactured exports: is Africa different? World Dev 37(6):1039–1050. https://doi.org/10.1016/j.worlddev.2008.09.014

Jakupec V (2016) Aid for trade: a critical analysis. In: Jakupec V, Kelly M (eds) Assessing the impact of foreign aid: value for money and aid for trade. Academic Press-Elsevier, London, UK, pp 45–57

Jakupec V, Kelly M (2016) Assessing the impact of foreign aid: value for money and aid for trade. Academic Press, London, UK

Jones S (2015) Aid supplies over time: addressing heterogeneity, trends, and dynamics. World Dev 69:31–43. https://doi.org/10.1016/j.worlddev.2013.12.014

Juselius K, Møller NF, Tarp F (2014) The long-run impact of foreign aid in 36 African countries: insights from multivariate time series analysis. Oxford Bull Econ Stat 76(2):153–184. https://doi.org/10.1111/obes.12012

Karns M, Mingst KA, Stiles KW (2015) International organizations: the politics and processes of global governance, 3rd edn. Lynne Rienner, Boulder, CO

Kaya O, Kaya I, Gunter L (2012) Development aid to agriculture and economic growth. Rev Dev Econ 16(2):230–242. https://doi.org/10.1111/j.1467-9361.2012.00658.x

Kaya O, Kaya I, Gunter L (2013) Foreign aid and the quest for poverty reduction: is aid to agriculture effective? J Agric Econ 64(3):583–596. https://doi.org/10.1111/1477-9552.12023

Kingsbury D, McKay J, Hunt J, McGillivray M, Clarke M (eds) (2016) International development: issues and challenges, 3rd edn. Palgrave, New York, NY

Kodama M (2012) Aid unpredictability and economic growth. World Dev 40(2):266–272. https://doi.org/10.1016/j.worlddev.2011.07.015

Langan M, Scott J (2011) The false promise of Aid for Trade. IDEAS Working Paper Series from RePEc. Retrieved from http://ideas.repec.org/p/bwp/bwppap/16011.html

Langan M, Scott J (2014) The aid for trade charade. Coop Confl 49(2):143–161. https://doi.org/10.1177/0010836713482880

Lee H-H, Park D, Shin M (2015) Do developing-country WTO members receive more aid for trade (AfT)? World Econ 38(9):1462–1485. https://doi.org/10.1111/twec.12258

Lof M, Mekasha TJ, Tarp F (2015) Aid and income: another time-series perspective. World Dev 69:19–30. https://doi.org/10.1016/j.worlddev.2013.12.015

Lopez L (2015) Corruption and international aid allocation: a complex dance. J Econ Dev 40(1):35–61

Martínez-Zarzoso I (2015) The trade effect of foreign aid: an empirical perspective. In: Arvin BM, Lew B (eds) Handbook on the economics of foreign aid, pp 179–196. https://doi.org/10.4337/9781783474592

Martínez-Zarzoso I, Nowak-Lehmann F, Klasen S, Larch M (2009) Does German development aid promote German exports? Ger Econ Rev 10(3):317–338. https://doi.org/10.1111/j.1468-0475.2008.00458.x

Martínez-Zarzoso I, Nowak-Lehmann F, Parra MD, Klasen S (2014) Does aid promote donor exports? Commercial interest versus instrumental philanthropy. Kyklos 67(4):559–587. https://doi.org/10.1111/kykl.12068

Mbekeani K (2010) Infrastructure, trade expansion and regional integration: global experience and lessons for Africa. J Afr Econ 19:88–113. https://doi.org/10.1093/jae/ejp021

Meschi E, Vivarelli M (2009) Trade and income inequality in developing countries. World Dev 37(2):287–302. https://doi.org/10.1016/j.worlddev.2008.06.002

Minolu C, Roddy S (2010) Development aid and economic growth: a positive long-run relation. Q Rev Econ Financ 50(1):27–39

Morrissey O (2006) Aid or trade, or aid and trade? Aust Econ Rev 39(1):78–88. https://doi.org/10.1111/j.1467-8462.2006.00399.x

Mosley P, Suleiman A (2007) Aid, agriculture and poverty in developing countries. Rev Dev Econ 11(1):139–158. https://doi.org/10.1111/j.1467-9361.2006.00354.x

Moyo D (2010) Dead aid: why aid makes things worse and how there is another way for Africa. Penguin, London, UK

Moyo JM, Bah E, Verdier-Chouchane A (2015) Transforming Africa's agriculture to improve competitiveness. The Africa competitiveness report 2015, 37. Retrieved from http://documents.worldbank.org.ezproxy.lib.monash.edu.au/curated/en/759341467995641147/pdf/96997-REPLACEMENT-The-Africa-Competitiveness-Report-2015.pdf#page=57

Naito T (2012) Aid for trade and welfare. Jpn Econ Rev 63(2):216–231. https://doi.org/10.1111/j.1468-5876.2012.00569.x

Nowak-Lehmann F, Dreher A, Herzer D, Klasen S, Martínez-Zarzoso I (2012) Does foreign aid really raise per capita income? A time series perspective. Can J Econ 5(1):288–313. https://doi.org/10.1111/j.1540-5982.2011.01696.x

Nowak-Lehmann F, Martínez-Zarzoso I, Herzer D, Klasen S, Cardozo A (2013) Does foreign aid promote recipient exports to donor countries? Weltwirtschaftliches Archiv 149(3):505–535. https://doi.org/10.1007/s10290-013-0155-4

Organization for Economic Cooperation and Development (2003) Glossary of statistical terms: official development assistance (ODA). Retrieved from http://stats.oecd.org/glossary/detail.asp?ID=6043

Organization for Economic Cooperation and Development & World Trade Organization (2009) Aid for trade at a glance 2009: maintaining momentum. Paris, France: OECD Publishing.

Organization for Economic Cooperation and Development (2011) Strengthening accountability in aid for trade: the development dimension. http://dx.doi.org/10.1787/97892 64123212-en

Organization for Economic Cooperation and Development (2013) Glossary of statistical terms: grants. Retrieved from https://stats.oecd.org/glossary/detail.asp?ID=1143

Organization for Economic Cooperation and Development (2016) Aid statistics at a glance to Africa. Retrieved fromhttps://www.oecd.org/dac/stats/documentupload/2%20Africa%20-%20Development%20Aid%20at%20a%20Glance%202016.pdf

Organization for Economic Cooperation and Development (2017) The 0.7% ODA/GNI target—a history. Retrieved from http://www.oecd.org/dac/stats/the07odagnitarget-ahistory.htm

Organization for Economic Cooperation and Development and World Trade Organization (2011) Strengthening accountability in aid for trade. https://doi.org/10.1787/9789264123212-4-en

Organization for Economic Cooperation and Development and World Trade Organization (2013) Aid for trade at a glance 2013: connecting to value chains. http://dx.doi.org/10.1787/aid_glance-2013-en

Organization for Economic Cooperation and Development and World Trade Organization (2015) Aid for trade at a glance 2015: reducing trade costs for inclusive, sustainable growth. http://dx.doi.org/10.1787/aid_glance-2015-en

Organization for Economic Cooperation and Development and World Trade Organization (2017) Aid for trade at a glance 2017: promoting trade, inclusiveness and connectivity for sustainable development. https://doi.org/10.1787/aid_glance-2017-en

Okada K, Samreth S (2012) The effect of foreign aid on corruption: a quantile regression approach. Econ Lett 115(2):240–243. https://doi.org/10.1016/j.econlet.2011.12.051

Ostenhaus A (2015) How to mitigate corruption risks in aid flow? Retrieved from http://blog.transparency.org/2015/06/15/how-to-mitigate-corruption-risks-in-aid-flows/

Oyejide TA, Bankole AS (2010) Aid for trade and regional integration in West Africa. Paper presented at the United Nations Economic Commission for Africa Expert Forum, Addis Ababa, Ethiopia. Retrieved from https://www.researchgate.net/publication/266454585_Aid_for_Trade_and_Regional_Integration_in_West_Africa

Peet R, Hartwick E (2009) Theories of development: contentions, arguments, alternatives, 2nd edn. The Guilford Press, New York, NY

Pettersson J, Johansson L (2013) Aid, aid for trade, and bilateral trade: an empirical study. J Int Trade Econ Dev, 1–29. https://doi.org/10.1080/09638199.2011.613998

Pieterse JN (2001) Development theory: deconstruction or reconstruction. Sage, London, UK

Pieterse JN (2010) Development theory. Sage, London, UK

Portugal-Perez A, Wilson JS (2012) Export performance and trade facilitation reform: hard and soft infrastructure. World Dev 40(7):1295–1307. https://doi.org/10.1016/j.worlddev.2011.12.002

Preston PW (1996) Development theory: an introduction. Blackwell, Oxford, UK

Rajan RG, Subramanian A (2008) Aid and growth: what does the cross-country evidence really show? Rev Econ Stat 90(4):643–665. https://doi.org/10.1162/rest.90.4.643

Razzaque MA, te Velde, DW (2013) Assessing aid for trade: effectiveness, current issues and future directions. https://doi.org/10.14217/9781848591646-en

Seers D (1970) The meaning of development. Ekistics 30(180):353–355. Retrieved from http://www.jstor.org.ezproxy.lib.monash.edu.au/stable/43616435

Shleifer A (2009) Peter Bauer and the failure of foreign aid. IDEAS Working Paper Series from RePEc. Retrieved from http://ideas.repec.org/p/hrv/faseco/8705862.html

Silva SJ, Nelson D (2012) Does aid cause trade? Evidence from an asymmetric gravity model. World Econ 35(5):545–577. https://doi.org/10.1111/j.1467-9701.2011.01431.x

Silverman D (2013) Doing qualitative research. Sage, London, UK

Skarbek DB, Leeson PT (2009) What can aid do? Cato J 29(3):391–397. https://doi.org/10.2139/ssrn.2261325

Skärvall L (2012) Does Swedish aid help or hinder bilateral trade: an empirical study on the effect of Official Development Assistance and Aid for Trade. Retrieved from http://www.diva-portal.org/smash/get/diva2:491628/FULLTEXT01.pdf

Stiglitz J, Charlton A (2006) Aid for Trade. Aussenwirtschaft 61(2):143–166. Retrieved from https://search-proquest-com.ezproxy.lib.monash.edu.au/docview/220796654?accountid=12528&rfr_id=info%3Axri%2Fsid%3Aprimo

Stockemer D, Lamontagne B, Charrette J (2011) Panacea, placebo, or poison? The impact of development aid on growth. Can J Dev Stud 32(1):3–16. https://doi.org/10.1080/02255189.2011.576133

Sumner A, Glennie J (2015) Growth, poverty and development assistance: when does foreign aid work? Glob Policy 6(3):201–211. https://doi.org/10.1111/1758-5899.12251

Tarp F (2006) Aid and development. IDEAS Working Paper Series from RePEc. Retrieved from ideas.repec.org/p/pra/mprapa/13171.html

Tembo D (2011) The private sector connection: EIF & aid for trade. Int Trade Forum (4):10–11. Retrieved from http://www.intracen.org/The-private-sector-connection-EIF-Aid-for-Trade/

Teravaninthorn S, Raballand G (2009) Transport prices and costs in Africa: a review of the international corridors. https://doi.org/10.1596/978-0-8213-7650-8

Thomas G (2011) How to do your case study: a guide for students and researchers. Sage, London, UK

Thomas G (2017) How to do your research: a guide for students, 3rd edn. Sage, London, UK

Turner L, Fink A (2013) Regional aid for trade and aid effectiveness: examples from East and West Africa. In Rassaque M, te Velde DW (eds) Assessing aid for trade: effectiveness, current issues and future directions, pp 211–233. https://doi.org/10.14217/9781848591646-en

Udvari B (2014, September) Aid for trade: does it enhance the intra-trade of Sub-Saharan African integrations? Paper presented at the 16th Annual Conference of ETSG, Munich. Retrieved from http://publicatio.bibl.u-szeged.hu/7088/1/etsg_2014.pdf

United Nations Conference on Trade and Development (2016) The Least Developed Countries Report 2016—the path to graduation and beyond: making the most of the process. Retrieved from http://unctad.org/en/PublicationsLibrary/ldc2016_en.pdf

United Nations Economic Commission for Africa (2015) Reducing trade costs to support Africa's transformation: the role of aid for trade. Retrieved from https://www.wto.org/english/tratop_e/devel_e/a4t_e/global_review15prog_e/uneca_final.pdf

Van Bilzen G (2015) The development of aid. Retrieved from http://www.cambridgescholars.com/download/sample/62308

Vijil M, Wagner L (2012) Does aid for trade enhance export performance? Investigating the infrastructure hannel. World Econ 35(7):838–868. https://doi.org/10.1111/j.1467-9701.2012.01437.x

Wagner D (2003) Aid and trade—an empirical study. J Jpn Int Econ 17(2):153–173. https://doi.org/10.1016/S0889-1583(03)00010-8

Wagner L (2014) Identifying thresholds in aid effectiveness. Weltwirtschaftliches Archiv 150(3):619–638. https://doi.org/10.1007/s10290-014-0187-4

Wang CC (2011) Aid for trade as a public good. J Int Trade Econ Dev 20(6):711–728. https://doi.org/10.1080/09638190903360220

Wickstead MA (2015) Aid and development: a brief introduction, 1st edn. https://doi.org/10.1093/acprof:oso/9780198744924.001.0001

World Bank (n.d.) History. Retrieved from https://www.worldbank.org/en/about/archives/history

World Trade Organization (2005) Ministerial declaration. Retrieved from https://www.wto.org/english/thewto_e/minist_e/min05_e/final_text_e.htm#aid_for_trade

Younas J (2008) Motivation for bilateral aid allocation: altruism or trade benefits. Eur J Polit Econ 24(3):661–674. https://doi.org/10.1016/j.ejpoleco.2008.05.003

Conclusion and Policy Recommendations: Creating an Enabling Business Ecosystem for Fostering Trade Opportunities in the Digital Age

Gbadebo Odularu, Babatunde Adetunji and Adenike Odularu

Introduction

> If African countries fail to invest in their digital and knowledge economies, they will face 100 million jobless citizens across the region by 2050.... But as countries scramble for resources to build their digital ecosystems, the continent is still struggling for electricity to power basic digital technology such that bridging the continent's infrastructure gap which is estimated at about $160 bn per year, without which, the innovation and digital hubs agenda will remain unachievable. (African Business Magazine 2019)

As Africa endeavours to continually strengthen its business ecosystems, this will set into motion a new direction in the business relations between its trading partners, based on the prevailing global dynamics as well as the mutual areas of interests and cooperation. Thus, the World Bank East of Doing Business remains one of the most effective barometers for measuring the level of Africa's business relations with its partners, as well as an invaluable opportunity to review and reflect on that relations and agree on mutual priorities.

G. Odularu (✉)
Department of Economics and Finance, Bay Atlantic University, Washington, DC, USA
e-mail: odularu@comcast.net; godularu@live.com; godularu@bau.edu

Socio-Economic Research Applications and Projects (SERAP LLC), Washington, DC, USA

Center for Research on Political Economy (CREPOL), Dakar-Yoff, Senegal

Trade, Economics and Agribusiness Division, SSCG Consulting, Birmingham, UK

American Heritage University of Southern California (AHUSC), Ontario, CA, USA

B. Adetunji
Department of Economics, University of Ibadan, Ibadan, Nigeria

A. Odularu
Federal Ministry of Industry, Trade and Investment, Abuja, Nigeria
e-mail: nikeodularu@gmail.com

G. O. A. Odularu et al. (eds.), *Fostering Trade in Africa*,
Advances in African Economic, Social and Political Development,
https://doi.org/10.1007/978-3-030-36632-2_10

Trade and economic relations as being enhanced by the AfCFTA among African countries will result in significantly favourable outcomes, despite the ups and downs in the socio-economic and political tensions if all AfCFTA members adhere to AfCFTA rules, and as all countries have confidence in the AfCFTA-led rules. Thus, trade disputes, like the increasingly recurring trade conflicts and reprisals between two neighbouring countries over agriculture produce should be peacefully settled within the AfCFTA window without resort to retaliation, escalation or force.

Digitalization will play an integral role in bolstering Africa's business relations with its trading partners. According to the AfDB, Africa should not rely on oil, gas or minerals to determine the competitiveness of their economies on the global level. On the other hand, it is the knowledge and the ability to innovate and create mega-businesses that are going to be like Google and Facebook of this world. African countries need to make their development ecosystem more enabling in order to capitalize on the global digital economy opportunities which is poised to rake in over $60 trillion in revenues by 2025 (African Business Magazine 2019). In other words, Africa's comparative advantage depends on nurturing its talents, the smart workforce full of bright ideas for a promising future and developing world-class innovation hubs, like the U.S tech capital Silicon Valley. Africa boasts of about 440 innovation hubs and centres which provide the ecosystem for access to the technology, financial instruments, digital tools and industrial expertise which are sine qua non to flourishing and scaling up their businesses. Within these innovation hubs, it is pertinent to note that cutting-edge research, science and technology are keys to enhancing competitive capacities in global businesses, especially in ever evolving and expanding business ecosystems.

Policy Solutions

According to the International Monetary Fund (IMF), Africa's growth prospects will be among the highest in the world by 2023. At the moment, six of the world's 12 fastest growing economies are from Africa. Africa is also the world's most profitable region, where digitalization will enhance the continent's capacity to generate more economic optimism that the next five years will be better than today. For instance, Rwanda is making frantic efforts to attract investors to its $1 billion innovation hub, the Kigali Innovation City, which will be co-financed by the Rwandan Government and Africa50, and which is aimed at making Rwanda an innovative, digital and expanding economy.

As Africa endeavours to adopt innovative tools in making its businesses relations with other countries more flourishing in this digital era, increasing number of African countries are establishing innovation hubs or Silicon Valleys. Thus, attracting national, regional and global talents and resources which are needed to transform these countries into digitally prepared and globally competitive knowledge-driven economies.

In addition to initiatives by the African Union Commission, African Development Bank (AfDB), African Export–Import Bank (Afreximbank), NEPAD Planning and Development Agency (NPDA) and other relevant platforms, there is increasing need for a global framework for the promotion of African digital capacity enhancement agenda, bringing together a wide range of stakeholders. This will contribute to improving its business ecosystems through innovation and private-sector engagements, as well as economic diversification and industrialization, investments in quality infrastructure and the blue economy, thereby accelerating economic transformation on the continent. In relating with its business partners, Africa is increasingly interested in trade and investments, and not aid, especially with the establishment of the $3.3 trillion African Continental Free Trade Area (AfCFTA),[1] thereby providing a 1.2 billion people marketplace for foreign investors in search of more cutting-edge technological solutions. However, there is a need for Africa to diversify its range of trade partners beyond the handful of countries that currently dominate its trade relations with other foreign countries, other than its traditional trading partners. AfCFTA will further enhance US–Africa trade and investment relations. Thus, the role of improving the ease of doing business and the enforcement of contracts cannot be overemphasized. The USA shares Africa's desire to jointly deepen dialogue and cooperation on strengthened trade and investment relations, thereby leveraging AfCFTA to promote a sound trade policy ecosystem, regional economies of scale and increased flow of trade and investment between the USA and Africa. This further requires pursuance of deeper business ties beyond the African Growth Opportunity Act (AGOA), which is scheduled to expire in 2025, eventually leading to a continental trade partnership between the USA and Africa (Odularu and Alege 2019).

Africa's anticipated infrastructural investments posit huge potentials for advancing its digital opportunities. For instance, the USTDA's feasibility study recommends ten investment plans in core ICT infrastructure and intelligent transportation systems, as well as digital security, inclusion and literacy. According to the World Economic Forum (WEF), Africa's e-commerce is rapidly booming, with an estimated 264 e-commerce start-ups operational on the continent (in 23 countries) and projected annual sales of $75 billion and 3 million jobs by 2025.

One of the most innovative digital apps in Africa, which has proven so impactful and innovative, is M-Pesa, as an innovative mobile money transfer service which was first launched in 2007. By May 2009, the app had more than 6.5 million subscribers. Currently, about 13 million users send and receive money via M-Pesa and without bank accounts. In other words, M-Pesa has proven to represent an innovative and spectacularly successful platform for poor farmers in the Rift Valley to bankers in Nairobi, where over 20 million Kenyans use the service to transfer money and apply for loans and receive wages. In April, African e-commerce company Jumia listed on

[1]The African Continental Free Trade Area (AfCFTA) is a tool for driving African industrialization, economic diversification and development. It helps to promote the type of trade that produces sustainable growth, creates jobs for Africa's youth and fosters opportunities for nurturing Africa's businesses and entrepreneurship.

the New York Stock Exchange has its shares soared 75% on the first day of trading, valuing the company at more than $1.9 billion (African Business Magazine 2019).

Critically important is the increasing capacities-strengthening roles of social enterprises that build and share digital technologies to help Africans become more active and increasingly digitalized citizens. For example, since the creation of M-Pesa, as an increasingly digital microfinance platform in 2007, related apps are now being fully embraced, and Africa's tech wizards are turning their focus on developing digital tools to improve governance, business, economics, democracies, health care, farming, banking, transportation, communication, etc.

With its mobile money market, being one of the most developed in the world, and about 70% of the population, using smartphones, only about 30% of the adult population in SSA have bank accounts, which is lower than in any other region, with the exception of the Middle East. However, these services are becoming increasingly accessible. Further, smartphones are now being leveraged not only for communication but also to access a bouquet of socio-economic services as central energy grids are unreliable as well as the expensive nature of long-distance travel.

The increased access to smartphones has resulted in Africa's rising digitalization. From 2007 to 2016, mobile phone ownership across the continent grew from 174 to 772 million, representing about 344% increase, compared to the global growth of 107% during the same period. Though mobile phones and their affordability are one of the bigger digitization stories on the continent, understanding the state of play and the opportunities that lie ahead for shaping Africa's future and its business landscape, apps and platforms are being fully embarked upon.

Digital finance solutions focusing on easy access to financial services, mobile banking services, mobile crop insurances, digital access to remittances and seamless cash payment will all allow for the transformation of Africa's business landscape and inclusive economic growth.

Leveraging digitization and innovation ecosystems towards complementing existing business development and facilitation options require basic infrastructure such as digital infrastructure (which include cheap broadband, supportive business and regulatory environments), good network of roads, efficient ports, technology and talented scientific and mathematical minds.

Over the next five years, African countries are likely to experience more regulations among which a few of them will be targeted at digital services, thereby restricting how African businesses will leverage on their expansion into parallel markets towards accessing relevant opportunities especially in trade, finance, education and health care.

Creating a Coherent Strategy

The blockchain technology industry and applications in Africa is in its infancy, being built by a few start-ups with limited capacities. Thus, creating a coherent blockchain strategy linked to its economic agenda will provide the critical momentum needed for Africa in this currently fragmented and competitive market. Since most of the future economic growth will be driven by Artificial Intelligence (AI), big data and blockchain technology, it will be important to communicate strong, consistent and workable strategies to drive implementation and impact. A key strategy in driving this is impact and pragmatism which can only be delivered through a consistent message. Web, data science, mobile and e-retailing will represent the most effective vehicles and platforms for strong presence and impact.

For Africa, there are exciting times ahead in the future of trade and the role of the government and private sector in serving the market. We should ask ourselves that 20 years from now, when a friend mentions the word ‘trade’ in a conversation, will we still visualize a physical building in a location? Or will we see an innovative system that embraces the needs of clients and addresses the multidimensional nature of Africa’s complex economy? The future starts with one thought, one conversation and one action: Is Africa ready to act and contribute to this global digital business opportunities space?

In an emerging surveillance society in which data sharing and surveillance systems allow others to know more about us than we do, AIs make sense of the floods of resulting data. Therefore, those in the know increasingly take advantage of that analysis, thereby creating conditions for a possible future where even as surveillance monitors our brains, quantum encryption breaks the last hope of privacy protection, and a digital backlash erupts.

Conclusion and the (Future) Research Opportunity Space

The objective of this sub-section is to identify the emerging challenges, and the likely policy research directions that will shape Africa’s trade in profound ways are over the horizon. Certainly, publicly funded research could help inform trade relations. business opportunities dialogue and policy development. Each challenge is multidisciplinary and requires proactive broad cooperation, academic research studies, foresight programmes and transdisciplinary exploration to surmount. The fact that these challenges confront the economy also presents the possibilities of opportunities and new directions for Africa’s economic trajectory. The trade relations and business opportunities for Africa will continue to evolve over the next decade as global trade becomes increasingly digitalized. The future of trade for Africa will be largely connected with its capacities to harness digital opportunities for job generation and wealth creation, especially for its teeming youth population (Odularu 2020; Odularu and Adekunle 2017). In addition to boldly adopting digitization policies as strategic enablers of inclusive development, efforts should be made to gradually digitize all the sectors of the economy, thereby generating business opportunities, especially for the underserved and shaping the future of our economies for a more global community.

References

African Business Magazine (2019) August–September 2019—African Business Magazine. [Online] Available at https://africanbusinessmagazine.com/magazine/august-september-2019/. Accessed 5 Aug 2019

Odularu G (2020) Strategic policy options for bracing Nigeria for the future of trade. Palgrave Macmillan, USA. Available online at https://www.palgrave.com/us/book/9783030345518

Odularu G, Adekunle B (eds) (2017) Negotiating south-south regional trade agreements. Advances in African Economic, Social and Political Development, Cham. Available online at https://link.springer.com/chapter/10.1007/978-3-319-45569-3_1

Odularu G, Alege P (eds) (2019) Trade facilitation capacity needs: policy directions for national and regional development in West Africa. Palgrave Macmillan, USA: Available online at https://www.palgrave.com/br/book/9783030059453

Printed by Printforce, the Netherlands